SERVING OLDER ADULTS:
Policy, Programs, and Professional Activities

ANDREW W. DOBELSTEIN
University of North Carolina

with Ann B. Johnson
Coordinating Council for Senior Citizens, Durham, Inc.

Prentice-Hall, Inc., Englewood Cliffs, New Jersey 07632

Library of Congress Cataloging in Publication Data

Dobelstein, Andrew W.
    Serving older adults.

    Bibliography: p.
    Includes index.
    1. Social work with the aged—United States.   2. Aged
—Services for—United States.   3. Aged—Government
policy—United States.   I. Johnson, Ann B.   II. Title.
HV1461.D62   1985   362.6'0973   84-17933
ISBN 0-13-806860-7

© 1985 by Prentice-Hall, Inc., Englewood Cliffs, New Jersey 07632

Printed in the United States of America

10   9   8   7   6   5   4   3   2   1

Editorial/production supervision
   and interior design: Virginia Cavanagh Neri
Cover design: Lundgren Graphics, Ltd.
Manufacturing buyer: Barbara Kittle

ISBN 0-13-806860-7   01

Prentice-Hall International, Inc., *London*
Prentice-Hall of Australia Pty. Limited, *Sydney*
Editora Prentice-Hall do Brasil, Ltda., *Rio de Janeiro*
Prentice-Hall Canada Inc., *Toronto*
Prentice-Hall of India Private Limited, *New Delhi*
Prentice-Hall of Japan, Inc., *Tokyo*
Prentice-Hall of Southeast Asia Pte. Ltd., *Singapore*
Whitehall Books Limited, *Wellington, New Zealand*

A DEDICATION—ELLEN BLACK WINSTON

Dr. Ellen Black Winston was the inspirational force for much that happened to improve conditions for older Americans and other vulnerable segments of the population in the last several decades. As teacher, social worker, organizer, leader, thinker, writer, and doer, she motivated and shaped curricula and services, conferences, organizations, caregivers, and agencies. Her dedication to quality services helped motivate the authors of this volume to share their experiences and insights with a new generation of helpers for the aging. In turn, this volume is dedicated to her.

Ellen was born, and spent most of her life, in North Carolina. More accurately she did not spend her life, she invested it on behalf of human concerns for people, carefully allocating her time and commitment to a broad range of issues and institutions where she felt she could make a difference. And she always did make a difference. Carefully prepared with thoughtful positions, knowledgeable about the issues and clear in her purpose, she became a leader in local, state, national, and international social welfare, often all at the same time.

After earning her Master's and Doctorate degrees (to which were later added six honorary degrees), she taught college and began an active involvement in community affairs. From 1944 to 1963 she served as North Carolina's Commissioner of

Public Welfare and began molding a modern welfare agency, honing her political skills and developing the personal strength to fight an issue through on the basis of principal knowledge and tenacity.

A woman, unique for the level of her influence in that period, a Southerner who was an acknowledged leader and creative worker for social justice as well as social welfare, President John Kennedy brought her to Washington to serve as Commissioner of Welfare in the Department of Health, Education and Welfare. She remained there from 1963 to 1967, overseeing programs designed to serve children as well as adults, helping shape national policy, and impacting on state welfare structures and multi and private social services everywhere.

She returned to her beloved Raleigh, North Carolina, a recognized national and international figure. Her interests and activities seemed boundless, yet she gave each organization and cause her undivided attention. Her own limitless energy inspired the organizations for which she worked. Each gained from her wisdom, her vision and her tenacity. She led the International Council on Social Welfare; she served as a founder of the local Wake County Council's Homemaker/Home Health Aide Service; she chaired the North Carolina Governor's Advisory Council on the Aging; she undertook one Presidency of the National Council on the Aging. In all these wide-ranging endeavors she remained involved and active—a commitment of herself. Those commitments were lodged in concern for women, in social work education, family planning and child welfare, home health services, and the arts and music.

Her contributions to the wide array of social organizations was her endless press for high standards, for quality of life. Standards of care and service delivery, she would point out, were needed to provide a goal for staff, a direction for training, and a basis for evaluation. "Only by careful adherence to standards . . . can the quality of care be assured," she wrote. Further, she would point out, as our knowledge and resources increase, the quality of care should be continually elevated by increasing our standards and being sure that those standards were adequately monitored.

Services to older persons, she pointed out, needed to be available, accessible, adequate, and acceptable. Those goals lent strength to her conviction that the most responsive services would emerge best if they were community-based and operated under voluntary auspices in cooperation with public agencies. Her adherence to these guidelines for social welfare services were strongly reflected in her support of community-based long term options for in-home services for the frail aged. While respecting the role of all the partners in the continuum of care needed in the community, it would be fair to say that she gave priority to homemaker/home health services.

To Ellen Winston, the development of such services were needed not just to respond to emerging demographic trends, but because those trends mirror and magnify individual circumstances, individual needs, individual problems, individual people. "To give overall statistics is not enough," she wrote. "It is necessary to look at the needs of a given individual at a given time." Dealing with social welfare on a national and international scale, she always remembered the significance of the individual and that the goal of major social movements was to enhance the options and opportunities for each individual.

Ellen Winston lived by example, as well as by word. She pioneered a leadership role for women long before it was considered acceptable. She unhesitantly spoke out against cuts in social welfare budgets and programs. She educated many state and national legislators about social need and public responsibility to serve that need. Unflappable in the face of challenge, she could with the tilt of her head and a quick wink convey her affection for a colleague.

Ellen Winston died in the summer of 1984, having seen almost each summer of this century unfold. She died after a brief illness in her home surrounded by a few friends and colleagues and a nurse from the agency she knew all along mattered most—the local home health agency.

She left new and stronger institutions, trained and dedicated workers a community and a nation more aware and able to respond to variations in the human condition. It is to honor Ellen Black Winston that this book is dedicated, and it is to inspire and motivate others to follow in her footsteps that it is written.

Jack Ossofsky, Executive Director
The National Council on the Aging

CONTENTS

chapter eleven   Serving Through Indirect Activities 205

**chapter twelve   The Working World of the Professional
Person 224**

Bibliography 234

Index 239

PREFACE

As the United States Congress examines the projected unacceptable budget deficits, which will plague the American economy to the end of the decade, educated "budget cutters" gravitate, instinctively, to the social security retirement program. Looked at in contrast to the whole of the federal budget, social security is an attractive candidate for the economic knife. Social security spending represents over one-third of all federal spending. It is a single program in which modest budget cutting could result in large reductions of federal outlays. From the "fairness" perspective as well, social security *ought* to be reduced, according to some. "Why," they question, "should independently wealthy retirees receive retirement and medical benefits from a federal program when they do not *need* them?"

The whole spectrum of concerns about older people—from policy issues, to the provision of helpful social services—have attracted increased public visability and debate. The older adult population is growing in size in relation to other population groups. Public resources appear to be shrinking at exactly the time when more resources seem to be needed. Professionals are acutely aware of growing commitments to serve older people, particularly among the personal helping professions such as social work. Like the larger public, professional people are often puzzled by debates over important programs for older people, such as those currently raised about social security. They often wonder how they should address these issues, and they struggle to keep their professional practices rèlevant to the changing expectations produced by the steadily growing older population.

This textbook prepares professionals for the challenging service to older people. This textbook has been developed on the premise that professional people must be able to understand the public issues and debates about older people as an important part of enhancing their professional helping skills at the same time. By combining an examination of older people and the significant public issues they face, with a series of practice skills needed to help older people, this textbook provides an important new dimension in professional education. In short, this textbook combines policy with practice, based on the assumption that effective practitioners understand the programs which form the basis of their helping activities.

This is an introductory textbook which leads the beginning professional through the policy and practice orientation in a series of four stages: The first stage, contained in Part 1, orients students to the problems which older people encounter in their lives. All older people face problems with income, housing, health, and their living environments. Students must understand how these problems complicate the lives of older people. The second stage, contained in Part 2, discusses differences in the ways older adulthood has been understood. Part 2 provides a theoretical foundation upon which most helping activity is based. One can identify the problems of older adulthood, but without theory to explain them—without some understanding about how and why these problems have developed—professional activity to do something about the problems is ineffective. Three theoretical perspectives are prescribed in Part 2: sociological, economic, and political themes.

The third stage, Part 3 of the textbook, describes theories and discusses the most evident public policies and programs which the nation provides to older people through its public and voluntary organizations. Once students understand the problems associated with older adulthood, and the reasons these problems develop, the student is ready to examine the structures which have been created to address the issues. The Social Security Act, the Housing Act, and the Older Americans Act provide the framework for identifying and describing, in detail, which programs are available to which older people under what kinds of special conditions if any. By the time the student has mastered Part 3, each student is well along the course to professional work with older adults.

The final stage, contained in Part 4, emphasizes methods of helping older people. The helping approach described, and richly illustrated in Part 4, follows a generic orientation. In the first place, many professions serve older people with sometimes unique professional applications, but commonality of problems facing older people, and the common base of service for them suggests methods of helping common to all professional disciplines. Secondly, because this is an introductory textbook, it is important for each student to master general helping methods as a foundation upon which further professional specialization can be built. Part 4, therefore discusses how a professional works with the formal systems of helping as well as the informal helping systems. In this approach Part 4 introduces the student to case management techniques as well as developing and using personal networks for older people, as part and parcel of an overarching helping process.

Most of Part 4, as through the textbook, emphasizes a "caring" approach for serving older people, somewhat in contrast with a "curing" approach. This textbook discusses policies, programs, and helping methods with a full realization that most older people are struggling with some handicapping social, emotional, or physical problem, but most older people are not handicapped. The approach in Part 4 emphasizes those helping methods which will enhance each older person's ability to live a better life, rather than exploring methodologies which might eradicate the problem itself. This focus is promoted in the belief that all persons, old and young, benefit from efforts to help them deal better with the difficulties which life promotes for all of us.

The field of services to older adults is growing as rapidly as the older population is growing. Many professions and many professional persons find that increasing amounts of professional activity are directed toward older people. A number of professional persons feel a need to re-orient themselves to older people. For example, many social workers providing public social services may find that they are working with more families regarding social planning for older family members—home making services, adult day care, and pre- and post-nursing home planning. These professional people will find this textbook a useful means to update and reform their well developed professional skills.

As students, when you complete your study of this text, you will be able to examine and debate, with confidence, problems such as whether social security funding should be reduced. You will understand, for example, that economic security is one of the most significant problems facing all older people. You will understand that the threat of economic insecurity is caused by a variety of economic and social forces. Earnings are decreased sharply for older people, and savings are not easily converted into usable economic resources. You will know that social security financing is separate and apart from funding other federal programs and thus "protected" from budget reductions. Furthermore, you will begin to understand that economic security is as much a psychological issue as an economic one. Middle- and upper-income older people feel just as threatened by the need to reduce their standards of living as do lower-income older people. Finally, from the perspective of the one-to-one helper, you will begin to understand that a foundation of stable and adequate income preceeds all efforts to assist older people with their other problems. From such a perspective, you will be able to question the wisdom of proposed reductions in social security programs.

This textbook is designed to get professional helpers off to a good start. It is a general orientation to learning how to help older people, but not so general that it does not offer specific ideas and methods for helping. The text follows a policy and method orientation which offers the opportunity to connect knowledge with skill in a professional helping approach. The text does not begin to present all that is necessary to know in order to serve older people, but it will get professional people a long way along the road. Now, it is time to get started.

ACKNOWLEDGMENTS

Andrew Dobelstein has been a social work teacher for eighteen years. Ann Johnson has been a social work practitioner for twenty years. We have worked together teaching about and working with older people for the last ten years. We have sat through endless meetings designed to improve services to older people. We have scurried about finding funds to improve educational experiences for students or to begin a new program. We have served on our share of State and National committees and task forces struggling with questions about how to make what we do with older people more effective.

We have talked often about the growing field of serving older people, trying to figure out what seemed the most helpful ou. of all the information that is being generated about this subject. We have come to some conclusions, which in turn encouraged us to write this book. We found that services to older people is a multi-disciplinary undertaking. Different professional people bring different perspectives to the tasks of helping older people, so that work with older people truly is a team effort.

We also learned that there are some common things all professional people ought to know about serving older people. There are theories of aging, there are an array of services available to older people, and there are some common working skills that all use, regardless of professional orientation. We also learned that older people are often their own best helpers. They have strengths and resources that emerge quickly in times of travail.

We must confess that we did not learn these things on our own. Our clients and our students taught us many lessons that are reflected in this textbook. We are grateful for the many things our parents taught us—even when they thought we were not listening. Andrew also thanks his children for their interest and ideas they offered. We are also grateful to Ron Toseland, State University of New York—Albany; Michael A. Patchner, University of Illinois; Margaret E. Hartford, University of Southern California; and Judith A. Altholz, Florida State University, who read this manuscript and made valuable suggestions to make it useful for students and practitioners.

Many of the vignettes and case examples came from interviews with persons in the field. Although they prefer to remain anonymous, we wish to thank them for their time and willingness to openly discuss their day-to-day professional tasks to bring the stark reality of operational concerns into this text.

Inspiration of a different kind came from older adults: the well, the struggling, the poor, those dedicated to serving others, and those whose coping abilities seem boundless. From them and more importantly, with them, we derived the strength and determination to produce a meaningful contribution to the published works in the field.

Although a book such as this owes so much to the help of others, we alone are responsible for any errors, omissions, or offenses that might be found in the book. We hope these will be few, and that each user will find in this book some measure of the knowledge that this textbook brings together in order to serve older people.

A.W.B.   A.B.J.
Chapel Hill, North Carolina

INTRODUCTION

Aging studies, often called gerontology, and the professional activity of serving older people, often called geriatrics, have been growing and changing during the past twenty years. Increasingly, persons educated and trained to assist older people live dignified lives are found in a wide array of occupational settings. Particularly in the fields of medical and social welfare, more and more persons are finding positions that involve working with older people in one way or another. The rise in the number of geriatric nurses, social workers, ministers, doctors, practical nurses, and recreation therapists indicates an expansion in this professional area. Older people now live longer. Older people have become an important political force in American life, acting as advocates for programs that will improve and protect what is becoming an entirely new way of life in America—retirement. All professions are seeking ways to prepare their members for the challenges posed by this new way of life.

It is no wonder that geriatric work is not restricted to a single discipline. Whereas the biological and social process of growing older once provided the core knowledge, now politics, economics, and social interaction factors also contribute significantly to understanding aging in America. Furthermore, these expanding bases of knowledge are applied in a wide range of situations by persons with quite different career preparation and skill levels. For example, nurse practitioners working in nursing homes not only need to understand the principles of the physical care of patients, but they need to understand how financial worries may cause patients to be less responsive as well. Likewise, social workers who counsel with older people and their families about living arrangements need to understand how the biological processes of aging may affect the choice.

Three themes dominate contemporary efforts to serve older people. First, education about aging and practice with older people is interdisciplinary. As a distinct field of aging emerges, a synthesis of knowledge about the aging process is obtained only from a composite academic and professional perspective. Second, those with professional education are less likely to be in direct service contact with older people than are those without professional degrees. For example, persons who help older people in senior centers most likely will range from older persons themselves to persons with specific professional training. The professional persons will be supervising, directing, and training others to become efficient in their work. Thus, professionals who work with older people must know how to help older people and know how to help those who help. Finally, public policies have generated programs designed to maximize the use of existing resources for older people, rather than to create new resources. For example, day care, originally developed as a service for children, has been adopted as a model for the care of older people. This model requires that professional people know what resources exist and how these resources may be called upon to serve older people. Moreover, all professionals who work with older adults must exercise skill in program planning and development in addition to the personalized helping skills they traditionally exercise.

As the specific practice of helping older people emerges as a new professional discipline, mastering the delivery of services to older people requires a textbook for professional persons from a variety of disciplines, at various levels of occupational education and training. While this text has been prepared with the social work professional in mind, the need for specific education on aging for health service professionals, and other professional persons, such as ministers, lawyers, and educators, has been given serious attention. Undoubtedly those who plan to work with older people will require education specific to their disciplines. However, a broad overview on serving older people provides an introduction to the programs and policies that shape the field of aging, and an introduction to methodologies for working with older people themselves. Such a focus for this textbook anticipates use by a variety of workers in different settings providing assistance to older persons who face many and complex life circumstances. This text also anticipates experienced workers educating others to work effectively with older people, while at the same time using their skills to build better services for older persons. Thus, it covers a wide range of material for a diverse audience, while providing sufficient detail to help professional people get started in an exciting and rewarding career.

For the most part, working with older persons is professionally satisfying. Although older people often have more than their share of problems, they also have a sense of patience and vision uncharacteristic of other population groups. Older persons also have been accustomed to doing things for themselves and for others. Therefore, they often accept help without feeling a threat to their sense of personal independence. When they do use help from others, they do so with a sense of appreciation that often rewards the helper immediately. Any text that introduces persons to providing services to older people should attempt to capture the spirit of excitement that comes from working with older people and that is generated by the many challenges this work presents.

Growing old in America is not an easy transition to the golden years. Much of the professional and popular literature on aging in America depicts older adulthood unglamorously, and life for many older people is not laced with the richness of "golden years." Older people are often socially isolated, economically exploited, restrained by their meager fixed incomes, rejected by their families, and uncertain how they will manage to live out the rest of their lives in their own homes and communities. The specter of the nursing home hangs heavily over their lives. Eleven percent of America's population is older than sixty-five. Most of these persons have retired from their jobs. Ninety-seven percent of them receive social security payments, yet twenty-five percent of them are living at a below-poverty level. For those who are sick, or handicapped, or frail, their lives are fraught with greater anxiety and suffering. These dreary statistics challenge the professional person to discover the older adults who live behind them and to develop the great potential that older adulthood holds.

Since the Older Americans Act was passed in 1965, much public attention has been directed to older adults. Social security, to supplement retirement income, legislated in 1935, and Medicare and Medicaid, to insure older people against health and hospital costs, legislated in 1965, were supplemented by an innovative approach to assisting older people under the Older Americans Act. The philosophy behind this legislation was not to create new social programs. Rather, it sought to provide public resources to assist older people to make better use of existing resources. Furthermore, the law promoted a spirit among existing service providers that would encourage adaptation of those services to the needs of older persons. Thus, the Older Americans Act stressed coordination of existing resources and conversion of those resources to greater usefulness by the older people who needed them. In so doing, the Older Americans Act has become the lever by which older people are reunited with their communities and reintegrated into the mainstream of American life.

Increased personal vulnerability accompanies growing old. Discontinuity of work, transitions in family roles, increased health concerns, changing housing needs, modifications in personal economic security, disruption of social and peer contacts, and increases in leisure time all add greatly to the pressure that people feel as they grow older in America. Some elderly run greater risks than others of living unsatisfying lives as a result of this increased vulnerability. The amount of social, emotional, economic, and physical support available from family, friends, and community organizations makes a crucial difference in how well older adults live within these constraints.

Helping professions—medicine, nursing, the ministry, social work, the law, and physical therapy—have a continuing commitment to assist people to live more satisfying lives. This commitment has been expressed through many efforts that have made it possible for persons to develop their resources. Now, with the growing numbers of older people, the helping professions have become committed to the development of professional skills that will improve the quality of life for older people. Serving older people requires a background knowledge of the psychological, social, and economic circumstances that define their lives. Professional persons must not only understand the complexities of older life and be able to assist older people in a complex social environment but also be able to help in the coordination of resources and programs that would make that environment conducive to a better way of life for all older people.

In this view, providing services to older adults requires broader preparation than most clinical programs can offer. Today the helping professions that serve older people are challenged by a variety of expectations. They appraise and screen personal care services that may be appropriate for older people, and that can be brought into reality by social planning and related efforts. They provide counseling to older people and their family members, primarily about emotional and interpersonal problems associated with aging, but also about the kinds of resources they may be able to use to improve the quality of their lives. They teach new self-management skills to older people to assist them in their efforts to remain in their own homes and communities. They collaborate with other professional persons to design programs that foster personal independence. They provide case management to insure that the services are focused on the older person's needs. They provide important linkages between the older person, agencies and organizations in the community, and institutions that determine policies that influence service developments. These same professionals also serve in policy-making organizations and set policy that has important influence on the lives of older people. Finally, they plan and carry out research projects to determine what needs are best met by what kinds of resources.

Growing old may be a normal experience, but America is not prepared to deal with it. As more and more people live longer, community institutions and support systems have not kept pace with the changing demands of older adulthood. Community support systems have developed in response to expectations from a younger, more heterogeneous population. During the twentieth century, the family has provided primary social and financial support for older Americans. But the widespread social and demographic changes that have swept America during the past two decades have also changed the nature of traditional family help for older people. Less and less frequently, older people live with younger children in extended households, freeing many younger couples from the financial burden and care of older parents. Yet, such changes in family life have caused concern among advocates for older persons, as families seem less willing to assist older persons. Thus, other social support networks must be made available as American social structures continue their endless changes.

In these times of fiscal austerity, the traditional social support systems will be even more important to older people if they are to live dignified lives. Alternatives to publicly-funded social resources exist within this traditional support structure, and professional persons increasingly will be called upon to strengthen the relationship between the older person and these resources. This will be accomplished by such tasks as identifying resources for older people, helping them over psychological and emotional obstacles that might prevent their use of these resources, and providing assistance to the resource providers to initiate and continue in newly developed relationships with older people and their families.

An effective social service system undergirds all community support structures for older adults. Available, accessible, adequate, and accountable social services require the integration of informal contacts—the family, the church, the voluntary social agency, and the public agency—in a focused, yet diversely applied, community-service network. Professional persons are called upon to improve this service structure while providing direct services to older people at the same time. Examining the service structure to determine what modifications might be suggested, working with organizations to assist them in focusing on new resources, providing consultation, education, and training to service providers with respect to the needs of older adults, and promoting new policies for social services among policy makers, complete the full circle of responsibilities professionals must undertake if they are to be successful.

As the field of services to older adults grows, more professional persons will be engaged in these numerous and far-reaching tasks. Greater specialization will undoubtedly reduce the scope of professional responsibility. Yet, even then, the professional person will have to gain a comprehensive knowledge of the issues in the aging process and will have to display eclectic professional skills in order to work successfully with such a diverse group of people as America's older adults. This text builds a framework that will help students in the helping professions meet these challenges.

CHAPTER ONE

COMPLEXITIES OF UNDERSTANDING THE FIELD OF AGING

Klieg lights heated the hallway and tightened the tension. Cameramen were shoving and jostling with the crowd for position in front of the door leading into the Empire meeting room. Only minutes before, people had completely choked the passageway. Now they were behind restraining lines held securely by plainclothes security guards. The chant, "We want Pepper! We want Pepper!," grew louder and more hurried as more and more persons were pushed tighter against the walls by the security guards.

WE WANT PEPPER!
WE WANT PEPPER!
WE WANT PEPPER!
WE WANT PEPPER!

Then he appeared at the end of the hallway. The lights swung in unison to frame him for the cameras, and a roar thundered in the crowded hallway. White-haired, slightly stooped, with large spectacles reflecting the light, Claude Pepper walked briskly through the crowd toward the door. At the door, he was met by two hotel security officers. They asked him for his credentials. No one was allowed into a session of the 1981 White House Conference on Aging without a delegate's or observer's badge issued for *that* session only. Even though Representative Claude Pepper was an honorary chairman of the White House Conference, even though he was a ranking and respected member of the House of Representatives and chairman of the subcommittee on aging, and even though, only the day before, he had given a stirring address to the conference participants in the opening session, eighty-two-year-old Claude Pepper was barred from the very meeting he had fought to establish. The irony turned the crowd to fury.

Let Pepper in!
Let Pepper in!
Let Pepper in!
Let Pepper in!

Pepper, red-faced and angry, turned away as his staff sought to argue with the security guards. Cameras captured the confrontation and goaded the crowd to its breaking point. Any moment, it seemed, the crowd might burst forth and storm the Empire Room. "Let Pepper in! Let Pepper in!" The pitch was higher and the pace quicker. A staff member was permitted to enter and another staff member left the Empire Room and returned quickly with Pepper and ushered him into the meeting room. The door was closed and barred by the security guards as cheers went up from the crowd.

Pepper was in. He was in the meeting room in which recommendations were being considered and discussion was continuing on matters of economic security among older adults. The specific subject was social security, and the concern among the delegates was that this White House Conference on Aging and the committee on economic security would become a forum to advance recommendations to alter social security. It seemed that the year of preparation for the White House Conference on Aging was reduced to this single issue. Will the social security system be preserved? Claude Pepper, in the unusual political position of advocacy, advanced as the white knight to save social security.

The complexities of growing old in America were dramatically acted out in Washington, D.C., during the four days when 1,500 delegates and observers, and a large number of hastily invited guests of the administration, met from November 30 through December 3, 1981 at the third official White House Conference on Aging. The *Final Report* of this conference, promoted as "A National Policy on Aging," tells how well-off older Americans are.

> There appears to be a misconception among some that the aged in America are: victims of poverty; abandoned by their families . . . ; living in deteriorated housing; victims of inflation; prisoners in their homes and neighborhoods; isolated from family, friends, and society; forced into premature retirement. . . . Indeed, emphasis on the problems of the elderly has obscured the single most extraordinary fact about the great majority of the elderly Americans: They are the wealthiest, best-fed, best-housed, healthiest, most self-reliant older population in our history.[1]

---

[1]*Final Report: The 1981 White House Conference on Aging,* 3 vols. (Washington: Department of Health and Human Services, June 1982), 1, 8.

The complexity of growing old in America is only partly reflected by the contrasting views about life in the older adult years. The glowing report of the 1981 White House Conference on Aging contrasts with familiar pictures of stooped and broken elderly who live in hovels and scrape to buy essential food. The complexity arises from the kinds of people who are older, the views Americans hold about what kind of society they want, and the actions that these now-retired older Americans undertook to create that kind of society. The 1981 White House Conference on Aging demonstrated the inherent complications as the delegates fought for recommendations they believed would best help older persons.

In 1979 Congress appropriated money for a third White House Conference on Aging. Then President Jimmy Carter appointed a conference director, deputy director, and a national advising committee. President Reagan brought to the presidency a different view of social problems and of the responsibility of government from that of President Carter, particularly as it related to the responsibility of the federal government to address social problems. Such a change, he affirmed, was a mandate from the electorate. Certainly seizing the political opportunity to alter national policies is in the best tradition of American government. But when it came to dealing with the social priorities of older adults, President Reagan's approaches clashed directly with the expectations of the older adults themselves.

Early in his presidency, Reagan accused the social security system of contributing to increased inflation and excessive government spending. When he publicly proposed social security reductions, Congress passed a resolution stating strong bipartisan support for the social security program. The new president also appointed a new director of the White House Conference on Aging. Mr. Rust had been the Republican counsel for the Senate Committee on Aging, and he brought considerable enthusiasm with him for the new job. Perhaps he was too enthusiastic because he was replaced, only a few months before the conference was due to begin, by a person previously unknown for work with older people.

As the time to begin the conference drew closer, considerable confusion developed in the planning process. The delegates were selected by the governors, according to strict formulas set by Congress. But several weeks before the conference was due to begin, state delegations were enlarged with additional White House appointees. In state after state, new faces appeared at state planning meetings with official letters from the White House Conference. There was no way to verify how these new delegates were chosen. New York had its delegation enlarged by sixty members; California's delegation swelled by one hundred and North Carolina's increased by fifteen.

Concerned that these efforts would destroy the opportunity to develop workable recommendations through the conference process, voluntary organizations that served older adults met to develop a set of objectives they would try to steer through the conference. The Leadership Caucus, as this coalition was called, developed eight recommendations that they called Eight for the Eighties. Jack Ossofsky, the executive director of the National Council on the Aging, chaired the Leadership Caucus. The eight recommendations were modest ones; the strongest was to preserve social security in its existing form.

As the beginning of the conference drew closer, the conference rules committee determined that there would be no vote on individual recommendations by all of the conference delegates. Anxiety increased. The reports of the fourteen working committees would comprise the conference recommendations. In other words, what each committee decided for itself would become the official conference recommendation. Concern spread that if key committees, such as the one on economic security, were dominated by delegates who sought to change such traditional programs as social security, the very fabric of government support for older people could be in danger. Indeed, the fear proved true. The committee on economic security, in its first meeting on December 1, received numerous recommendations that social security be drastically revised. One of the most damaging recommendations was made by Bruce Nestande. His recommendation called for extensive changes in social security, including a gradual phasing out of the system.

Nestande was a Republican member of the California legislature from Orange County. He had been one of the coordinators for the Reagan presidential campaign in southern California, and his disdain for government welfare programs was well known. He was also a last-minute, White-House-appointed delegate. After he offered his recommendation, he returned to California. He was not interested in the rest of the conference. The damage had been done, however. The recommendation was on the table and due to be voted on sometime the next day.

Word of this manipulation spread quickly through the conference, and delegates told one another about similar tactics in other committees. There appeared to be an effort to stack the committees against liberal proposals. The committee chairpersons were all chosen by the White House. Most committees passed rules limiting debate on issues and limiting who could submit recommendations. The Leadership Caucus acted quickly. It held an open meeting in the Great Ballroom of the Shoreham Hotel, right across from the headquarters hotel. The meeting was advertised as a "speak-out" session in which people could tell what was going on in various committee meetings. It was chaired by Charles Schottland, a well-known social welfare administrator, himself retired. Delegate after delegate came to the microphones and described the abuses in the conference sessions. Some complained that they were not allowed to speak. Others complained that recommendations were ruled out of order. Others complained that ultraconservative delegates, like Nestande, were given special privileges in some meetings. All the speakers called for action.

Finally, as midnight approached, a black woman from New York, her face deeply lined from years of toil, rose and asked the group to call Representative Claude Pepper to intervene. "Mr. Pepper," she declared, "believes in old people. Ask him to come to this meeting so we can ask him to help us. Certainly, Congress won't let us down!" She returned to her seat amid cheers and chants. "We want Pepper!" The tone of the meeting changed; complaints changed to appeals for action; speaker after speaker pleaded for Pepper to come to the rescue. Shortly before midnight, the crowd was clamoring for Pepper to appear. He had spoken strongly earlier in the day. At last he came. When the cheers died down, Pepper gave an impassioned plea for an open conference, pledged the support of Congress for social security, and vowed to attend the session of the committee on economic security, thus setting the stage for the following day's confrontation. The crowd left the Shoreham Hotel singing, "*We shall overcome!*"

The final recommendations on social security adopted by the White House Conference on Aging were mild compared with recommendations like Nestande's. Most called for changes to give older people more options to work and maintain social security coverage. What seemed to be an effort to manipulate the conference collapsed as the original, state-appointed delegates held strongly to their positions. Rather than ending in acrimony, the conference closed with some optimism. The recommendations have been printed and distributed and, for practical purposes, all but forgotten. What has not been forgotten, however, are the politics of aging demonstrated by the conference. As such, the 1981 White House Conference on Aging illustrates many significant features that must be considered in any study about older Americans.

AGING AND POLITICS

Older people have political power they are just beginning to exercise. They represent a numerically important segment of the population, and they are wise to the ways of politics. Many participated in and learned from the civil rights struggles of the 1960s. Others have been administrators and political officials. Some, like Claude Pepper, still hold political office. Most vote and are better informed about government than the average American. This political sophistication has helped older adults understand that through political efforts, public programs can be undertaken that will benefit the whole community. In other words, older Americans today are increasingly likely to strive for public policies that address a broad range of issues facing older people. They are less interested in seeking their own, more individualized solutions to individual problems, but it is not unusual for older people to be able to come together in a coalition, such as the Leadership Caucus, as they did prior to the White House Conference. They realized that collective action on eight issues was preferable to countless actions on multiple issues. And they realized that one issue was more important than any other: income security and the social security program. Furthermore, they were able to agree to work together to achieve success on the issue they chose.

The political maturity and skill of older people is impressive and effective. While it is difficult to identify an "aging coalition" as such, the politics of aging and the policies that this political involvement has generated have aided, greatly, the well-being of older people. If our older Americans are "the wealthiest, best-fed, best-housed, healthiest, and most self-reliant" of any generation of older Americans, it is because their political maturity has stimulated the development of public policies and public programs that have made them so. Thus, in order to serve older people well, it is important that policies be developed that continue to provide a foundation for broad-based social programs, not only to maintain the present social and economic position of older people, but to improve that position as well. Older people may be well-off as a group, or when compared to the elders who preceded them, but there is still too much poverty, unhappiness, and desperation among far too many. Thus serving older people requires that older people be supported in this political tradition.

AGING AND ECONOMICS

Older people are very concerned about their personal economic security. This was evident at the White House Conference on Aging both from the recommendations developed in the committee on economic security and from the unusually high number of recommendations in other committees that also related to economic concerns. More than 40 percent of the recommendations dealt with matters of personal economics. This concern is generated less by avarice than by the realization that most older people are independent and want to remain so. The heavy emphasis on independence derives from ideological preferences deeply rooted in this generation of older people. For example, most older people object to accepting government aid, and many even dislike accepting their social security checks, although their right to these checks was established by their own contributions as workers. While older people desire strong ties with children, they want their financial independence even more. And because their incomes are fixed, they are vulnerable to economic cycles. Even as children struggle for economic and personal freedom independent of the larger family, so too older adults cherish the same sense of personal freedom that comes with financial security.

Unfortunately, older people as a group are not well-off financially. In 1979 the mean family income from all sources, for all families, was $22,375 per year. In families headed by someone age sixty-five or older, the mean yearly income was $14,727. Even granting the usual caveats—that older people have fewer fixed expenses, their families are smaller, and they have special tax advantages—the discrepancy in income remains a striking characteristic of older adulthood. Yet there is optimism among older people, even among those with the tightest incomes. Provided that those incomes can be maintained to meet a modest standard of living, older people are satisfied with their lives. Helping older people requires an understanding of the delicate relationship between personal economic security and personal independence. When income falls, older people quickly lose a sense of personal security. Thus, efforts to assist older people to maintain their financial stability are basic to all other efforts to assist them.

AGING AND SOCIETY

Older people form a socially heterogeneous group, and their interests and abilities are as wide-ranging as American society itself. At the most recent White House Conference on Aging, the delegates and observers represented every imaginable segment of American society. There were women and men, of all nationalities and all races, from all parts of the country, with all levels of wealth and social standing and with a wide range of physical capacity—from people with serious illnesses to those who jogged daily along Rock Creek Parkway. Most seemed like "normal American people."

But with this diversity comes the diversity of need. The 600 recommendations produced by the White House Conference on Aging represent an unfinished American social agenda. Moreover, there are older people with very special problems and needs. Some need special medical care. Others need special counseling for mental problems. Others have anxieties and concerns for which they seek special services. Some need more special assistance from public programs than do others. Some older people can drive; others require innovative forms of public transportation.

The major questions that ran through the White House Conference on Aging concerned the society or the culture in which older people live. Whether American society is ready for its older population was a central theme of much of the discussion. Maggie Kuhn, who formed the Gray Panthers, held her own Conference on Aging while the 1981 White House Conference was in session. Ms. Kuhn and many of her followers believe that without radical social and structural change, American institutions will continue to discriminate against older adults. The efforts of Ms. Kuhn, as well as those of contemporary scholars, have suggested that America is growing older. *The Graying of America* is the title of one such study.[2] In 1890, the median age in America was twenty-two. Today it is thirty. Not only are people living longer, but more people are living longer. While the American population is aging, it is also becoming more complex. All forms of change are more rapid. New technologies, new social customs, new social institutions, such as new family forms, and new ways of understanding our environment move rapidly through the lives of young and old alike. Transitions to these new ways of thinking and doing are difficult for everyone, but they present special challenges for older people for whom the view of the future had always been conditioned by views of the past.

Older people face new social challenges for which there has been no preparation. Family life is different. Children leave home when parents are in their late forties or early fifties. The postparental period has lengthened for many older people. With this comes longer periods of marriage than most older adults ever dreamed when they first married. A longer postparental period means that many older women begin seeking rewarding non–family-related vocations without much preparation, and in an increasingly tightening labor market. Many older persons will also experience some period of single living, due either to separation, divorce, or death. Retirement carries with it a prolonged period of time when gainful employment is no longer essential to sustain the living standard. However, older people are concerned about whether they will have enough postretirement income to live frugally. Social displacement and uncertainty about the future contribute to the unresolved concerns of growing older in America.

[2] James A. Jorgensen, *The Graying of America* (New York: Dial, 1980), p. 32.

America is changing rapidly, but whether these changes will be supportive of older people remains a very uncertain question. For example, at the same time that older people need the security that comes from income support systems such as social security, some in society are suggesting that social security is too costly and should be abandoned or significantly changed. These forces come together to present a complex social mosaic for today's older Americans. The social transitions in older adulthood today are more challenging than they have ever been, while at the same time there is serious concern as to whether sufficient social institutions exist to ease these transitions for older adults. These questions provided the underlying sense of urgency at the 1981 White House Conference on Aging.

THE LIVES OF OLDER AMERICANS

It is almost impossible to convey the political, social, and economic circumstances affecting the lives of older people through a discussion of them. The circumstances themselves are complex, and they impinge differently on different people. Older people represent such a diverse group that patterns are hard to identify. Perhaps the best way to illustrate the social, economic, and political impact on older people is through their own eyes. Here are some examples of how older people live and how life events condition their lives.

The Davises

Mr. and Mrs. Davis live in Miami, Florida. They moved there, like so many others, seeking fulfillment of their lifelong dreams of retirement. Mr. Davis was a salesman for a large industrial toolmaker. He is seventy-six years old. Mrs. Davis is seventy-two. She never graduated from high school, but she held well-paid jobs as an accountant after educating herself sufficiently to meet the requirements for those positions. They were married in 1929 and suffered through the Great Depression with no steady work, little money, and a young child. Mr. Davis had a childhood illness that disqualified him from military service, and during World War II they were able to develop some social and economic stability and to move ahead financially. They built a house after the war in a northern city and raised their family.

Ever since they visited Florida in 1952, they dreamed of returning there. The mild climate and easy lifestyle was in sharp contrast to the hard work and cold winters of Philadelphia. So when Mr. Davis reached age sixty-five and his company unceremoniously discharged him, after an initial hesitation, the Davises sold their house at a nice profit, bought a small travel trailer, and set off for Florida.

They felt more like vagabonds when they reached Florida, and to feel "rooted" again, they purchased a house. But they were unsettled socially, and the house seemed like a burden, so they sold that house at some financial loss and bought a share of an apartment complex that had complete recreation privileges.

Here they seemed content for the next several years. Mr. Davis played shuffleboard and Mrs. Davis became involved in the many club and social activities organized for and by the residents. In his younger years, Mr. Davis had some serious medical problems requiring surgery. Shortly after they settled in the apartment complex, Mr. Davis' ulcer became troublesome, requiring him to be hospitalized. Medicare paid $5,000 worth of bills, and the Davises paid about $1,000. Follow-up visits with the doctor left Mr. Davis anxious about his medical condition. The doctor recommended surgery, but Mr. Davis did not feel it was necessary. He found a new doctor after a search of several months.

Mr. Davis also learned that the company from which he retired had been acquired by a new firm. Although his pension would be continued because of federal legislation, it was reduced to the minimum amount. Social security payments became more important as the Davises tightened their belts to try to protect their meager savings. Then they learned that the owner of the land on which their cooperative apartment was built was raising the land rent substantially. The Davises thought they owned their apartment but learned that they had only bought "shares" in the entire development; these shares were offered by the owner, who had the right to raise land rent as he saw fit. Thus, instead of supporting them adequately in an inflation-safe retirement home, the Davis' fixed income was being eroded quickly by inflationary pressures.

Mrs. Davis was active in local politics, and through her contacts with local and state political figures she was helpful in organizing a residents' association that attempted to litigate the problem of escalating land rents. But after a series of legal setbacks, the residents became frustrated and the association began to fall apart. About the same time, Mr. Davis needed further surgery. He was hospitalized for five days at a cost of $12,000. Fortunately, Medicare paid about $9,000 of these costs, yet the balance owed drained the Davis' resources further. Mr. Davis went into a state of depression after the operation, but after six weeks he began to get back his old spirit.

After much soul-searching, the Davises decided to leave the apartment complex and buy a small house where prices were more affordable. They have put their apartment up for sale, and if they get their asking price, the move will not result in a financial loss. They are looking forward to leaving the complex. After ten years they had become very disillusioned with the glamor of retirement. They found living with other older people uninspiring, even though some of their closest friends were among this group.

The Davis' two sons who, with their families, live in northern cities and visit several times a year. The Davises often wish for a closer relationship with their children, but, on the other hand, they have come to enjoy their freedom to come and go without the responsibility of an extended family. Mr. Davis enjoys small woodworking and glassmaking projects. His new house will give him more space to work on these. Their friends in the complex think they are foolish to make such a move at the present time. They seem to have everything they want—a nice place to live with complete leisure and recreation facilities. They are taking major responsibility for maintenance of a house in addition to entering a financial venture that could prove costly.

Mr. and Mrs. Davis represent a common set of circumstances that are the subject of discussions about policy for older people. Retirement environment often determines the quality of life for many older adults. Housing, in turn, determines the type of housing environment, but older peoples' largest source of retirement assets are tied into housing. Therefore, people like the Davises must risk a loss of assets if they want to change their retirement environment, or if they prefer to protect their assets, they must often accept retirement environments that no longer seem to satisfy their retirement needs.

Mrs. Apple

Mrs. Apple celebrated her eighty-fifth birthday last month in the Presbyterian Home for the Aged. She is in very good physical health, although she is quite cautious about venturing out on her own. She has lived there for fifteen years, since her children convinced her to sell her house and move. Mrs. Apple does not resent the move, although she wishes her children would spend more time with her.

Mrs. Apple is wealthy. Her husband did very well in the retail drygoods business, and together they were well-known contributors to worthwhile local projects. Mrs. Apple has four sons and two daughters, and a total of thirty-one grandchildren and great-grandchildren. Most of the family live nearby, and someone is likely to take her out for dinner each week. The remaining time Mrs. Apple spends with her friends at the home. She reads, but she also watches television most of the time.

Mrs. Apple has her own room at the home, and in it she has many personal items, each part of the family heritage. She has her writing desk, a lamp she and Mr. Apple bought for their first house, and a small collection of figurines given to her by her grandchildren over the years.

Mrs. Apple is friendly and quick-witted, and she loves to talk about the past years of the Apple family. She knows, or knew, most of the outstanding people who participated in the events that shaped local history; and she loves to talk about this history and its people, with scrapbooks spread out in front of her. Occasionally a professor from the nearby college visits to ask questions about the past. This is always an occasion for Mrs. Apple. With the help of one of these professors the family published a private edition of the history of the Apple family in the community. All the family members were presented with copies several Christmases ago.

Mrs. Apple seems happy with her life at the Presbyterian Home, although there are days when she is very lonely and would like to be a more active part of the life around her, particularly the life of her children and grandchildren. During these times she often talks with the attendants about her home with longing for the days past. As she talks, the attendants grow restless and allow the ever-glowing television to draw her deeper into the world of fantasy.

Mrs. Apple represents some of the problems of life in institutional care facilities. People like Mrs. Apple are often isolated from the substance of family life, even when family members maintain contact. Life in even the best retirement homes quickly becomes an artificial life form. To the extent that older people can remain in their own homes, they have a better chance of meaningful experiences with family and loved ones.

The Pruits

Mr. and Mrs. Pruit also live in a church-sponsored retirement center, the Mount Digbee Christian Home. They moved there five years ago when they decided to sell the house they had owned and lived in for thirty-five years. It was a lovely little house built right after World War II and packed with all the treasures of fifty-three years of married life. The three children, who grew up in the house, were sorry to see their parents sell it, but none felt they should challenge their parents' decision.

Mrs. Pruit grew up on a farm in the Midwest and married Mr. Pruit, who worked for a utility company. Later they moved east at the convenience of the company. Mrs. Pruit carried with her all the customs of the Midwest; she was a wonderful "down-home" cook, excellent seamstress, award-winning needlecrafter, and devout churchwoman; she was also generous and unassuming. In her quiet but deliberate way, she molded the family, including Mr. Pruit, in her own image. It was Mrs. Pruit who decided they should sell their home and move. Mrs. Pruit was concerned about Mr. Pruit. He had had a heart attack ten years earlier, and although he had recovered, Mrs. Pruit knew there were too many things to do around the house. They had a greenhouse, a vegetable garden, a yard full with flowers, and a workshop with a power saw, a drill press, and a wood lathe. They made hundreds of pounds of candy at Christmas time to be sold to raise funds for the church. There was just too much to do; and Mrs. Pruit decided they needed a change.

They bought a two-room suite, for life, at the Mount Digbee Home. The price was equal to the proceeds of their home, and the agreement they signed with the home was that they would be able to live there for life and receive whatever care they needed, for a set monthly fee. Upon their death, their equity would remain with the church that sponsored the home. With Mr. Pruit's retirement pension, their savings, and social security, they were quite happy and comfortable in their new surroundings. Mrs. Pruit directed the craft program at the home, and they traveled extensively without the responsibility of a household. They adjusted painlessly to separation from their possessions, which were divided among the children.

Two years after they entered the home, Mrs. Pruit had minor physical problems that frightened her. She withdrew from her active schedule with the full support of her physician. Mr. Pruit began to exhibit a variety of physical complaints, and he made occasional visits to the hospital for observation. The Pruits became afraid to travel for fear they would become ill away from home, and they cut down on social contacts.

The Pruits are still active with the church, but they seldom go to services, preferring to attend services in the building. They take most of their meals in the group dining room and visit outside the home only occasionally. Their children live out of town but maintain contact with them by telephone. They hope this year to have a good old-fashioned Thanksgiving with all the family and the commotion of earlier days but, so far, none of the children has made any plans about it.

The Pruits are a lot like Mr. and Mrs. Davis, to the extent that the kind of housing determines the environment in which they live. The Pruits were willing to exchange their independent form of living for a total-care environment. Quality professional services are the key elements to the success of retirement centers like Mount Digbee. Because people like the Pruits no longer have an option about where they live, if the professional services begin to deteriorate, the living environment becomes unsatisfying.

Mrs. Judson

Mrs. Judson is almost ninety years old—she thinks. Her mother was a slave on a large southern plantation, and when she was born is not quite certain. Mrs. Judson was born on a farm less than one hundred miles from where she now lives. During Reconstruction and with the help of the Freeman's Bureau, her family was able to obtain land from the Bureau and, surmounting difficult struggles, to hold the land on which Mrs. Judson still lives. Her twelve children, sixty grandchildren, and many great-grandchildren are spread over the country. Some are professional people. Others are hard workers and simple people like Mrs. Judson.

Mrs. Judson lives by herself. The children added a bathroom to her two-room house ten years ago, and she still feels spoiled by the luxury. She manages a small garden, cooks some of her own meals, and sits on her porch deep in thought. She looks forward to visits from the social worker and the woman from the white church who occasionally brings her a hot lunch. Her hands are tough and calloused, and her face is deeply lined. In the summer, the sun bakes the house and the land around it. In the winter, the harsh winds whip through the frame house. Mrs. Judson's stamina must protect her from the harsh elements of the world because she is one of the warmest and kindest people one can meet. She is happy, and she continuously rejoices that the Lord has blessed her so abundantly.

During the week at least one of her granddaughters usually comes to deliver some food and fix up around the house. On special occasions more of the family comes. These are happy times for Mrs. Judson, although she often forgets who is who in the large family. Since she still lives on the family land, everyone comes home when they visit Mrs. Judson.

Mrs. Judson was examined by a doctor about five years ago. The social worker thought she should be "checked." That was the only time Mrs. Judson remembers seeing a doctor. She complains occasionally about pain in her legs and stomach, but she would never think of seeing a doctor, and the social worker would probably not recommend it after all the stress of the last checkup.

Mrs. Danforth

Mrs. Danforth is eighty years old. When she is home, she lives in her own house in Columbia, South Carolina; but Mrs. Danforth is not home very often. Her travel schedule keeps her out of town more than half of the year, and when she is in town, she is just as busy with local and state issues. She also finds time to assist in and enjoy a wide variety of local cultural affairs, from the visiting-artist program sponsored by the local university to participation in the local chapter of the Woman's Club.

Mrs. Danforth is a former administrator of a large federal social welfare agency and also former administrator of the state's social welfare programs. She has been past chairman or past president of most of the national social welfare organizations, and she continues in important leadership roles with a number of them. She is an imposing force in state politics. Most people who have worked with her and for her comment on her continuing influence and her ability to realize goals that would be impossible for others. She is a hard-driving person, and during her career, she has earned the respect of enemies and friends alike.

Mrs. Danforth's husband died about twenty years ago. He was a teacher at the local university. Old friends report that they were very close despite Mrs. Danforth's own demanding career. The social occasions at their home were full of music, good conversation, and laughter. Born in a small mountain community and educated at a large metropolitan university in the Midwest, Mrs. Danforth is a charming person whose imposing presence cannot be overlooked in any group setting.

Last year Mrs. Danforth contracted influenza and developed complications from it, including pneumonia. She had to be hospitalized at one point for a couple of days, and her friends became quite concerned for her. Her recovery was slow. She lost weight and her active schedule was severely limited. She continued her numerous projects from her living room, and gradually, as her health built up, her pace of activity increased; she is now working at her previous level.

One of Mrs. Danforth's current commitments is to assist in the development of quality home-based services for older people. Her work with the National Home Caring Council has been a pioneer effort to develop standards for home-based services, to identify local public and voluntary organizations that successfully provide these services, and to certify these organizations as a means of insuring public safety in the use of such services. Since this effort began, organizations have been certified in every state, and the movement is growing, particularly as greater emphasis is placed on developing alternatives to institutional care for older people.

Mrs. Danforth talks very little about herself, but when she occasionally lapses into personal conversation, she reveals a generous spirit and a kind heart. She is very happy with the way she lives. She feels that she has made an important contribution to society during her years of public service. When friends ask why she works so hard, she replies that she would not have it any other way.

Mrs. Danforth is a successful example of an older person living at home without the need for outside resources. But, in the case of Mrs. Danforth, back-up resources are necessary if and when she has some difficulty. The informal support system is very important to older people like Mrs. Danforth because older people who are not dependent on a formal support system may, from time to time, need some social supports. It is not unusual that, lacking an informal support system, older people who live independently are placed in nursing homes or in hospitals at the slightest provocation, because often less formal resources do not exist.

A PERSPECTIVE ON AMERICA'S ELDERLY

Finding a common theme in the lives of America's older people, as diverse as Claude Pepper and Mrs. Judson, may be impossible, unless the theme itself is diversity. No single factor—degree of activity, level of health, amount of income, place of residence, type of post-employment interests—seems to define America's older adults. They are all different. To some extent, the society in which they live gives some direction to the course of their lives, but change is the most common social experience for all older people. Moreover, for reasons to be explained later, older people themselves cling to individualism. They are fiercely independent and want to be seen and treated as individuals. Thus, despite all efforts to generalize about older people, the most that can be said, to assist professional helpers understand older people better, is that older people cannot be understood as a group.

A product of this phenomenon of uniqueness in older adults is the growing trend of individualized and personalized policies, programs, and professional helping techniques. The tradeoff in this trend toward personalized assistance is a decrease in dependency among older people, and older people and their families. All current portraits of older adulthood show a network of support that includes family and friends to some degree but does not depend upon the family as the primary foundation of support. Whether this pattern is the product of changing family relationships and responsibility, or whether the pattern itself contributes to changing forms remains an endlessly debated question. On the one hand, current efforts strive to re-engage older Americans with mainstream society, but on the other, the provision of social resources, from income maintenance to in-home services, removes intimate forms of interdependent obligations from older people and permits a different kind of social isolation to prevail.

The final section of this book discusses some of the important questions that remain as America struggles to provide better resources for its older people. Certainly evaluating the shift in dependency in older adulthood from the family to the society is one question that will have to be examined. At present it is important to recall that the challenge presented by the diversity of older adults requires a greater and more extended helping approach than has been attempted previously by American public policy. This approach includes efforts to insure the independence among older people that they are seeking, while at the same time strengthening the assistance-providing capacity of traditional institutions, such as the family, all without placing burdens of dependency on any of the parties. The task is difficult to achieve and perhaps even more difficult to understand.

The first part of this book is designed to provide a base for understanding why older people are as diverse as they are. The three themes addressed are social explanations, which include a review of theories explaining older adulthood; economic explanations, which show the important interplay of personal and social economics in the lives of older people; and political explanations, which suggest how a growing political astuteness among older people has helped forge the present public response to them and their problems. The social theories of older adulthood, discussed in Chapter 2, provide a base for the chapters that follow.

CHAPTER TWO

UNDERSTANDING OLDER PEOPLE

Complexity and change mark the world of older Americans. Adults who are now sixty, seventy, and eighty years old experienced two world wars, an economic depression that altered the political fabric of our nation, an explosion in human rights that changed the social context of their lives, and developments in technology, the impact of which it is still impossible to measure. Few older Americans ever anticipated the relative security they enjoy, yet by all objective accounts, older people are poorer and more socially disadvantaged than the vast majority of Americans. Older people fall below the median in all social-demographic statistics except age. The paradox of older adulthood in America may well be that the only similar characteristic among older people is their inferior status in American life. The great social changes that today's older people have experienced, and even helped create, seem to have left them behind rather than in the forefront of the quest for the benefits of life in America.

Partly because older people have had different experiences and react differently to the rapid changes in their lives, a growing number of theories have been proposed to describe and explain why older people are the way they are, in the hope that through a better understanding of older people will come more effective means of helping them live satisfying and dignified lives. This chapter provides a survey of those theories developed to explain aging and to attempt to shed some light on the many debatable characteristics of older adulthood. The purpose of any theory is to provide a framework for understanding better the subject of study. A theory provides a means to organize a variety of observations into an orderly explanation. Thus theories about aging and older adulthood provide professional people with a deeper knowledge about what kinds of activities will be helpful.

This chapter explores five contemporary theoretical approaches to aging and older people: cohorts, life experience theories, developmental theory, sociological theories, and medical-biological theories, including some current theories of aging advanced by mental health specialists. This long list suggests two important features of theories on aging. First, each professional discipline presents a view of aging unique to its professional orientation. Second, there is no consensus, no single theory of aging. Thus professional people are cautioned to view these theories with an open mind, and when appropriate, to explore some of them in greater detail.

CURRENT EXPLANATIONS OF THE EXPERIENCE OF AGING

Growing Older in Cohorts

Older people must be understood both in today's context and in the context of major historical events that have shaped their lives. The social and political contexts that have influenced older people's lives and how they thought about life remain crucial to what they think about life as they live it today. Older people often criticize younger people for not doing things the way older people have been accustomed to. Conversely, younger people often show surprising impatience with older people when they do not accept contemporary ways of life. Moreover, older people may differ in their attitudes and opinions, depending on just how old they are—some in their eighties may have raised younger people who are now in their fifties and sixties. Thus, growing older in America cannot be understood very well without understanding *cohorts.*

The word *cohort* means "an enclosed company." Cohorts might be thought of as classmates. At a university, for example, the class of 1973 is very different from the class of 1983. The people in one class get to know one another, some begin life-long friendships, and a sense of kinship develops. The experiences of this group have a certain similarity, even though they were lived individually. There might have been an important football game, or perhaps there was another campus-wide event that became a focal point around which other experiences shaped a generalized sense that this or that graduating class has a uniqueness about it that separates it from the others. When that group leaves the university it carries with it characteristics of the particular class. This is a cohort: a group of people enclosed by a common experience.

The idea of cohorts is very useful to understanding older people. Examining cohorts of older people around just one major social, economic, and political event, the Great Depression of the 1930s, illustrates the significance of cohorts in understanding older people (Table 2-1).

TABLE 2-1   Selected Aging Cohorts: Age at Time of Critical Events

WORLD WAR I (1914–1917)	GREAT DEPRESSION (1929–1935)	WORLD WAR II (1942–1945)	BABY BOOM (1946–1950)	TODAY (1985)
16–18 years old (possibly in war)	35–37 years old (young families)	45–47 years old (possibly in war)	45–47 years old (steady period)	85 years old
6–8 years old	21–26 years old (older children in depression families)	35–37 years old (probably in war)	37–41 years old (raising families)	75 years old
	11–16 years old (younger children in depression families)	25–27 years old (probably in war)	27–31 years old ("Now" generation)	65 years old
		14–17 years old	17–21 years old (Living with depression-era parents)	55 years old
			7–11 years old ("Baby boom" generation)	45 years old

Everyone who is sixty-five years old today, or older, experienced the Great Depression in some way. As will be discussed later, the Great Depression had a profound influence on most policies and programs that exist today to serve older people. The Great Depression was of such significance that it had some influence on all who lived through it, but that influence was different for each, depending on whatever else was happening when the Great Depression struck. Those who are now sixty-five years old would have been about eleven years old during the most severe part of the depression. They probably remember their parents struggling to make ends meet, and they may recall all the personal sacrifices exacted from them during those difficult times.

Those who are now seventy-five years old, however, had different experiences with perhaps more chilling and more devastating effects. These people were young adults, possibly married, perhaps even with a family of one or two small children. Already on tight personal budgets, with great responsibilities, these people faced the depression under severe personal stress due to total loss or serious reduction of income. They had babies to feed and clothe, without any public resources. For assistance they may have stood in line for free food. The specter of hunger, sickness, and perhaps even the death of loved ones was not fantasy for this cohort. Having some personal financial security before the depression, and suddenly being without, through no fault of their own, left a profound psychological impression on many of them. Because they experienced loss of independence in a most personal way, it is easier to appreciate the fierce sense of personal independence that this cohort of older people places foremost in their lives today.

Those who are fifty-five years old today and just facing the prospect of retirement were small children during the depression. They had few personal experiences of the depression that were bad enough to have a lasting effect on their lives. They heard stories from their parents, perhaps, but they are a cohort with a different orientation. Instead they probably recall—vividly—World War II. That event made a strong impression on them and will likely influence the way this cohort views the problems and challenges of older age as the time for more life change draws nearer.

Cohorts help explain the wide variation in the way older people live and the varied explanations about why they live as they do. Much has been said, for example, about older people who want to live in retirement communities where all amenities are provided for a fixed monthly rate; yet about 65 percent of all people over the age of sixty-five have bought and paid for their own homes.[1] Closer examination reveals that it is the youngest cohort of older people that prefers the retirement communities, while the older cohorts prefer living in homes they have lived in most of their lives.

Thus, understanding aging cohorts helps explain why older people do not think and behave as a single group. Not only is each older person different in life experiences, but older adults gained these experiences at different times in their lives and thus developed different reactions to the events. Older people have vastly different expectations for themselves, which are rooted in a personal psychology that evolved within the context of these important life-shaping historical events.

Life Events and the Aging Individual

One theory of aging attempts to explain the aging process and the subsequent behavior of older people as a product of life changes that create pressure, challenge, and stress for the individual. In contrast to the significance of historical events that defines a cohort of older people, life event theory explains aging as a product of the way people have adjusted and adapted to the usual life experiences. For example, marriage, divorce, and sudden financial or career reversal, or an important education experience, are events that leave a lasting impact on anyone's life. These events do not occur in a vacuum, however, but in ever-changing combinations with other personal, social, and historical events. Although it is easy to understand how a single life event causes stress and strain for the individual, we still know very little about how to judge the effect of several, varied events in interaction. For example, the interaction of personal life events such as marriage and financial loss may leave a different imprint when the nation is in a depression than when the nation is highly prosperous. In the former case a sense of hopelessness and helplessness may prevail; in the latter, a sense of personal responsibility may develop. Moreover, the life event itself may be perceived differently by different persons depending upon

---

[1]U.S. Department of Health and Human Services, *Income of the Population 55 and Over, 1978* (Washington: Social Security Administration, 1981), 40–48.

personality factors. For some, retirement is a dreaded experience, but for others it is looked forward to with great relief. Finally, people possess different capacities for adapting to and integrating life experiences. A financial loss may be accepted much more easily by someone with adequate financial resources than by someone who has none. Thus, this theory of aging, which relies upon life events to explain the aging process, presents a complex model, but one that closely replicates the reality of older adulthood.

Although the model is complex, the theory itself remains very general. It does not identify general patterns that would suggest guidance and predictive ability. In other words, given that life events interact with personal characteristics and other factors in a person's life, are there any *patterned* personal and social characteristics that would suggest that an older person would be likely to behave this or that way if this or that event interacted with this or that personal characteristic? Linda George, a researcher at the Duke University Center for the Study of Aging and Human Development, suggests that if the life-event theories are combined with life-cycle, developmental, theories of aging, some patterns may be found that offer better explanations of the nature of older adulthood. Dr. George and other life-cycle theorists assume that life events are age-related. "Clearly," she says, "certain life events are closely linked with age or stage of life cycle. Different family-based events are likely in late life than are typical in early adulthood."[2] In other words, important life events also happen at certain ages. For example, marriages take place at certain ages, rearing a family is an age-relevant experience, and so on.

To the extent that it is organized and presented as a theory, the life-event theory differs significantly from the cohort approach to understanding older people. The cohort approach recognizes that events occur independent of the age of the individual; the life-cycle theory suggests that events occur with respect to age. Through application of the idea of cohorts, patterns become evident, and the predictive value of a traditional life-event theory greatly expands. Considerable attention has been given to age-specific characteristics of the aging process. The problems with age-specific theories should become clear as these theories are discussed below. The cohort approach proposes that older people within a single cohort project similar, rather than different, characteristics. A cohort theory of understanding older people, which is not an age-specific theory, may be best understood by examining some age-specific theories such as life-event and developmental, or life-cycle, theories, which are the most widely discussed of all theories of growing older.

Developmental Theories of Aging

Developmental theories of aging contrast with the idea of cohorts. Simply stated, developmental theories hold that aging is part of a life process that begins at birth and ends with death, a cycle composed of several stages, periods, or "bench-

[2] Linda K. George, "Models of Transition in Middle and Later Life," *Annals of the American Academy of Political and Social Science* 464 (November 1982), 29.

marks": infancy, early childhood, puberty, adolescence, young adulthood, maturity, and old age. Each of these stages is associated with particular life events that have something to do with mastering certain life tasks. Mastering these life tasks leads to personal fulfillment and capacity to move successfully on to the next stage.

Perhaps no one has explored developmental theory more thoroughly and understandably than Erik Erikson. Like most general psychological theories of growth and development, Erikson's approach to understanding aging through development views life as a progression from incompleteness to completeness over some period of time. In his book *Identity, Youth and Crisis,* Erikson proposes specific personal tasks that must be mastered for successful progression from one life stage to the next.[3] For example, the school-aged child, usually eight to twelve years old, struggles to master the tensions between new-found social and physical abilities, represented by increased industry, with an emerging sense of inferiority stemming from earlier childhood experiences of helplessness. Departing somewhat from the benchmark terms listed above, Erikson calls the final stage in life *maturity,* a stage in which the person struggles with issues of integrity on the one hand and despair and disgust on the other:

> Only he who in some way has taken care of things and people and has adapted himself to the triumphs and disappointments of being by necessity the originator of others and the generator of things and ideas—only he may gradually grow the fruit of seven stages. I know of no better word than *integrity.* . . . Despair expresses the feeling that the time is short, too short for the attempt to start another life and to try out alternative roads to integrity.[4]

The sense of despair, that life has passed by, a fixation on the earlier, youthful days when life seemed fullest, is often the depression that captures older people, and leads helpers to urge older people to "accept their age." In the context of Erikson's life-cycle theory, this despair among older people is a result of long-standing struggles to achieve personal completeness; it is not a matter of facing a reality that one is no longer physically or mentally capable of doing things that were important during earlier life periods. Consequently, remonstrations to accept the realities of reduced functioning in maturity entirely miss the point, which is the *quality* of the struggles that despairing older people face.

Though most helping professions today accept developmental theory as an explanation for existing human social, psychological, and biological states, there are elements of that theory that should be examined critically by those who work with older people. First, developmental theory assumes a progression to completeness and expects movement toward a specific known, human state. This idea of progression suggests some design in life which, if followed, leads to a better human state than when the design is not followed. Developmental theories also assume that

---

[3] Erik Erikson, *Identity and the Life Cycle* (New York: International Universities Press, 1959), 120.

[4] Ibid., 98.

there are times in the growth of the human being when social, psychological, and biological forces have a differing impact on the human state. Finally, developmental theory assumes that there is a time when these forces come together in such a way that the human state reaches its most exalted form, or, as is sometimes observed, the person is at the "peak" of life. Conversely, developmental theory assumes that after the peak of life, particularly in the later years, progressively less exalted states are the expected course of affairs.

Erikson's scheme of human development has its antecedent in the "epigenetic principle," an abstract conception that has to do with the development of theories: "The principle states that any theory that grows has a *grand plan*, and that out of this grand plan, the *parts* arise, each part having its *time* of special ascendancy, until all parts have arisen to form a *functioning whole*."[5] It is from this context that Erikson identified the special timing of ascendancy in human life, which he called *stages*. He likewise believes that developmental theory leads to that special time that he calls a functioning whole, when everything seems to come together. From that point, growth stops, and its antithesis, *aging*, begins. "Metabolism" is reached with the prime of life, then "catabolism" increases until death. Thus according to Erikson and similarly inclined developmental theorists, aging is the downhill part of life, until life ends. The life cycle is said to be complete in death.

The epigenetic theory of life also suggests that the "grand plan" has a particular time span, somewhat less than one hundred years. Technology may make the aging process less noticeable but will not extend the length of the cycle to any appreciable extent. Hence it is possible to plot a *life curve* that shows how, as technology reduces the significance of social, biological, and psychological trauma, a perfect aging curve becomes more a reality (Figure 2-1). Developmental theory emphasizes progressive biological deterioration as the main element in the aging process. In this view, the popular biological model of aging suggests that as people age they lose "reserves" or capacity to react favorably to events or to ward off illness and forms of social and psychological trauma. Diminished ability, in this view, is part of a normal aging process. As a result, the combination of increasing incapacity with unanticipated illnesses, or trauma, produces problems in that the older person is unable to manage life's usual tasks without assistance. Sometimes when this combination occurs, the individual, after a period of repair and recuperation, achieves a plateau and is able to continue relatively independent of assistance. Such a cycle is called a *crisis* situation. But when reserves have deteriorated to the extent that the individual cannot recoup sufficiently to manage life's tasks, the situation is said to be *chronic*. In the extreme form, chronic situations require prolonged nursing care, often until death.

Although developmental theory relies heavily on stages of life through which people pass, it does not necessarily suggest that these stages always take place at the same age in every person's life. In general, however, developmental theory holds that personality changes emerge from the individual and that these changes are

---

[5] Ibid., 52 (emphasis in the original).

universally recognizable. Though developmental theory may not be age-specific, it does suggest that stages, or periods in life, are sequential, each requiring mastery of certain tasks as preparation for the next stage. Successful aging would thus result from successful mastery of life's earlier stages. In this view, physical and psychological degeneration may also be part of successful aging, when the older person accepts it as a normal part of life.

There is considerable difference among developmental theorists over the relevance of developmental theory in explaining older adulthood. Developmental theory does explain the behavior of infants and children quite well. Particularly when developmental theory is applied to cognitive growth, it is very useful in explaining how children mature. However, when applied to later periods of life, and particularly to older adulthood, developmental theory loses much of its explanatory authority. In the first place, by adulthood each individual has already amassed a great variety of experiences, most different in quality than the experiences of anyone else. These different experiences complicate efforts to identify or forecast the individual's successful mastery of life's tasks. In the second place, adulthood is not as sequential as early childhood. Not only do adult social experiences vary in their patterns, but psychological processes also vary among adults. Thus, though it is quite possible that infants and young children face similar developmental stages and tasks of mastery, particularly in the early months and years, the variety of adult experience makes generalizations about later life stages and integrative tasks seem very superficial.

In fact, according to the psychologist K. Warner Schaie, a well-regarded researcher of aging lifestyles: "Because of the multiplicity of situations that elicit meaningful adult behavior it is the *sine qua non* of adult development models that behavioral variability will *increase* over the life span."[6] Variation depends in great measure, as discussed above, upon personal interaction with particular life events, and social events at certain periods or stages of life. Developmental theory does not account very well for the great variety of lifestyles among older adults, and it may well be that excessive life experiences in earlier years account for the limitations that some older people place on their lifestyles in later years. Schaie concludes his discussion with the observation that "as old age is reached a return may occur to greater structural simplicity [in lifestyle] if only to counteract experiential overload."[7]

Perhaps most frustrating, developmental theory fails to explain the downward side of the human life curve. Developmental theory is concerned with growth—growth at one stage in preparation for growth at the next. Particularly in Erikson's model, developmental theory does not satisfactorily account for decay, loss of function, or even long periods of instability as elements of *growth* move toward an end. Developmental theory may in this sense be compared to the massive booster rockets

[6]K. Warner Schaie, "Mid-life to Old Age," *American Journal of Orthopsychiatry* 2 (1981), 201.
[7]Ibid., 205.

on a space satellite. It gets out of the atmosphere, but has no function in controlling the ride in space or returning the vehicle to earth.

The popularity of developmental theory as an explanation of aging and older adulthood has caused some stereotyping of older people and contributed to negative attitudes toward older people among both the general population and helping professionals as well. Developmental theory assumes that increased deterioration is a normal process. It also holds that aging is the prelude to death; a recent rush of literature has suggested that professionals should help older people face and accept death as the final life stage. These prescriptions raise serious professional and personal questions. Should someone be prepared for death, and, if so, how does this preparation take place? Furthermore, in a society that values youth, prefers disposable products to reusable ones, and seeks new models in preference to the old, social values combine with developmental theory to portray a dismal view of the aging process. To the extent that all older adults are seen as being in their final stage of life, they are stereotyped, often in the most negative ways. This attitude is what Robert Butler has frequently called "agism."[8]

Aging and Socialization

Considering the fact that developmental theory is handicapped in explaining older adulthood because of its emphasis on growth, some theorists suggest that adulthood and older adulthood are more likely to be understood in terms of changing personal roles and changing social status. Rather than seeing older adulthood as either a growth period or a steady state, this sociological explanation of aging interprets the changes that take place as modifications of the older person's position in society. For example, as children leave the family to develop independent careers and lifestyles, the parents are still mothers and fathers, but their position as mothers and fathers has changed relative to the mothers and fathers who are still supporting their children. Now they may have more money and time to engage in more personal activities. These parents' role has changed.

Socialization theories, therefore, are concerned with explaining why adults do or do not accept and integrate with the new social roles expected of them. Socialization theories are likely to examine how society provides support for role changes, so as to ease the transition from one set of roles demanded by society to another set of roles.[9] In this view, the rapidly changing diverse society of today presents a wide range of acceptable social roles but places great emphasis on the pace of change in moving from one social role to another. For example, today it might be socially sanctioned for older people to retreat to retirement communities or otherwise maximize personal enjoyment from post-retirement time. In a period of economic insecurity, however, older people might be expected to economize, to sacrifice personal pleasure, and to accept family responsibility, perhaps through car-

[8]Robert Butler, "Psychiatry and the Elderly," *American Journal of Psychiatry* 132 (1978), 9.

[9]Irving Rosow, *Social Integration of the Aged* (New York: Free Press, 1967).

ing for grandchildren so that adult children could be gainfully employed. Role expectations may change rapidly in a dynamic society, and the study of older adulthood from this perspective suggests that different older people have different capacities to move from one set of role expectations to another.

The problems with socialization theories lie in their reliance on socially determined behavioral norms. If society places particular emphasis on one set of behaviors, the focus of social institutions shifts to support the adoption of that set of behaviors among the population. This socialization process is necessary for a well-ordered society but carries a risk: the dominant social norms may not be the right ones for particular population groups. Some situations, such as those that lead to agism, may not serve the welfare of specific populations, such as older people, no matter how well the norms may serve the larger society. In this sense, increased political activity among older people could be explained as an effort to modify social norms that affect them adversely.

Perhaps one of the most puzzling theories of aging to emerge from socialization theory is "disengagement theory." It suggests that as older people continue on the downward side of the life cycle, they begin to withdraw themselves from various forms of social interaction. As chronological aging increases, social activity decreases, social roles change, and social norms support increased isolation of older people; friends are lost through death, and new social relationships are difficult to form and maintain due to the increased incapacity associated with normal aging. The theory thus proposes that older people voluntarily retreat more and more from active social contacts, and consequently the theory assumes that the social isolation often discovered among older people is part of the usual process of aging.

Though now widely disputed, disengagement theory was highly regarded during the 1960s, and it is not difficult to imagine the impact this type of understanding about older people had on the kinds of programs and services that were developed then. In particular, the use of nursing and rest homes increased dramatically. It was also an era of rapid development in housing units specifically designated for older people. The housing patterns for older people that took form during that time have had lasting consequences. It was truly believed that because of role changes older people enjoyed life better in segregated communities, and great efforts were made to promote such communities. Congregate housing and retirement communities were very popular. Retirement was seen as the major role change required of older people. Accepting the new role of retirement meant accepting golf courses, swimming pools, clubhouses, social directors, and many other amenities associated with resort living. Obviously, many older people were completely unprepared for such role changes, and many spent a lot of money trying to do what seemed expected of them, only to find that that way of life was not for them.

Leisure theory is another sociological theory closely related to disengagement theory. Somewhat as a corrective to many negative consequences of disengagement theory, leisure theory suggested that retirement demanded social roles that older people were not prepared to assume; more significantly, the theory argued that retirement brought considerable amounts of leisure time to older people who did not know how to manage it to best advantage. Thus it was important to prepare older people for retirement and for a better use of leisure time. Otherwise, leisure time, particularly for very active people, would lead to depression and social withdrawal.

Not only were older people encouraged to develop recreation skills, but they were encouraged to participate in a wide range of post-retirement activities. Max Kaplan, who has studied the relationship between aging and leisure, has called leisure that activity which is pleasant, covers the full range of commitment and intensity, and provides opportunity for recreation, pursuit of growth, and service to others. In Kaplan's view leisure contributes substantially to health, longevity, happiness, personal security, emotional and personal growth, and contentment.[10] Thus by teaching people how to use leisure, substantial contributions can be made to the lives of older people.

As it has become clear that retirement is not a vacation and that many older people do not wish to live their lives isolated from the larger community, questions have been raised about many sociological theories of aging. In large measure, subsequent reexamination of sociological theory suggests the danger of stereotyping older people in terms of any sets of behavior they might display. Sociological theories of aging have made clear the fact that older people are not comfortable playing roles established for them by the larger society. The reexamination of social role theories also publicized the prejudice often directed toward older people, which stems from a fundamental fear of aging and death that most people harbor. In other words, those who fear aging personally also express strong negative views about older people, and they tend to see old people as feeble, withdrawn, physically unattractive, in need of constant activity to keep them happy, and emotionally difficult. In a perverse way, these attitudes are returned by older people, who frequently find younger people insensitive, uncaring, and too self-involved. These stereotypical orientations toward older people may be encouraged by sociological theories that highlight socially rewarded behavioral norms that do not fit with the way older people want to behave. In this way, stereotypes such as "the generation gap" become another social condition to which older people are expected to adjust, rather than an opportunity for bringing young and old together.

Biomedical Theories of Aging

From an intellectual orientation similar to developmental theory, biomedical theories of growing older declare that old age is a time of declining biological functions. These theories promote the idea of a cellular aging process, not causing death, but making the body and the mind increasingly susceptible to diseases. Somewhat in evidence of this viewpoint are statistics that show conclusively that the leading causes of death are diseases most likely encountered among older people: cardiovascular accidents, heart attacks, vascular accidents, and cancer, in that order. More-

---

[10]Max Kaplan, *Leisure: Lifestyle and Lifespan* (Philadelphia: Saunders, 1979), 141-167.

Actual Survival Rates in the
United States by Number of Years Lived

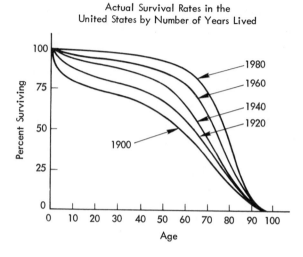

FIGURE 2-1
Life curves, 1900–1980.
Source: Department of Health and Human Services, Office of Health Statistics.

over, biomedical theories of aging support the idea of a fixed lifespan, such as depicted in Figure 2-1, and these theories argue with good statistical authority that despite advances in medical technology, the human body just wears out after about one hundred years if nothing terminal happens before that time.

For these theorists, older adulthood is understood as increasing physical limitations and increasing need for long-term care as the older person becomes unable to care for personal needs unassisted. The biomedical literature abounds with an emphasis on special practices for older people. For example, dental health for older people takes on new significance as failing teeth produce eating problems and appearance anxieties. Diet and nutrition are given special consideration for older people. Attention is drawn to special sight and hearing concerns of older people, and additional attention is drawn to the changing mental health of older people, often precipitated by organic changes. The purpose of this special attention is to provide a medical and social safety net for older people, so that their remaining years will be as satisfying and as "normal" as possible. But these biomedical interventions are not presumed to extend the life cycle.

There is no doubt that biomedical theories of aging have contributed considerably to enhancing the quality of life for older people. Yet biomedical theories of aging, like developmental theories, present the unglamorous elements of growing older. These theories emphasize deficits and dysfunctions as products of age. Yet it is abundantly evident that deficits do not occur regularly with age, and with some persons, deficits and dysfunctions do not occur at all. While it is true that aging produces biomedical changes, it is also true that aging is a life-long process, and the changes often attributed to age may indeed be consequences of events that took place at younger years.

Carl Eisdorfer and his colleague Donna Cohen argue that many of the biomedical symptoms associated with old age may not be part of an aging process as such. Through longitudinal research they suggest a cohort phenomenon may be a more likely explanation for many biomedical symptoms than an aging process.

The importance of the cohort effect is illustrated by the significant increase in the prevalence of Parkinson's disease with advancing age followed by a fall over time in the prevalence of the disease. It was subsequently discovered that many people showing the symptoms were among those who had been infected in 1917–1921 with a viral flu strain causing central nervous system destruction. Thus many people who were alive in the 1920s and were affected by the toxic virus lived long enough to display Parkinson's deficits later in life. For a time, clinicians and scientists were misled and mistakenly attributed the disease to aging.[11]

Eisdorfer and Cohen acknowledge that deficits are more likely with age even if age is not the causal factor. In this view, if age does not produce the deficit, then age should not be the crucial factor in dealing with the deficit. For example, they point out that biological loss in the central nervous system remains associated with age, but little thought has been given to how an older person can adapt and compensate for this change without functional losses. Whereas biomedical losses mediate the quality of life throughout the lifespan, unusual efforts are often undertaken to assist children and younger adults to adapt to these losses. The same efforts are not made for older people. Eisdorfer and Cohen refer to this phenomenon as therapeutic nihilism among the health professionals, a product of values placed on older adulthood, not a product of biomedical science.

Summary

The various theories of aging discussed above do not explain satisfactorily the constituent factors in the experience of aging. The notion that people age in cohorts, in response to important shared experiences in earlier stages of life, is a valuable key to some aspects of the psychology of aging. It also serves as a reminder that older people are not all alike—older and younger cohorts may have vastly different experiences and attitudes, and subsequently they may respond to older adulthood in vastly different ways. Cohort theory, however, does not explain individual differences in the aging process and generally ignores the importance of contemporary life experiences among the elderly. Socialization theories, by contrast, are very much concerned with how older people integrate with contemporary society. But the idea of "socialization" carries with it strong behavioral expectations, which may be especially unsuitable for dealing with the extremely varied lifestyles and attitudes among the elderly; disengagement theory, with its long-range effects on our concept of housing for the elderly, and leisure theory, with its emphasis on filling up older people's time with activities, are two cases in point. Developmental theory, to its credit, has built up an integrative perspective on life that includes maturity and old age as part of a continuing process, much the same for all, that each individual works through in his or her own way. But important as it may be for explaining behavior and psychological growth in childhood, developmental theory is inade-

[11] Carl Eisdorfer and Donna Cohen, "The Issue of Biological and Psychological Deficits," in *Aging and Society*, eds. Edgar Borgatta and Neil McCluskey (Beverly Hills, Cal.: Sage Publications, 1980), 53.

quate to explain mature, adult behavior. Though it is true that physiological and cognitive changes are likely to occur predictably with chronological age, or in stages, it is equally true that age alone is not sufficient to predict the behavior of older people, whether anticipated changes have occurred or not. Biomedical theories have directed attention to the deficits likely to occur in older adulthood, but these deficits are approached with professional attitudes and programs aimed at accommodation rather than adaptation. By describing older adulthood as the downward side of the life cycle, biomedical theories and developmental theory, like some socialization theories, inevitably imply that the elderly are past the most rewarding parts of life.

Because these theories cannot adequately explain older adulthood, they provide only limited direction to professionals about the kinds of actions that enhance the aging process. Studying older adulthood is an eclectic science. Research and theory-building in the field of aging is limited because the type of analysis and study varies vastly from discipline to discipline. The diversity among older people frustrates the development of any theory about the aging process that can be applied universally. Older people have accumulated a vast range of life experiences, and older adulthood may be a time of sifting through and choosing old and new experiences that are the most satisfying in the individual's present circumstances.

Taken together, the various current theories about aging and older people tend to reinforce popular ideas about older people and often obscure the extent of individualism among them. Most of all, growing older is a selective experience in survival. Change is characteristic of all age groups in society, and human development theories relevant to the unique changes in older adulthood have been slow to develop. Only when such relevant theories are developed will it be possible to undertake worthwhile efforts to enhance the quality of that time of life. Most of all, a sound conception of *successful* aging must be developed. Ideally, successful aging would seem to be a time of reflection, opportunity for heightened spontaneity, a golden time of life, a sense of personal satisfaction, and increased personal flexibility and independence. Thus far, most theories have concentrated on explaining observed realities—a necessary step, but one that may encourage a short-sighted, unnecessarily pessimistic view of the nature and potential of older adulthood.

SUCCESSFUL AGING AND THE QUALITY OF LIFE

A concern for successful aging shifts attention away from attempts to develop a theory of aging and older adulthood. Instead, it is equally useful for practitioners to consider the social circumstances and activities that enhance life for older people. By identifying the components of positive experiences in older adulthood, helping professionals can gain a better understanding of the state of older adulthood itself and also begin to appreciate the range of professional activities that might be employed to serve older people. In some ways, quality of life might be thought of as another theory that attempts to explain part of the older adult experience.

Just what does it mean to "enhance" life? No general description of quality of life exists, nor can it be measured. Yet personal well-being and personal satisfaction contribute greatly to the success of older adulthood and how well older people live with the resources available to them. A sense of safety and security, the opportunity for personal choice, and a sense of contentment, independent of economic need, are significant elements of a high-quality emotional and social environment.[12] Quality of life can only be defined very subjectively by each individual, but several important social conditions contribute to circumstances that improve the quality of life for older people.

Physical Environment

Where older people live determines the context of quality of life. Most older people own their own homes.[13] In 1980, there were 11,749,000 owner-occupied housing units with owners age sixty-five or older. As many as 65 percent of older adults live in their own homes, and 85 percent of these homeowners have no mortgage debt. Most owner-occupied and rental property in which older people live is older housing; 95 percent is fifteen years old or older. This housing is likely to need repair or renovation to enhance its comfort to the aging resident. Lacking special architectural features, such as grab-bars, handrails, accessible light and wall outlets, wide doorways, and special-height toilet bowls, older housing may not always contribute to the quality of older adulthood. Instead, rather than enhancing life, this housing often presents a series of problems with which older people must learn to live. All in all, as many as 20 percent of older people live in housing that is not appropriate to their present needs. With a 15 percent poverty rate among older people, many lack financial resources to purchase appropriate housing.

About 70 percent of older people live in urban areas, 35 percent specifically in central city areas. The urban elderly are more likely to live in older urban sectors, so that even if the housing in which they live is adequate and appropriate to their needs, the surrounding neighborhood may be undesirable or unsafe. It is not uncommon that older people remain virtual prisoners in their city homes and apartments, not because of physical limitation, but because it is not safe to venture out on the streets. Even when the threat of crime is minimized, many urban environments challenge older people. Congested sidewalks, which may be cracked and crumbling, wide, busy streets without monitored crosswalks, and complex access areas to public transportation all contribute to stressful living conditions. Lack of access to public facilities may be more troublesome for these older people than for their counterparts in rural areas who have never had such resources to rely upon.

[12] White House Conference on Aging, "Report," Technical Committee on the Physical and Social Environment and Quality of Life (Washington: Government Printing Office, 1981), 1.

[13] All data presented in this section are based upon 1980 Census data, unless otherwise noted, as reported in U.S. Bureau of the Census, *Statistical Abstract of the United States,* 102nd ed. (Washington: Government Printing Office, 1981).

Housing contributes to or detracts from quality of life in another way. Housing is more than shelter. It constitutes a base for emotional security, a feeling of being home, close to one's own. It accords a sense of independence and mastery. Unfortunately, repair, maintenance, high utility costs, and rapidly escalating taxes force many older people to relocate to housing that is presumed to meet their economic needs but often fails to meet their emotional and aesthetic needs. Even when older people move from less to more appropriate and desirable housing, they may suffer a sense of dislocation and emotional trauma and loss. Thus there are no clear-cut choices for improving the quality of housing for older people. On the one hand, an undesirable physical environment may be offset by the sense of familiarity and emotional security associated with the present housing. Conversely, relocation to more adequate and physically desirable housing may present undesirable emotional trauma, which at the same time may be more than balanced by the added comfort, convenience, and security. As in most circumstances in which older people must make choices, flexibility and available options that can satisfy personal preferences are the fundamental building blocks for enhanced quality of life.

Use of Time

As one of the most complex issues in quality of life for older people, the use of time has provoked wide-ranging discussion. In most cases older people suddenly find inordinate amounts of extra time in their daily lives. They may retire, or their spouses may retire, from full-time employment. In such circumstances, not only is more time available, but it is available during periods of the day that previously had been occupied by other activities. All too often pre-retirement dreams of unfettered leisure are quickly transformed into a post-retirement reality of boredom, aimlessness, and depression, followed by frustration and personal deterioration. Many older people are unprepared for these increased amounts of personal time, and they are also poorly equipped to use time independently without external structures. The breakdown in daily routines that provides therapeutic effects of vacations may provoke anxiety when extended over long periods of time. Thus many older people have come to realize that retirement is not a long vacation, as they may have anticipated during their working years. Unfortunately, many other older people have not come to this realization, and they struggle to use post-retirement time as they use leisure time; the two are not the same.

Much of the difficulty revolves around the issue of work. As will be explored in greater detail, work gives definition to personal life in American society. The question most frequently asked of new acquaintances, "What do you do?" anticipates a quick personality sketch from the answerer. Work also provides a measure of value of the individual. "What did you do?" is the question older adults frequently ask each other. As if speaking about another life, by telling what they did, older people communicate a sense of value. Therefore, it is not surprising that work may define quality of life in older adulthood just as it does at other life stages. Older people want and need work opportunities to enhance the quality of their lives. Work for wages has been discouraged by public and private employment policies, yet many older people would prefer to continue working at their jobs—and many do. Many others seek and find second careers by going back to school and by exploiting hobbies and productive activities and transforming them into vocational pursuits. For many older people, especially craftsmen, writers, artists, and various professionals, some of the best, most creative, and most useful work comes in later years when some of life's pressures are reduced. In fact, for many older people real creativity and making more rewarding contributions to society only begin in the later years of life.

Preretirement planning helps older people appreciate increased time. Whether as part of a comprehensive program, or the occasional opportunity to discuss with friends and family what choices are available after retirement, preparation for increased amounts of time can reduce anxiety and occasional periods of depression. Preretirement discussions that explore all opportunities can enhance the use of retirement time. Preretirement planning may also help identify personal and interpersonal problems that might arise: one spouse may anticipate retirement as a means to increase recreation time; the other may view the additional time as an opportunity to pursue a new career. Without discussion and planning, different expectations about the use of this time may conflict during the early retirement years. Quality of life for older people would be improved considerably if firms undertook efforts to counsel employees about the use of time after retirement. Such counseling would, on the average, cost less than the traditional watch and retirement luncheon, but it would be much more valuable to the older person.

In general, those who adapt successfully to retirement use their new time in three ways: in social and recreational activities, in maximizing new or second career opportunities, and in personal growth activities. All three require some degree of understanding and some personal skills that may not have been necessary before retirement. The social and recreational uses of retirement time are those traditionally associated with retirement. However, the use of social and recreational opportunities to promote quality of life requires preparation and skill. From playing golf to hiking and skiing, preparation is necessary to engage in these activities in meaningful ways. Similarly, though many older people desire greater social contact with others, often they have not developed useful interpersonal skills. Social exchanges under such circumstances can be disappointing. Maximizing new and second career opportunities also takes preparation and skill, and here again frustration and disappointment are likely products if goals are attempted without preparation. Education, training, and advice from qualified experts is very important. Extra time for pursuit of personal growth likewise enhances quality of life, but even opportunities to read or engage in cultural events, or expand one's understanding through formal education, such as Elderhostel programs, require preparation and planning.

The Family and the Social Support Network

The family forms the cornerstone of social organization in American society. Everyone has a family, even though not everyone has the "ideal American family," whatever that may be. A social support network grows from the family and eventually establishes the context for all productive social interaction. The "real" American family defies a single description. Husbands, wives, children, parents, brothers, sisters, aunts, uncles, cousins, step-parents, step- and half-brothers and sisters, all in various combinations, constitute a definable kinship system for everyone. Our present understanding of the family focuses on the system of mutual dependency that develops among people within a kinship system. In some instances, those dependency relationships are defined by law. Parents, for example, are required to care for children by providing them with financial support. In other instances, dependency relationships are socially sanctioned. Children are expected to support their elderly parents, although they are not required to do so by law as they once were in certain circumstances.

Although most professionals may tend to think of the family as two parents living in marriage with two dependent children, fewer than 7 percent of all families in the United States are so constituted.[14] A wide variety of family types characterizes American society; single parents with dependent children, children with dependent older parents, and blood relatives living together are but a few of the possible combinations. In fact, the type of family varies so widely that the United States Census Bureau defines a family simply as persons "related by blood or marriage and living together." The variety would be even greater if those related by blood or marriage but living in different places were included in the definition. For most purposes, all of these units of kinship organization are included in discussions about the family.

An older person's family, therefore, may be quite diverse. Although substantial numbers of older people live alone, particularly older women, most older people have family ties. Often these ties have deteriorated over the years, so that it may no longer make sense to think of some older people as having active and interdependent family relationships. On the other hand, a full examination of the diversity of the older person's family structure may reveal interdependent family relationships that might otherwise go unnoticed. For example, nieces and nephews may be actively interested and involved with older people in cases where the sons and daughters are in different parts of the country. Siblings often link up in older adulthood in meaningful interdependent relationships, even when in earlier periods they may have been preoccupied with their own families and children.

The family adds immeasurably to the quality of life of older people. Yet the warmth, support, and assistance that family members frequently provide may often be offset by tension, anxiety, and friction among family members. While family systems support, they demand as well, and some older people may not be able to meet those demands. Careful analysis of the family system can aid decisions about who should be involved and when they should be involved. The fact remains, however, that the family network provides resources for older people that, if properly cultivated, can improve their quality of life.

---

[14] Anita Farel and Andrew Dobelstein, "Supports and Deterrents for Working Women," *Journal of Marriage and the Family*, 14:2 (1981), 57–63.

Other Social Support Networks

Even when older people do not have viable interdependent family ties, it is likely that there are other supportive relationships that contribute greatly to the quality of their lives. Interdependent relationships among close friends are not at all unusual among older people. In fact, one of the compelling reasons for remaining in one's own home, even when that housing is far from adequate, is the significance of these social networks. Neighbors and friends may contribute security, assistance, and social support that would be disrupted in the wake of a move.

Neighborhood organizations such as senior centers, churches, schools, clubs, beauty and barber shops, neighborhood taverns, and grocery stores help create a network of social structure that interlaces with neighbors, friends, and family relationships. The significance of such networks was emphasized many years ago by the psychiatrist Harry Stack Sullivan, who suggested that such networks were essential to a sense of personal security. "Security operations," as Sullivan called these supportive networks, are "the operations which maintain our prestige and self-respect which are dependent upon the respect of others for us and the deference they pay us."[15] In Sullivan's view, security operations provide orientation in time, place, and identity and are as important as personal psychology in determining the ability of the individual to live a normal, happy, and healthy life.

Summary: Serving the Elderly Who Are Well and Capable

Though it is true that physiological aging has been documented in biomedical theories, and though to a certain extent increasing loss of physical and cognitive functions are associated with older people, not all older people experience these changes in the same way, or to the same degree, or even at the same chronological age. Medical science has not been able to arrest or reverse physical aging, but it has offered alternatives for mediating the quality of life as defined by older adulthood. As a result of medical advances, the life curve for all people has become much flatter, as demonstrated in Figure 2-1. As a result, professionals today are concerned less with identifying the stages that previously gave some definition to older adulthood than with promoting the continued interaction of older people with the environment in satisfying ways. In this view, developmental theory and the stages it forecasts have become deficient as a means of guiding professional helping activities. Moreover, as physical aging becomes less and less associated with chronological age, to a large extent other theoretical orientations to older adulthood are insufficient to suggest what can be done to assist older people. New theoretical orientations based on interaction between older people and their environment are only now beginning to emerge.

To the extent that people in the helping professions emphasize assistance to the physically and emotionally infirm older persons, existing theory can assist pro-

[15] Harry Stack Sullivan, *The Collected Works*, ed. Helen Perry et al., vols. (New York: W. W. Norton, 1953), 2, 218.

fessionals in their work. Yet most older people who seek assistance are not infirm. Furthermore, public policies and programs to serve older people are increasingly directed toward elderly who are well and capable. To serve this group earlier theoretical perspectives often required professionals to approach them as if they were infirm, correcting the infirmities, and in doing so, establishing a plan for more comfortable living. Such approaches are completely out of character with contemporary public policies.

Many early psychiatrists were sensitive to social conditions as the source of quality of life, and it is instructive to recall Harry Stack Sullivan's views of maturity. Sullivan calls maturity "the appearance and growth of the need for intimacy—for collaboration with at least one other, preferably more others"; and he goes on to say that "the life of the mature is always increasing in . . . importance. . . . the greater the degree of maturity, the less will be the interference of anxiety with living. . . . and when one is mature, anything which even infinitesimally approximates the complexity of living in the world as we know it today is not about to become boring."[16] Although not a prescription specifically for older adulthood, Sullivan's definition seems to capture the dynamic quality of full maturity that older people are increasingly seeking. Only by an examination of the quality of the world in which older people live can the helping person assist the great majority of older people who are likely to ask for help.

While all theories on aging to date have serious deficiencies for explaining older adulthood, theories that reflect quality of life do offer some meaningful explanation for the way older people live and face everyday life tasks. A quality-of-life approach suggests that when older people are well-adapted in their environment, they live better, more satisfying lives. A key element of any quality-of-life theory must be the importance of personal choice and alternatives. Because older adulthood is not an easily defined stage in life, older people need an environment that is diverse, and that can be adapted to them.

CONCLUSION: MYTHS AND REALITIES OF AGING

Quality of life is an elusive idea. It cannot be easily defined by objective standards, but rather it takes its definition from individual, personal viewpoints. Thus the best way to define the quality of life of older adulthood is to ask older people how they view their lives and what parts could be improved. That is what Louis Harris and the National Council on Aging did in 1974, and again in 1978.[17] These surveys drew information from national samples of older and younger adults on issues concerning older people. The polls showed that, in general, young people and the general population tend to overestimate the problems of older adulthood, a finding consist-

---

[16] Sullivan, 1, 310.

[17] National Council on the Aging, *Myth and Reality of Aging* (Washington, D.C.: The National Committee on the Aging, 1981).

ent with the popular view that older adulthood is an unpleasant period of life. But this was not the view held by the older people themselves.

Respondents eighteen to sixty-four years old believed, in 1978, that older people were worse off financially than they had been ten years earlier; but older respondents themselves did not believe they were worse off financially. Moreover, the older people believed that they were better educated and that their health was better than it had been for older people ten years before. At the same time, however, the poll found that older people were less satisfied with life in 1978 than they were in 1974; the reasons most commonly cited were the rising cost of living, fear of crime, the rising costs of medical care, and loneliness and isolation. The 1978 opinions of older people also suggest that, as a group, in addition to being more likely to suffer from the high cost of living than other groups, they are much more likely to experience criminal victimization, loneliness, and difficulties with getting adequate medical care. (Even so, the 1981 poll reported that although 74 percent of the respondents younger than sixty-five believed that crime is a very serious problem for older people, only 25 percent of those over sixty-five believed the same; and only 13 percent reported that they were lonely.) Interestingly enough, both older and younger respondents rated poor housing least important on the 1978 poll's list of the problems facing older adults.

It also appears from the Harris reports that ideas about aging changed considerably in less than a decade. In 1974, most respondents thought people grow old at age sixty-three (men) or sixty-two (women), but in 1981 they believed people grow old at age sixty-six or sixty-five. It is especially worth notice that 28 percent of the people surveyed in 1981 gave no chronological answer to the question about when a person grows old, preferring to say "it depends" or "when someone slows down." These results reflect a more realistic view of older people in American society and also popular acceptance of the notion that aging is a different experience for different people.

The quality of life in older adulthood is measured in part by personal satisfaction with it. Despite evidence that, overall, quality of life is improving for older people, the Harris surveys reveal several areas for serious concern. In general, older people have become less satisfied with their lives than they were in 1974 and express more negative attitudes about their circumstances. In 1978, most older people agreed that their lives could be happier than they are at present, and almost half agreed that life was getting worse, not better. When dissatisfaction with life was contrasted with actual life situations, the Harris survey found greater satisfaction among the younger elderly, the elderly with higher incomes, better-educated elderly, and elderly who were employed, at least part-time. Thus it seems that though life satisfaction is still negatively associated with age, this is not due to chronological age as much as it is to a shortage among older people of resources that contribute to the quality of life.

Perhaps one of the most significant findings of the 1981 Harris report concerns the use of time among older people. The older respondents spent less time in recreational activities and hobbies, socializing, sitting and thinking, caring for others, exercising, and listening to the radio than did their younger counterparts. On the other hand, the older people spent more time watching television, "doing nothing," and reading. They also went to church more often than young people, ate out more often, and visited neighborhood social organizations more frequently. In general it appears that older people are using social resources, in place of personal resources, as the contexts in which they spend their time. Since use of time is such an important factor in the quality of life, the quality of these resources takes on added importance. For example, neighborhood social organizations should provide more than card tables and checker games; they might offer opportunities for personal growth among their activities. Similarly, restaurants that cater to older people should try to offer well-balanced, nutritious meals. Religious organizations should be attuned to dealing with older people's spiritual needs beyond those usually addressed on Sunday mornings.

Because it is impossible and undesirable to attempt to regulate the wide range of social and neighborhood organizations that increasingly serve older people, knowledge, through education, is about the only way of insuring high quality in these organizations' services. Older people must be helped to develop and apply their own standards of quality in these organizations. Some of this ability might be encouraged by preretirement counseling programs. Much of it, however, will have to be provided through the usual educational organizations in the community.

The important factor in every case is that the strongest explanation of older adult behavior is not age, physical condition, or a stage of life often euphemistically called "golden age," but the quality of the environment in which older people live. Successful aging requires high-quality housing, a safe and familiar community, sufficient family and friends to provide a secure interpersonal social network, and neighborhood organizations that offer a range of activities that promote curiosity and growth.

Growing older in America is a challenge, for ours is a society that places high value on the new and the young. The social and personal pressures of a youth-oriented society are extensive for an older person. From theories explaining older adulthood, to decisions that commit public resources to the service of the elderly, older people themselves have not been primary concerns of this society. To the extent that older people are most dependent on adequate financial resources, older people without sufficient personal finances are the most disadvantaged in this society. The economics of growing older is our next major subject for exploration.

CHAPTER THREE

ECONOMICS AND GROWING OLD IN AMERICA

Aging and economic security represent a great American paradox. Successful aging should establish economic security, but this is not the case. While the Harris surveys show that older people are not primarily concerned about their incomes, older people in higher income brackets find life more satisfying than elderly in lower income brackets. Moreover, statistics show that older people are more likely to be poor, and regardless of how older people view their life circumstances, objectively, being poor in American society is a serious disadvantage. As Chapter 2 suggested, quality of life is related to the amount of income available to the older person. While the amount of income is important to economic security, the type of income, its source, and its reliability, as well as non-income-producing wealth, all contribute to economic security. This chapter examines economic security from various positions in order to provide helping persons with a better understanding of the economics of aging.

Economic disparities among older people are striking. Of the top wealth holders in America, 28 percent are men over fifty, and 22 percent are women over fifty.[1] There are approximately 55,000 men and women who are worth more than $1 million. Yet the most recent statistics indicate that slightly more than 15 percent of

---

[1]Unless otherwise stated, all data presented in this chapter are drawn from U.S. Bureau of the Census, *Statistical Abstract of the United States,* 102nd ed. (Washington: Government Printing Office, 1981).

all Americans over age sixty-five are in poverty, up one percentage point since 1978. Considering the fact that 11.6 percent of the entire population is below the poverty level, and about 17 percent of American children are in poverty, the amount of poverty among older people compared to the number of very wealthy older people or to the number of young people seems puzzling. The inequitable income distribution among older people is a further example. In 1979, about half the men over seventy had incomes of $8,000, which is hardly a respectable income, but even more striking, the average income of women over age seventy was only $5,800.

While there are serious economic inequities for all groups of people in America, these inequities are more striking for older adults. Of the total national assets, about one-third is in real estate; another third is in corporate stock; about 12 percent is in cash; the remainder is in other forms of assets. The assets of most older people are likely to be in real estate, but wealthy older adults are likely to have considerable holdings of corporate stock. While only 10 percent of the real estate is controlled by the top .5 percent of the most wealthy, half the corporate stock, half the bonds, and 80 percent of all trusts are controlled by this small group of individuals. Those older adults represented among this small group are very well off, but most older people must depend on cash or real estate as a source of wealth.

Earnings from work are a minor part of the income of older people; this is another source of economic disparity. While older people need proportionally as much income as their younger counterparts, they are denied the main source of income available to most Americans. Most older people are retired and are not part of the labor force. They live on prior savings, income from stocks, bonds, or rents, money from children or family members, or government income transfer programs. In fact older retired people receive a greater share of government funds, in the form of income transfers, than any other single group in the population. Tax money forms so great a part of the income of older people that the most delicate questions are raised about the quality of life for all older people. There is little argument that tax money should be used to assist old people who live in poverty or who have very small incomes. Whether tax proceeds should be used to help older people keep up a standard of living that may be considerably higher than that of many who are working and paying the taxes has prompted acrimonious political debates.

In practical terms, older people present greater diversity with respect to economic need and economic security than other groups of Americans. Whether rich or poor, older adults have problems protecting their incomes even though these problems are different for the wealthy older person than for the lower-income older adult. Maintaining a consistent standard of living is the common quality-of-life issue for all older people. Yet, as Table 3-1 shows, older people face economic discrimination when compared to younger counterparts.

Discussing the economics of growing older from the quality-of-life perspective requires a few words of explanation. While Americans believe in democratic ideals that support equality, wealth and income inequities abound. If any person, through legal means, develops and maintains a particular level of wealth, income, and standard of living, Americans accept that standard of living regardless of the level of the

TABLE 3-1 Comparison of Income From Work For Selected Age Cohorts

1979 MEDIAN FAMILY INCOME OF MARRIED COUPLES

	ALL MARRIED COUPLES		MARRIED COUPLES ONLY HUSBAND WORKED		MARRIED COUPLES HUSBAND & WIFE WORKED	
	NUMBER PER 1,000	MEDIAN INCOME	NUMBER PER 1,000	MEDIAN INCOME	NUMBER PER 1,000	MEDIAN INCOME
TOTAL	48,180	$21,503	11,336	$18,735	25,442	$25,119
Under Age 35	14,088	$20,080	3,796	$17,048	9,894	$21,352
Age 35-54	18,811	26,321	4,057	21,047	11,648	28,515
Age 55 and over	15,280	16,365	3,483	17,800	3,901	26,816

Source: *Statistical Abstracts of the United States.* United States Department of Commerce, 1981, Table 738.

standard. For example, if a person has the resources to own a home, maintain a membership at a country club, travel, and meet obligations to the family, Americans respect that standard of living for that person, even though many other persons do not live as comfortably. In the quality-of-life approach to understanding older adulthood, a reduction in standard of living, due to age alone, is not fair. In other words it is not fair to adjust economic inequalities, or inequalities in standards of living of older adulthood, when these inequalities are sanctioned for other cohorts of the population. The argument of some, that income and wealth equality should be a public policy goal of public income support programs for older people is anthetical to a quality-of-life philosophy.[2] Older people should not be forced to bear the brunt of economic inequalities endemic to the American economic system. Therefore, the point of view prompted in this discussion is clear. Economic security for older people means maintaining a standard-of-living level maintained prior to reaching older adulthood.

Whereas there must be a public obligation to assure a decent level of economic security for the very poor older person, even to the extent of improving that person's standard of living, the standard of more affluent older people must not be lowered if quality of life is to be maintained. In simple terms, this approach to economic security in older adulthood is different than economic security approaches for other portions of the population. The ratio of pre-elderly economic security to post-elderly economic security, for all classes of people, should remain the same. This point of view is consistent with the theoretical positions discussed in Chapter 2. In summary, these positions argued that the quality of old age is not a time of sudden change, but rather older adulthood continues patterns of living developed over a lifetime of experience.

THE AMERICAN ECONOMY AND OLDER PEOPLE

Personal Economics

Older people face loss of earnings from work as the most serious economic problem. Due to retirement or decreased work for wages, the primary source of income in old age shifts rapidly. The American economic system is based upon work, and wages from work are the chief source of economic support for everyone. Consequently, when someone stops working, income must come from other sources. In order to understand how this shift can take place requires an examination of the American economic system. The American economy functions both as a system of personal economics and as a system of national activities. Both personal and national economics continue to affect older adults.

The major share of income for non-retired persons in the labor force is earned income from salaries, business, and farming. For individuals and families under age

[2]Gary Nelson, "Support for the Aged: Public and Private Responsibility," *Social Work* 27, no. 2 (March 1982), 137–46.

fifty-five, as much as 93 percent of all income is earned in the work force. The remaining 7 percent is from other sources, and as discussed below these sources become significant for older people. For the person age sixty-five and over, earned income decreases as a percentage of total income to the point that it comprises only about 30 percent of total family income. Depending on the health and previous employment pattern of the older person, earned income may be an unstable and unreliable source of income at best. More than 95 percent of all old people have worked at some time or have, or had, spouses who have worked in the past. This degree of work force attachment suggests the extent of loss of earned income that must be made up by personal savings from previous work periods, other forms of non-work producing income (interests and rents), and social security and other government income transfer programs. To some degree all three of these sources of income for older people require previous work force attachment.

There are sources of income for older people that are not related to a previous attachment to the work force. Contributions from family members, government welfare programs, both in cash and in kind, and special tax advantages, may supplement income for older people who had not worked or for those who had worked but had not earned enough from work to save for a comfortable retirement. These sources of income will be examined later, and because social security is such a unique form of employment-related, government-administered income replacement, it will be discussed in a special section.

The sharp loss of income from earnings which comes with most retirement decisions is unlikely to be replaced from other sources. Particularly for the higher earners, the reduction in earned income undoubtedly requires some reduction in the standard of living. Most savings for older people are in real estate, their own homes in most instances, and therefore these savings are not available to replace lost earnings. Company pensions, a growing source of replacement income for older persons, generally constitute about 20 percent of pre-retirement income. Social security also substitutes for pre-retirement income, but the higher the earning, the smaller the amount of pre-retirement income replaced by social security. For the $900 per month earner, for example, social security would take the place of about 30 percent of that person's pre-retirement income.

In some respects low earners are better off than high earners when they retire. Although lower earners' savings may be less, and benefits from company pension plans may be lower, social security may replace a greater share of pre-retirement income, and thus some persons may have more retirement income than they had before retirement. Table 3-2 provides some perspective on this issue. In those situations where a low- or average-income couple receive social security, the replacement rates are sufficiently high so that, given modest sources of other income, older people may not have to change their level of living in major ways. Even so, the low earners may still be in economic hardship, close to the poverty line or below it. Either way, older people are not likely to have an abundance of financial resources, even though the shock of a switch from income earnings to nonearned income may not be as great for the low earners. Table 3-2 demonstrates that presently, social

TABLE 3-2 Social Security Replacement of Pre-Retirement Income

	LOW EARNED (3,400)*		AVERAGE EARNED ($8,600)		MAXIMUM EARNED ($16,500)	
	INDIVIDUAL	COUPLE	INDIVIDUAL	COUPLE	INDIVIDUAL	COUPLE
1976	62%	93%	42%	63%	30%	46%
1978	61	92	42	64	32	48
2000	75	113	49	73	36	54
2050	108	162	61	91	43	65

*Based on 1976 dollars, percentages based on last year of earnings.

Source: Social Security Administration, Office of the Actway. *The President's Social Security Proposals* (Washington, D.C.: U.S. Government Printing Office, 1976), p. 30.

security does not replace all income that had been earned before retirement. Social security replaces a greater share of pre-retirement income for lower-income beneficiaries, and as time goes on, some low-earning social security beneficiaries may have more income from social security than they had before they retired. Even though many persons believe that social security will take care of their income needs after they retire, this is not true. Bringing such facts to light is another good reason why pre-retirement counseling can help improve the quality of life for older people.

As far as the individual older person is concerned, post-retirement living costs might be reduced without a reduction in the standard of living. For example, if savings have been invested in housing, there will be no monthly mortgage or rent payments to make. There are tax advantages given to older people. Some states exempt a large share of property taxes on homes. The federal government gives a double tax exemption to older people, and it excuses many of them from paying further social security taxes. Some forms of income, such as social security, may be exempted from state and federal taxes, and there are a larger number of government supported in-kind programs available to older people which reduce their cost of living. For example, Medicare, and in special cases Medicaid, reduce the costs of medical insurance, and special housing programs may reduce housing costs for older people who do not own their own homes.

On the other hand, there are unusual costs associated with growing older which may make living more costly. Health care and illness among older people is of great concern. Despite the existence of Medicare and Medicaid, a much larger share of the older adult's income is needed for these purposes. Older people are much more likely to need assistance in a variety of living tasks. They may need household assistance, particularly if they own their own homes. It is not desirable for a seventy-year old person to be up on a ladder cleaning gutters, for example. Older people may need help preparing meals, cleaning homes, getting to the grocery store, and doing the many errands required in everyday life. If family and friends are available to help with these tasks, fine, but more often outside assistance is necessary and must be purchased.

In an interesting study about household expenditures by older people, Yung-

Ping Chen and Kwang-Wen Chu found that there are important and significant differences between the way older and younger households spend their incomes. Older persons spend more of their household incomes for food and medical care; less is spent for shelter and recreation.

> Compared with other aged groups, the aged spend relatively more on household utilities, medical care, personal care, and gifts and contributions; they allocated relatively less to clothing, house furnishings and equipment, automobile purchase, education and recreation. . . . For the aged as a whole, food remains the largest budget item and is greater than for any other age group.[3]

Aside from the extra costs, the various forms of personal assistance in daily living which older people need have another important economic aspect. Even in those cases where older people can afford to pay for personal assistance services they might not be available. Because the number of persons who may need certain of these services is small, the demand is not sufficient to generate interest in the private sector to provide them. Simply stated, there may not be enough older people in a community who need shopping assistance, for example, to make it financially worthwhile for grocery stores to offer it as a special service. Because there is not sufficient aggregate demand to excite the free enterprise system into action, regardless of how much older people may need these services, they just do not generate profits. In such circumstances, the public sector must provide these services if they are to be available at all.

At the personal level, income for the individual older adult decreases as older people are squeezed out of the work force. Although mandatory retirement ages are no longer legal, strong pressures to retire persist as persons advance in years. In most cases, lost income from wages is not completely replaced from other sources. For most older people, a post-retirement income gap requires changes in living patterns. Savings in cost of living in some areas of life are likely to be lost by greater expenses in others. Most older people are faced with the reality that they must reduce their standard of living. These are the realities of personal economics of growing older. Whether it is fair that reduction in standards of living accompany older adulthood remains a debatable question. Whether reduction in standard of living is wise, also continues to be debated, particularly when health and welfare may be jeopardized by lower standards of living. These debates will be explained in the book's conclusion. For now, however, the fact of reduced personal income among older persons is one of the life issues with which professional helpers must deal.

National Economics

The American economic system does not operate only in a personal way. There are larger national and societal consequences of this economic system. On the one hand, individual economic decisions have an important influence on the nation-

---

[3] Yung-Ping Chen and Kwang-Wen Chu. "Household Expenditure Patterns: The Effect of Age and Family Head," *Journal of Family Issues* 3, no. 3 (June 1982), 245.

al economy. On the other hand, the American economy is directed by government decisions that in turn influence individual economic choices. Generally the American economy is a "free-market" economy. In such an economy, markets operate in a manner to generate a full range of economic choices. However, there are times when markets fail, as during periods of depression, and there are instances where markets do not operate efficiently for some groups of people. The failure of markets to meet the need for special services for older people, discussed above, is an example of market inefficiency.

The personal economics of older adulthood are linked very closely with a free-market system. Despite the persistent belief that the American economy operates with free markets, independent of regulation, where, "the economic system possesses a very special mechanism to reconcile the many conflicting interests,"[4] the American economy is managed to a large degree by the feueral government. The efforts to resolve the problems of the Great Depression ushered in a period of increased governmental involvement in what were previous autonomous economic activities. At the end of World War II the Congress extended further responsibility for managing the American economy by passing the Full Employment Act of 1946.[5] This law and subsequent revisions established the Council on Economic Advisors and assembled federal power to promote an economic climate that would insure full employment for the labor force. From this authority and from the significant expansion of the taxing and spending powers of the federal government, the federal budget has become the primary mechanism for developing and achieving American fiscal policy.

National fiscal policy, as provided by law and as evolved during the past four decades, sets forth three broad objectives: economic growth, balance, and equity. Economic growth, as measured principally by changes in the Gross National Product (GNP), provides the measure of economic well-being. In the simplest explanation, in order to live well and to improve the standard of living, the economy must grow faster than the population. During the last ten years, the population has been increasing steadily at a rate of 1.1 percent per year while the GNP has fluctuated, actually decreasing some of the time (see Table 3-3).

There is debate among economists about the amount of growth necessary to achieve particular social objectives. As reflected in the GNP, economic growth must remain well above population growth since it is the surpluses from growth that can be used to improve the level of life in America. Government spending for general welfare purposes is allocated from surplus in growth, after the population has settled on some standard of living. In American society today, there are a number of publicly financed sectors which Americans accept as a way of life. Transportation, roads, parks, public safety, education, as well as income-maintenance programs are all forms of government activity made possible by the relative affluence

---

[4] Robert Havenman and Ken Yon Knopf, *The Market System* (New York: John Wiley & Sons, 1962), 2. (Represents the classic explanation of American economic activity.)

[5] Stephen Kemp Bailey, *Congress Makes a Law* (New York: Columbia University Press, 1950), Chapters 1 and 3.

TABLE 3-3   Population Change and Growth in the
Gross National Product 1970-1980

	POPULATION CHANGE	GNP CHANGE
1970	1.3	3.1
1975	1.0	−1.1
1976	1.0	5.4
1977	1.0	5.5
1978	1.1	4.8
1979	1.1	3.2
1980	1.1	− .2

Source: *Statistical Abstract of the U.S.A.* Tables 3 and 4.

of American society. Provision of these amenities at public expense provides solid justification for fiscal policies that seek to sustain and stimulate economic growth.

Economic balance is every bit as significant as economic growth. Uneven growth, even to the modest extent reflected by the GNP figures in Table 3-3, produces waves of economic instability. During periods of negative growth, for example, government commitments for public products can be continued only by borrowing, which places a drag on economic growth in subsequent years. Sometimes, in severe economic times government commitments have to be reduced, as has been the situation during the most recent federal administration. When growth is rapid, other problems occur. If surpluses exist one year, they must be used with the thought in mind that they may not be available in subsequent years. For example, if surpluses exist to build a highway system during one period of time, will the resources be available to maintain it in later years?

Fiscal policy, therefore, attempts to achieve steady growth. By varying taxing and spending activity, the federal government tries to maintain a steady rate of growth. Taxes may be raised or lowered, and the federal government can spend more than it collects in taxes when necessary. Growth fluctuations are particularly troubling to the labor force. Since government activity is used to speed or retard economic growth without wide-ranging cycles, the labor force is particularly sensitive to the trends set by fiscal policy.

In order to reduce the adverse effects of economic growth in the labor force, a number of social programs have been developed that will moderate the impact of growth cycles on the domestic population. Called "counter-cyclical," these programs are designed to work in opposition to prevailing economic trends. Unemployment Compensation (UC) is the most carefully designed counter-cyclical program. As more and more workers are unemployed, established unemployment benefit programs are extended automatically. Two results are achieved through this program. Unemployed workers receive government payments until they are reemployed. Thus UC operates as a type of welfare program. UC also pumps money into the economy, and this acts as a modest stimulus to prevent further economic slippage. UC allows wage earners to keep paying mortgages, buying food, and obtaining consumer goods, countering the expected slowdown during poor economic times. Social security has counter-cyclical elements built into it as well. Benefit increases are attached to changes in consumer costs, or "indexed." As costs rise, benefits rise, counteracting the negative consequences of uneven growth on a population with fixed incomes.

Fiscal policy also seeks economic justice. Not only must there be growth, and balance, but both should occur in a framework such that, at the least, those who become better off do not do so at the expense of others who, subsequently, become worse off. At best, economic justice might even suggest that the lot of the worse off becomes better at the expense of the better off. Obviously, personal values are important to a discussion of economic justice, as economists, political scientists, and policy makers attempt to define justice from different perspectives. In any event, economic justice objectives exist in law and in economic practice. For example, the tax rates increase with increases in income.

Economic justice is an important issue for older people because of the sharp decrease in income upon retirement. The poverty rate of about 15 percent among older people suggests the extent of social justice which present fiscal policies must reflect. The debates over social security in the White House Conference on Aging revolved around legitimate economic justice issues of American fiscal policy. Through fiscal policies which have distributed income, the current poverty rate among older people has been cut in half during the past two decades, attesting to the significance and the capacity of American fiscal policy to implement economically just programs. Yet the dilemma remains in definitions of economic justice for older people in light of the income changes they experience. Reflecting on the statements at the beginning of this chapter, issues of economic justice ask whether older people must expect a reduction in the standard of living, and whether public funds should be used to help supplement income of relatively wealthy older people so that their standard of living is not reduced. Obviously, such questions have no exact answers.

THE FISCAL POLICY FOUNDATION FOR PUBLIC PROGRAMS

All three objectives of fiscal policy have relevance for older persons' economic status as decisions are made to tax and to spend funds to achieve fiscal policy objectives. Spending decisions are more straightforward in their impact on older persons' economic status. Two types of public programs are available to older people: programs that distribute cash and programs that distribute benefits in kind. Each type of program has two distinct functions: to assist the financially needy or to provide benefits to which the recipient is entitled by law regardless of need. This scheme is shown in Table 3-4, and the specific programs that fit the squares A, B, C, and D in Table 3-4 will be identified and discussed in Chapter 8. The fiscal policy issues of the varying types and kinds of programs are discussed here.

**TABLE 3-4   The Kinds and Types of Programs
Available for Older People**

PROGRAM KIND	PROGRAM TYPE	
	CASH	IN-KIND
Need Tested	A	B
Entitlement	C	D

The free-market idea fails for most older people. Older people are forced out of the labor market for many reasons: failing health, increasing inability, biases against older people, public policies and practices, and retirement incentives such as income support plans. A governmental response to market failure is consistent with fiscal policy objectives. The inequalities created by these market failures are most evident in the reduced income available in older age and in the subsequent efforts by government to protect income for older people. Table 3-5 shows the aggregate sources of income by shares, for the older adult population. Retirement income for all groups comprises over half of all income. Social security provides most of that income. Private pensions contribute less than 10 percent of the aggregate income, whereas earnings continue to provide meaningful amounts of income.

Cash programs, such as social security, are desirable types of public programs since they provide maximum autonomy to older people. With cash, the older person can exercise individual preference with respect to particular needs, wants, and desires. The use of cash is compatible with the entire economic system. With cash, older people are like other consumers: they maximize their individual preferences

**TABLE 3-5   Percentage Distribution of Money Income From Particular Income Sources, 1978.
(Persons Aged 55 and Over.)**

SOURCE	ALL UNITS	MARRIED COUPLES	NONMARRIED PERSONS		
			TOTAL	MEN	WOMEN
Total percent	100	100	100	100	100
Percent of income from					
Retirement pensions	54	50	61	58	62
Social security	38	34	46	40	48
Railroad retirement	11	1	1	2	1
Government employee pensions	6	5	7	6	7
Private pensions or annuities	7	8	6	9	5
Earnings	23	30	12	20	9
Income from assets	19	18	21	17	22
Public assistance	2	1	3	2	4
Other	2	1	3	3	3

Source: U.S. Department of Health and Human Services, Social Security Administration, *Income of the Population 55 and Over,* 1978. Washington, D.C.: U.S. Government Printing Office, 1982, p. 49.

in the marketplace. In some ways, cash programs are more efficient fiscal policy mechanisms since cash is provided directly to the older person, without an intermediary.

In-kind programs distribute goods and services to older people. The justification for in-kind programs lies in the ability to focus the resources carefully on the need. Since cash can be used to purchase a wide variety of goods and services, the purchased products may not fit the need exactly. This is particularly true in those circumstances in which markets are likely to operate imperfectly, as is the case for older people. Housing may be purchased, but it may not be standard housing. Older adults might like to purchase household assistance, but if there are no household assistance services to purchase, and the aggregate demand is not great enough to excite the market into operation, the purchasing power is ineffective. Therefore, in-kind programs are important to assist older people to live satisfactory lives. The exact value of in-kind services is difficult to estimate since they cover so many products. Public housing may be equal in value to a $2,000 per year supplement, for example.[6]

Both cash and in-kind programs may be need tested or available as a result of statutory entitlement. Need-tested programs are available only when financial need is established. These programs, therefore, are available only when personal financial resources are not sufficient to enable older people to function at some established economic level, such as the poverty level. On the other hand, entitlement programs are available to older people regardless of economic need. Eligibility for entitlement programs is guaranteed by law, after older persons have met the conditions set forth in the statutes. For example, older people are entitled to social security if they worked in social security covered jobs and if they are retired, regardless of post-retirement income level. The elderly nutrition program is available to all older people regardless of personal income. Particularly in the case of social security benefits there has been increased public discussion about entitlement programs. For example, social security benefits are paid to older people even though they may have adequate income from savings and prior investments. In the free market system, there is much less debate about the use of means-tested programs than about the use of entitlement programs as a way to achieve fiscal policy objectives.

The interface of public-spending programs with the free-market system is by no means smooth. There are a number of areas where effort to achieve compatibility with fiscal policy goals and the free market produce ambiguities, conflicts, and inconsistencies for the individual older person. Perhaps the most significant is the extent to which provision of retirement income discourages work among older persons if and when work is available. At present, only about 12 percent of all persons age sixty-five and older are employed at all including part-time employment. The four most important reasons for retirement are factors relating to personal health, the state of the economy, demand for older workers, and sources of retire-

---

[6]For estimates of cash values of in-kind programs, see Andrew Dobelstein, *Politics, Economics and Public Welfare* (Englewood Cliffs, N.J.: Prentice-Hall, 1980), 199–224.

ment income. Available sources of adequate retirement income, and particularly "social security benefits [are] responsible for almost half the reduction in labor force participation of elderly men since 1950."[7] A worker with average earnings who retired at age sixty-five in 1980 has social security benefits valued at more than $124,000. Thus, the incentive to retire and begin collecting these benefits should not be underestimated, even when these benefits may provide only a modest source of monthly income.

Reduced labor force participation among the elderly has a number of undesirable features. First, there is a loss of national productivity as older people are no longer engaged in the production of goods and services. Second, the more older people who retire, the greater the public burden, and as the older adult population grows in size the ratio of workers in the labor force who must support retired older people grows smaller. From a ratio of twenty workers to one retiree in 1960, the ratio has shrunk to three to one at present. Thus there are fewer people available to support more. Third, older people themselves want to work, but the provision of retirement incomes and the related structural factors that discourage older people from working, make work options for older people limited.

A second area of lack of fit between free-market principles and fiscal policy concerns savings. An efficient free-market system would suggest that during periods of employability, workers would save for those times when they were no longer employable, as for example, in older age. There are market conditions that drive older people out of the labor force, such as depressions, recessions, poor health, and advanced age. The known existence of means-tested and entitlement programs, some argue, discourages people from saving to meet these unproductive periods. The existence of this protection, largely in the form of social security for the aged and disabled, not only discourages personal savings but also diverts funds that otherwise might be used for investments and further national economic growth.

The single greatest source of savings for older people is their homes (see Figure 3-1). While this form of savings does provide some protection in old age, it does not contribute to the overall national pool of savings. It is a static form of savings that cannot be used to improve national productivity through capital investment and development. Moreover, this form of savings lacks liquidity, and from the personal standpoint it is not a reliable form of income support in old age. For people whose savings are mostly personal real estate, social security is a much better investment. Today's retired worker with $124,000 in social security benefits contributed $11,500 during actual employment. The same investment of $11,500 in a home, would have a retirement asset value of less than $50,000.[8] In this view, "contributing" to social security is more valuable than building other retirement assets.

A third factor that suggests a lack of compatibility between fiscal policies and

[7]U.S. Congress, Congressional Budget Office, *Work and Retirement: Options for Continued Employment of Older Workers* (Washington: Government Printing Office, 1982), 19.

[8]Joseph Friedman and Jane Sjogrem, "Assets of the Elderly as They Retire," *Social Security Bulletin* 44, no. 1 (January 1981), 16-31.

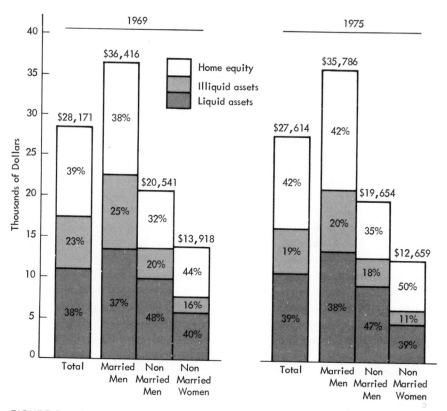

FIGURE 3-1 Source of assets in retirement, 1969 and 1975. *Source: Social Security Bulletin 44, no. 1 (January 1981): 29.*

free-market principles concerns the whole problem of defining income. Many programs make sharp distinctions between earned income and income from other sources. Since so little of the income of older people is earned, they are often eligible for many means-tested programs even though total income from all sources would make them ineligible for them. Other income, "unearned" income, may or may not be related to previous labor force attachment. As a result of definitional problems, older people may be worse off or better off financially, and may or may not need public support. The matter is not always clear.[9] For example, most social security income is untaxed, but it is counted in determining eligibility for need-tested programs, such as Supplemental Security Income (SSI) and Medicaid. At the same time, income from earnings may disqualify an older person from receiving social security benefits, but income from stocks, bonds, investments and savings

[9] Marilyn Moon, *The Measurement of Economic Welfare* (New York: Academic Press, 1977).

may not. Therefore, the transfer of cash or in-kind resources to older people, as a means to adjust market inequities does not insure equity. Public cash transfer programs are necessary to fiscal policy objectives, but in themselves they may not satisfy issues of individual equity.

Fiscal policies and related public programs include not only direct cash and in-kind expenditures, but they include tax expenditures as well. Fiscal policy objectives can be achieved either by public spending or through selective taxation. Although the federal income tax is progressive in the way the income tax is levied, there are wide ranging exceptions, or exemptions, from paying tax. Many of the tax exemptions favor older people. For example, older people get an extra personal exemption of a fixed amount. Income from social security, the single most important source of income for older people was included as taxable income beginning in 1983. Mortgage payments on personal, individually owned housing are tax deductible. These deductions represent savings for older people who may be exempted also from state and local government property taxes. The main tax savings for older people are summarized in Table 3-6.

Despite the fact that it is difficult to calculate exactly the amount of tax expenditures that benefit the elderly, using conservative estimates, and adjusting the tax expenditures to the size of the older adult population, as much as $45 billion in tax benefits may go to older people. Based on current population of older people if distributed equally, this would amount to $1,181 per year for each older adult. Added to direct federal expenditures for social security benefits and a proportionate share of health expenditures, the total federal benefit to older people may well average between $8,000 and $10,000 per year per older person. Thus, American fiscal policy does attempt to take into account the fact that older people are disadvantaged in the market economy, and to the extent discussed earlier, direct expenditures, in-kind products, and tax exemptions provide some measure of economic equity to older people.

TABLE 3-6 Tax Savings for Older People, FY Ending September 30, 1981

SELECTED ITEMS IN MILLIONS OF DOLLARS

Mortgage payments	$19,805 (Million)
Property tax	8,918
Interest on credit	5,260
Deferred capital gains on sale of items	1,110
Tax exemptions for elderly	2,260
Exclusions from other retirement benefits	10,270
Exclusion of social security for retired, survivors and dependents	25,710
Tax credit for elderly	125

Source: Office of Management and Budget, "Analysis of the Budget," Washington, D.C.: U.S. Government Printing Office, 1983, p. 87.

ADEQUACY, EQUITY, AND EQUALITY

In the closing section of his most popular economic treatise, John Maynard Keynes, the architect of contemporary American fiscal policy, argued that an unregulated economic society neither provided work for all who wanted and needed it, nor did it distribute income and wealth in an equitable manner.[10] Keynes's theories, adopted in the policies of the New Deal Democrats and reaffirmed in post-World War II efforts to return the nation to full domestic productivity and growth, remain at the foundation of American fiscal policy. This policy advocates government intervention in private markets to promote growth, stability, and economic justice.

As far as older Americans are concerned these economic objectives have become essential to their well-being. As retirees, often through forced retirement, older people are no longer labor market participants. Moreover, inequitable distribution of wealth and income, characteristic of lifetime patterns reflecting long-standing social and political inequalities in a variety of economic markets, are carried into older adulthood. Without fiscal policies that realize just economic goals, personal economic stability would be impossible for most older people to maintain. In 1959, 25 percent of all persons age sixty-two and over were below the poverty level. By 1979 only 12 percent of older persons were below the poverty level. This stunning reduction in the poverty rate among older persons is due almost exclusively to pre-tax cash transfers. Without this fiscal assistance there is little doubt that poverty would increase dramatically among older people; the fiscal assistance is entirely consistent with American fiscal policy objectives.

Many contemporary political economists are obsessed with the income inequities in America. Income equity is concerned less with equal shares of income among older people than with whether the distribution is fair. Income inequities do exist. The United States consistently has shown a distributional inequality in which Americans remain between 35 and 40 percent between measures of perfect income inequality and perfect equality (.35 to .40 Gini Ratio). In other words, America is only 35 to 40 percent of the way to perfect income equality. Since no nation would ever reach perfect income equality, the questions are: What is a fair income distributional ratio; and is the American ratio fair? Thus it is difficult to examine income distribution without raising other issues of income equity. For example, distributional inequality may be less significant when relative consumer power among older people is measured instead of the amount of cash available to them. Such measures, however, would have to take into account family size and personal obligations, or the measures would have to be based on post-tax, post-transfer economic resources such as savings or stocks and bonds, in order adequately to reflect economic equality. Whether an older person were richer, or whether an older person

---

[10]John Maynard Keynes, *The General Theory of Employment, Interest and Money* (New York: Harcourt, Brace & World, 1936), 372-77.

were better or worse off after retirement, cannot be determined by only examining income distribution patterns. One would want to know what financial resources were available for what kinds of consumption. If, for example, an older person had a large portion of total wealth invested and not available for consumption, that person might not be economically equal to someone with full social security and a supplemental pension. Thus income equity is difficult to evaluate when thinking about economic stability among older adults.

Equality is a politically active ideal. Politics, more than economics, are likely to define economic equality or to set some standard of economic equity. Irving Kristol observed, "Every inequality is on the defensive and must prove itself against the imputation of injustice and unnaturalness."[11] Inequality is more than the opposite of equality, however, and it is not self-correcting. Perfect income inequality would be as unlikely as perfect income equality, even if uniform definitions of equality existed. Thus there is more concern with economic equity, that is, economic justice or fairness, than with economic equality, despite proclaimed American ideals. The American government provides recognition for a wide variety of particular, individualized interests. Pluralism is the political climate in which public decisions are debated and decided. The tendency to have one's own way or to exert one's own view of what is right and good is maximized in American political life. Thus there is usually vigorous political debate over problems such as income equality and economic fairness. As older people have developed greater political power, and as levels of poverty among older people have decreased, debates over whether older people have equal shares of income have given way to debates over whether the income distribution is fair. Older people are less concerned about whether income is distributed equally than with whether they have something which they recognize as their "fair share." For this reason, older people interviewed in the Harris surveys were generally satisfied with their incomes, even though statistically their incomes were very modest.

The growing political significance of older people is discussed in detail in the next chapter. The close interface between politics and economics in the lives of older people, however, is an important issue in understanding the economics of older adulthood. The lines between older people are less likely to be drawn between the rich and the poor. Instead they are much more likely to reflect preferences in living style and the ability to maintain accustomed standards of living, whatever meanings these standards have for the older people themselves. The concern for politically defined fairness, rather than for economic equality, is the context for contemporary social security debate. As a politically defined group, older people have promoted a social security system that will treat them fairly with respect to what they understand social security to be.

[11]Irving Kristol, "Equality as an Ideal," *International Encyclopedia of the Social Sciences* (New York: Macmillan, 1968), 110.

SOCIAL SECURITY: THE ENIGMA OF ECONOMICS
AND OLD AGE

No discussion of the economics of old age could be complete without an examination of social security. As the most significant income-maintaining program for older people, social security holds a critical position in both the economics and politics of old age. The largest share of the federal budget is consumed by social security payments. Yet there is persistent concern about this program by opponents and proponents alike. Social security is a distinctively American system for assuring income for older people in retirement. Yet it is much more than either an insurance program or an income-distribution program. Thus, social security is as confusing and as puzzling as any American public program. The purpose of this discussion of social security is to provide the professional person with a background of the most pressing social security issues. A more detailed explanation of social security programs appears in Chapter 6.

Change is the most striking characteristic of social security. Despite rhetoric to the contrary, Congress constantly changes social security. Spurred by a nonpartisan task force appointed by President Reagan, chaired by the former chairman of the Council on Economic Advisors Alan Greenspan, the 98th Congress, like its predecessors for almost fifty years, undertook to resolve the serious, growing economic problems of social security in perpetuity. The first, most puzzling social security issue emerges: Americans believe the income needs of older people must be calculated and financed for at least half a century into the future, but during the past fifty years the social security program has never operated within the fiscal boundaries projected for it. Either there has been too much or too little money, and consequently study commission reports and congressional modifications of social security abound. Never would an American business attempt to predict its economic future for fifty years, nor would Americans expect such performance from any other public program. Social security is an exception; and by believing that social security benefits are calculated for fifty years, Americans believe social security is economically sound.

The 98th Congress reduced the many recommendations of the Presidential Task Force into legislative changes in both financing and administering social security. The Congress deferred the automatic cost of living increases. Cost of living increases were made "automatic" by Congress in 1972 to prevent political tampering by Congress with social security benefits. The 98th Congress also approved an escalation of social security tax increases in order to resolve the short-range social security financing deficit. In 1977, the present social security tax tables were set and, after much political pain, legislated to prevent political tampering with social security taxes through 2050. According to the 1977 law, social security taxes established then would have made social security financially sound until the year 2050. With the severe recession of the 1980s and with some demographic changes, things did not work out as planned. The 98th Congress also required that federal employees participate in social security and that social security benefits provided to wealthy retirees be taxed. Both decisions contrast sharply with previous social security commitments.

Despite these changes, the 98th Congress did not address social security's central problem. This problem is not inexact economic forecasts or changing national economic situations, nor is it the real concern that social security might fall into the wrong political hands and be destroyed. As serious as these problems are for social security, the real problem is the changing expectation of the purpose social security should serve for older people. Without agreement over the purpose for social security, no amount of economic or political reform will produce a satisfactory solution to social security's current and future problems.

The center of the struggle over social security's purpose revolves around the fairness, or equity question. Specifically the debate has raged over whether social security should operate like a welfare program (or an income distribution program), or whether it should operate as an insurance program. Insurance programs and welfare programs are not compatible. Insurance programs provide benefits with some relationships to the contribution. The economic status of the recipient is not an issue, but the basis of the benefit is related directly to prior economic status: the more contributed, the greater the present benefit. Conversely, welfare benefits are provided on a noncontributory basis, usually from undesignated public funds. The welfare beneficiary need not have contributed, and eligibility as well as the size of the benefit are dependent upon the beneficiary's current economic condition. The benefit is determined entirely by need. Moreover, economic need is defined relative to a variety of noneconomic factors: household size, place and type of residence, and often capacity and willingness to work. The incompatibility of these two types of programs is seen in Figure 3-1 and the earlier discussion of that figure.

Social security was legislated as part of the Social Security Act of 1935. This comprehensive, far-reaching legislation contained a variety of public programs including both entitlement (insurance) programs and need-tested (welfare) programs for older people—Social Security and Aid for the Aged (now Supplemental Security Income, or SSI), respectively. Both President Roosevelt and the Committee on Economic Security, which developed the legislation, were clear on the two separate means for providing income security for older people, and the division of those separate means into separate programs. For example, President Roosevelt ordered a complete recalculation of social security benefits and taxes the day before he was to present the act to Congress, when he learned from his secretary of the treasury that after the first thirty years, the program might not have enough worker contributions to pay anticipated benefits.[12]

From the outset social security opponents were skeptical that the insurance

[12] F. S. Drowley, "Financing the Social Security Program—Then and Now," in U.S. Congress, Joint Economic Committee, *Issues in Financing Retirement Income,* Studies in Public Welfare, 18 (Washington: Government Printing Office, 1974), 21–158.

features of the program would be able to resist welfare pressures. Business and industry groups charged that social security was a fraud and that the tax levied against employers and employees was a thinly disguised effort to support a federal welfare program. However, President Roosevelt was clear on social security's purpose and was able to convince the skeptics.

> President Roosevelt's desire to place chief reliance on wage-related contributing social insurance meant not only the rejection of uniform old age pensions but also a sharp separation between insurance benefits related to past contributions and assistance benefits payable on the basis of individual need.[13]

This was what people believed they were buying when they supported social security in 1935 and the years following.

Yet many careful observers of social security thought that either social security was more of a welfare program than administrators admitted, or if it were really an insurance program, it competed directly with private insurance retirement programs that could do a better job for middle and upper income wage earners. One of the great conservative spokesmen, Senator Robert Taft of Ohio, was particularly sensitive to the anomalies of social security. Taft was concerned that while President Roosevelt and his administrators, principally Arthur Altmeyer, defended social security as a strict insurance program, they were liberalizing it as well. The required amount of employment for eligibility was reduced, and the benefit structure expanded. Thus a gradual shift to include welfare features in social security was promoted as early as 1937, when the first benefits were paid to the first retiree, who had not participated in the system long enough to have "earned" his benefits.

One of the most acrimonious arguments over whether social security was "fair," as it became more like a welfare program, took place between Senator Taft and Altmeyer in 1950.

SENATOR TAFT: The additional benefits you would get [from social security] would not be equal to the taxes you would have to pay. Is that not right?

MR. ALTMEYER: ... the formula is weighted to give the lower wage earners a larger benefit in proportion to their wages ... than higher wage earners.

SENATOR TAFT: That is not an insurance principle, of course, that is a social-welfare principle.

MR. ALTMEYER: That is a very sound social-insurance principle.

SENATOR TAFT: It is a social-welfare principle. It has no relation to insurance.[14]

---

[13] Arthur Altmeyer, *The Formative Years in Social Security* (Madison: University of Wisconsin Press, 1968), 257.

[14] Andrew Dobelstein, "In Quest of a Fair Welfare System," *Journal of Social Welfare* 2, no. 2 (Summer/Fall 1975), 37–38.

Taft, of course, was right. The distinction was made clearly again twenty-five years later by Preston Bassel, then the president of the United States Chamber of Commerce, when he told the Congress:

> It is our understanding and belief that in a social security system individual equity yields to social adequacy, and that in dealing with the broad social and economic problems we face widows, children and other retired people. We have to devise a system as a broad social service to take care of them.[15]

Robert Ball, U.S. Commissioner of Social Security from 1962 to 1973, and still an outspoken expert on social security, stated recently that "in spite of what is sometimes said, there have not been major departures from the original purposes of the American social security system." Yet in the same breath, Ball also recommends: "Social security benefits should continue to be weighted in favor of those with low wages, and benefits for dependents should be retained."[16] In fact Ball's whole explanation of social security, today and tomorrow, testifies to the confusion over whether it treats older people fairly. Indeed, social security has become a complex structure reflecting a wide variety of expectations, rather than the consistent system of economic support for older people, which it is purported to be.

Martha Derthick, among others who have studied social security, discusses the struggle for fairness as competitive efforts to achieve adequacy and equity in the same economic program. Derthick suggests that the program was made politically appealing by allowing confusion over the two conflicting objectives.

> A program that gave benefits in return for contributions could plausibly be said to give benefits "by rights," whereas in a program financed by general revenues, entitlements would have been much more open to debate.
>
> The confusing mixture of purposes and benefits principles, the widely appealing symbolism of insurance, the low initial cost, the assurance of benefits as a matter of right, immune to debate, all help to explain the popularity of the old age insurance program. In making the choice for a program that based benefits on contributions rather than some other type of program, the executive founders intended to avoid politics as conflict. That was one of their principal reasons for preferring it to other alternatives.[17]

CONCLUSION

The problem with social security represents the important issues inherent in the economics of growing old in America. The problem with social security, therefore, is not its economics, as such, but its politics. The issue is whether social security and

[15] U.S. Congress, Joint Economic Committee, Subcommittee on Social Security, *President's Social Security Proposals* (Washington: Government Printing Office, 1974), 225.

[16] Robert Ball, *Social Security Today and Tomorrow* (New York: Columbia University Press, 1978), 460, 484.

[17] Martha Derthick, *Policy Making for Social Security* (Washington: The Brookings Institution, 1979), 227.

the American economic system are treating older people fairly. This is not an economic issue of setting standards for retirement pensions, or social security benefits, or income transfer programs; it is a political issue of deciding whether social benefits should be provided with respect to what contribution has been made, regardless of post-retirement economic status, or whether social benefits should provide income maintenance for older people based upon what they need. The problem is a political struggle over what is fair. It is this problem that sparked the intense debate at the 1981 White House Conference on Aging. In this context, the economics of older adulthood is not a series of attempts to provide exact sums of income to persons but rather an effort to reach some compromise with respect to assisting older people to maintain the level of living to which they were accustomed before retirement. This is the essence of the quality-of-life issue raised by the economics of growing older in America. The political complexities of achieving this quality of life are examined next.

CHAPTER FOUR

THE POLITICS OF AGING IN AMERICA

Politics, it has been said, decides who gets what, when, where, and how.[1] Politics is concerned with how resources are distributed and why they are distributed as they are. Government is the means by which political decisions about the distribution of public resources take place. As older people become a larger portion of the population, they seek greater shares of the public resources. Older people claim public resources because of their numbers, their needs, and as a fair share of part of the public resources. In its most simple language, older people base these claims on the argument that if they did not work hard, invest their savings, build the physical world in which we live—the buildings, the streets, the railroads, the parks—there would be nothing for others to use and enjoy. Thus older people claim a fair share of the public heritage they created.

The politics of growing old in America reflects those activities by older people directed at claiming resources they need to live with respect and dignity. The politics of growing old includes both personal as well as institutional politics. Simone de Beauvoir captures the implications of the personal politics of aging:

> It is in an underhand, sly manner that adults tyrannize over the dependent old man. . . . If persuasion and artifice fail to make him yield, they do not

[1] Harrold Lasswell, *Politics: Who Gets What, When, How* (New York: Meridan Books, 1958).

hesitate to use lies or a bold decisive stroke. For example, they will induce him to go to a rest home "just to try it," and then abandon him there.... He is a mere object, useless and in the way: All they want is to be able to treat him as a negligible quantity.[2]

On the personal level the politics of growing old represent the struggle for individual rights: the right to know, the right to decide the course of one's life, the right to self-respect, and the right to dignity.

American social institutions are not finely tuned to promote equitable distribution of public resources to older people, mostly because Americans have not valued aging or the contributions that the aged make to our society. Thus the personal politics of aging in America is often a struggle to maintain sufficient independence and personal power so as to control decisions affecting one's own life and to avoid those situations where personal choice is subject to institutional policies. The tyranny of which de Beauvoir speaks is no less repressive in its personal form, as experienced by the older adult, than the institutionalized forms of political repression that Americans have always resisted.

The institutional politics of growing older has been characterized by traditional public struggles over the division of scarce resources by competing claims of various groups. Older people, however, have become a politically identifiable group in their own right. As the population over age sixty-five has increased, older people have become a significant force in organized politics. Unlike children, for example, older people vote in greater proportion than others.[3] Older people have also formed identifiable and separate interest groups that have had an important part in the development of all social welfare legislation, particularly that related to older people. As the 1981 White House Conference on Aging clearly showed, many of today's older adults developed and administered contemporary social programs, thereby bringing into retirement important political knowledge and experience. Through these and other efforts older people have emerged as an important political force in their own behalf.

The Great Depression was the first political milestone for older people. Before this time, old people who managed to outlive their ability to work were either maintained by their families or placed in institutions. The "county home," the "poorhouse," or the "old folks' home" were all euphemisms for the deplorable almshouses that provided "indoor" relief to those without other resources. As this form of relief came under more and more direct public criticism during the early decades of the twentieth century, localities and states gradually developed programs that provided cash assistance to needy older people as a substitute or replacement for the county homes.

Although states passed laws to provide assistance to needy children and the needy blind in 1911 and 1907 respectively, it was not until 1923 that Montana and

[2]Simone de Beauvoir, *The Coming of Age* (New York: G. P. Putnam Sons, 1972), 217.
[3]Alan Campbell, Philip Converse, Warren Miller, and Donald Stokes, *The American Voter* (New York: John Wiley & Sons, 1964), 157–250.

Nevada became the first states to enact effective laws that provided cash assistance to the needy aged. Although Arizona had passed such a law in 1915, it was quickly declared unconstitutional. By 1935, when the Social Security Act was legislated, only twenty-eight states had old-age assistance laws. Even then, only sixteen states actually spent any money on these programs, and the total expenditures were a mere $35,000.[4] The median age of the population in 1935 was about twenty-eight years, and less than 5 percent of the population lived beyond the age of sixty-five. Since most older adults lived in families, where there was some care available, the lack of public response might be more understandable. Dependent children, who lost financial support due to the death of a parent, were a much more visible public concern than were old people who had learned, somehow, to eke out an existence in a world of harsh realities, for the few remaining years of life.

THE TOWNSEND MOVEMENT

The first significant political expression of older adults' needs was begun by Dr. Francis E. Townsend. A physician, born in Illinois, educated in Nebraska, retired in California, Townsend died at the age of ninety-three in Los Angeles in 1960. The success of what has been called the Townsend Movement reflects the political potential that older people now realize and that has now gained public respect. When Townsend retired to Long Beach, California for health reasons in 1920, he reflected on why an older person like himself, after a lifetime of work, should be unprotected against loss of income. Loss of job due to health reasons, or an economic calamity such as the Great Depression, quickly erased a lifetime of economic independence. Townsend wrote a pamphlet outlining his ideas about an old-age income security plan. In this plan, Townsend proposed a uniform $200 per month pension to everyone who would retire at age sixty, providing the recipient *spent* the $200 every month. The pension was to be financed by a 2 percent tax on all business transactions.

Townsend reasoned that it was important to get older workers out of the labor force to make room for younger, more productive people. He also reasoned that if the $200 were spent every month, the economy would be stimulated. He never considered his plan a retirement plan, as such, but he saw in it "a national economic pattern, a broad-scale to the aged and young alike, and on that basis I shall fight for it with all the energy that remains at my command."[5] Fight for it he did. As his idea gained momentum, as many as 80 percent of the registered older voters signed his petitions to Congress, pushing the total number of signatures to above twenty-five million. Five thousand Townsend clubs were created across the country, boasting of five million members. These clubs were designed to lobby congressmen in their home districts for the plan. It was not long before this organized political ac-

---

[4] Josephene C. Brown, *Public Relief—1929–1939* (New York: Henry Holt & Co., 1940).
[5] Quoted in *New York Times*, September 3, 1960, 25.

tivity, almost unheard of in that day, was branded as socialism, and Townsend himself was summoned before a congressional investigative committee. When he refused to answer some questions, he was sentenced to thirty days in jail, a sentence Congress was too timid to make him serve.[6]

The work of Francis Townsend produced immediate results with lasting political consequences. The Social Security Act, which included the social security retirement program as Title II, was a direct response to Townsend's pension idea and the political furor it stirred. The conditions of the Great Depression made it necessary to develop some type of government income protection programs. The political influence of the Townsend movement must be seen in that perspective. There is conflicting evidence about President Roosevelt's personal commitment to a national retirement insurance program in contrast to commitments that were politically expedient. Arthur Altmeyer reports that Roosevelt's "advocacy of social insurance and related forms of what we call social security antedated his presidency."[7] Biographical materials of Frances Perkins, Roosevelt's close political ally in New York and his secretary of labor, suggest otherwise. In one speech, Roosevelt questioned whether a federal old-age security plan was appropriate. Referring to pressures of the Townsend movement, Roosevelt suggested that the goals of such a program were impractical. Perkins' materials also suggest that Roosevelt was reluctant to urge Congress to move ahead on any national retirement plan.[8] Whether or not Roosevelt was personally committed to social security and a national retirement program, there is general agreement that the pressures of the Townsend movement kept retirement and pension proposals before the president and the Congress as the Social Security Act was drafted.

Another significant effect of the Townsend movement on the development of social security derives from the highly political character of the movement itself. During the early days of the Great Depression, Louisiana Senator Huey P. Long developed a "share the wealth" plan, and Upton Sinclair proposed a program to end poverty in California. These programs became political platforms for both Long and Sinclair, and Townsend and the Townsend movement quickly became embroiled in colorful partisan political activities. Townsend himself was a principal backer of the third-party candidacy of William Lemke in 1936, which included the support of the outspoken and influential Detroit "radio priest," the Reverend Charles E. Coughlin. Even though more overt political activities fragmented the Townsend movement, its political influence on policy affecting older people was strongly felt long after World War II. When social security was reviewed for modification in 1954, 160 Congressmen signed a petition to substitute the Townsend plan of a *universal* pension program for the administration's proposals of improving social security by expanding benefits only for those covered under the program.[9] Mrs. Perkins herself acknowledged the political significance of the Townsend movement.

[6]Abraham Holtzman, *The Townsend Movement* (New York: Harper & Row, 1963).
[7]Arthur Altmeyer, *The Formative Years of Social Security* (Madison: University of Wisconsin Press, 1968), 11.
[8]George Martin, *Madam Secretary* (Boston: Houghton Mifflin Co., 1976).
[9]Ibid., 117.

When I saw that old Dr. Townsend had died just this last winter, I could not help but say to myself, "God rest his soul; he was a good old man!" . . . In particular, he startled the Congress of the United States, because the aged have votes . . . If the unemployed didn't stay long enough in any one place, they didn't have a vote. But the aged people live in one place and they have votes, so every Congressman heard from the Townsend plan people.[10]

THE WHITE HOUSE CONFERENCES ON AGING

Although the Townsend movement never broadened its base of social concern beyond old age pensions, it did demonstrate the significant political potential of older adults in a time when interest-group politics was relatively unknown. Neither the enthusiasm of older adults nor the realization of their political potential abated with the passage of the Social Security Act in 1935. Title II of this act, which established the social security retirement program, was a prelude to a growing political movement among older people. It was not uncharacteristic, therefore, that in 1947 Congress appropriated funds to study the problems facing older people. At the conclusion of this study, President Truman convened a National Conference on the Aging in Washington, in 1950. Spurred by the recommendations from this Conference, in 1951 Congress created a Committee on Aging and Geriatrics that was to be responsible for coordinating federal programs that served older people. In 1956, Congress created the Federal Council on Aging and provided resources to the Department of Health, Education and Welfare (DHEW) for a special staff on aging. As DHEW directed special attention to problems of older people, within the context of the programs under its administrative authority, states began to create their own special staffs devoted to the interests of older people. Voluntary associations of older people also developed from the growing public attention. The National Retired Teachers Association was established in 1947, the National Council on the Aging was founded in 1950, and the American Association of Retired Persons was founded in 1958.

In 1958, John Fogarty (D. RI) introduced the White House Conference on Aging Act. The purpose of this legislation was "to convene a national forum of the most knowledgeable people in the field of aging to distill their combined experience into a blueprint for action on aging."[11] A U.S. Senate subcommittee busied itself with developing information through hearings and special reports under the leadership of Senator Pat McNamara (D. Mich.).[12] A significant feature of the Fogarty legislation was the authorization of $15,000 to each state that agreed to participate in the conference and that held a pre-conference study of the problems and issues facing older people in that state. These funds enabled every state to establish a state committee for the White House Conference, conduct factual surveys, and convene

[10]Frances Perkins, *The Roots of Social Security* (Washington, D.C.: U.S. Government Printing Office, 1963), 10.

[11]U.S. Congress, Special Committee on Aging, "Hearings on the Elderly Bill" (Washington, D.C.: U.S. Senate, 1958).

[12]Ibid., 118.

local and state conferences. A wealth of information was generated for the formal meeting in Washington, and against this background the first White House Conference on Aging met in Washington in the second week of January 1961.

The highly successful White House Conferences on Children, begun in 1910, provided the format for planning the White House Conferences on Aging (WHCOA). The White House Conferences on Children, as significant as they were in establishing child welfare policies in this country, never quite developed the political sophistication evidenced in the first White House Conference on Aging. The persons who participated in the activities of the WHCOA were the direct beneficiaries of the policies they recommended. Unlike children, the participants were also members of interest groups that had other access to the political process. Political structures already existed in the Congress to respond to concerns of older people, and a base of social legislation already existed that could be built upon fearlessly. Most significantly, as Senator Barry Goldwater observed, the participants in the WHCOA voted. Thus the WHCOA constituted a new base of political organization for older people and has remained an important feature in subsequent aging-related social issues.

Reports from the state conferences were presented at the WHCOA and subsequently assembled by the special Senate Subcommittee on Aging.[13] Although the form and content of these state reports varied, they did strike themes that echoed in Washington. There were, as expected, calls to improve social services for older people, to improve retirement income, to improve health care, and to expand housing programs for older people. But several new themes found expression from the state meetings and attracted congressional attention. Repeated grumbling that DHEW had not given sufficient attention to the needs of older people was accompanied by recommendations that older persons were not getting a fair share of public resources and services that were already in place. Thus there was a sentiment that developed from this first WHCOA that older people would benefit from existing programs if the programs were better organized around older people's interests and if older people's needs were emphasized.

THE OLDER AMERICANS ACT AND MEDICARE

The excitement stirred by this WHCOA was not lost on Congress or the new president, John F. Kennedy. In the Senate, the special subcommittee on aging busied itself with conducting hearings, mostly on retirement income, and in preparation of studies and special reports about older people's problems. For thirty years, pressure had been building for a health care plan for older people, but this idea had become embroiled in politics by the American Medical Association, which had declared these proposals a form of "socialized medicine." One of President Kennedy's first

---

[13]U.S. Congress, Committee on Labor and Public Welfare, U.S. Senate, "Background Studies Prepared by State Committees for the White House Conference on Aging" (Washington, D.C.: U.S. Government Printing Office, 1960).

tasks was to lend the support of the presidency to resolving this long-term issue of adequate health care for older people.

Kennedy, as well as other leaders in the Congress, understood the increasing political visibility of older people advocating for a large number of improvements in social programs. This political pressure might be turned to break the logjam over health care issues. Early in 1963, President Kennedy sent a message to Congress, "Elderly Citizens of Our Nation," in which he strongly supported medical care legislation as well as a more comprehensive approach to satisfying many social wants of older people. Among these he proposed "a five-year program of assistance to state and local agencies and voluntary organizations for planning and developing services for older people."[14]

Two bills reflecting the president's interests in older people were introduced in 1963. One was the administration's bill (S 1375 and HR 5840). The other was a bill developed under the guidance of the special Senate subcommittee on aging (S 200 and HR 7959). Both bills were designed to improve social services for older people. Medical care legislation had also been introduced and was pending. The main difference between these two bills was a proposal in the Senate subcommittee's bill that would create a new administrative agency, an Administration on Aging. Anthony Celebrezze, secretary of DHEW and a former mayor of Cleveland, Ohio, testified against the Senate's proposals. He argued that a new agency was unnecessary since DHEW could provide the special focus on older adults' issues needed to develop better services for them. The Senate, however, was not persuaded. The Senate remained convinced that older adults' problems had to be dealt with separately. A compromise was reached, providing for a new division within DHEW, called the Administration on Aging (AOA), with an Administrator on Aging who would report directly to the secretary of DHEW. This compromise kept the special focus on the problems of older people without creating a new organization, while preserving overall program development within the DHEW structure. The legislation failed to work its way through the elaborate legislative process of Congress before adjournment, and it died with the 88th Congress. The importance of this legislation rested on the strong agreement that something special should be done for older people.

John W. McComack, former speaker of the House of Representatives, once called the 89th Congress "the Congress of fulfillment." The social legislation adopted by this Congress, as a tribute to the memory of John F. Kennedy, and as a testimony to President Johnson's parliamentary skills, is even more staggering when gauged against the caution of the 1980s. Unlike the 97th Congress, which convened in 1980 with a strong conservative mandate, the landslide victory for the Democratic party in 1964 was believed to carry a liberal mandate for a broader federal role in the nation's social concerns. President Johnson put medical insurance and older Americans' problems at the head of his domestic legislative agenda. The National Council of Senior Citizens brought 1,400 older people to Washington at

---

[14]John F. Kennedy, "To Support Our Older Citizens," *Messages of the President*, 23, 154.

the opening of Congress to watchdog both the speaker of the House of Representatives and other congressmen until it appeared there was sufficient support for programs for older people.

If it was not by design, it was not accidental either that the Older Americans Act (HR 3704) was introduced in Congress early in 1965. It sailed through the House of Representatives on March 31 and passed the Senate unanimously on May 27. Such strong support for aging programs and presidential legislative initiatives was essential if medical care for older people was to be acted upon favorably. The Senate was very narrowly divided on Medicare, so the support for the Older Americans Act provided some of the momentum the Senate needed when it finally acted favorably on Medicare in June. Medicare won Senate approval sixty-eight to twenty-one and became the eighteenth title to the Social Security Act. Thus the 89th Congress smiled favorably on older adults early in the session.

THE POLITICAL IMPLICATIONS
OF THE OLDER AMERICANS ACT

A full discussion of the programmatic features of the Older Americans Act is provided in Chapter 6. The political features of this act are important to discuss now. The Older Americans Act is different from most federal welfare legislation, thus contributing some new understanding of the politics of aging policy. First, the act established a separate Administration on Aging in the Department of Health, Education and Welfare, to give special emphasis to older people and their problems. Second, the act emphasized coordination and planning of existing resources as an alternative to developing new service programs, on the assumption that through such efforts the elderly might receive a fair share of social resources. Only modest direct service programs were funded under the original act, and these programs did not require the development of new structures or new social agencies. Services like information and referral were to be offered through traditional social agencies. The emphasis on coordination and planning politicized service provisions for older people by setting in motion a process by which funds and resources allocated for one population and traditionally used for one set of purposes were now to be used by the aged. For example, day care, always considered to be a service for children, was now a service that also should be available to older people. Through better "coordinating and planning" it was assumed that shifts in resource allocation would be accomplished in local communities.

As a third, unusual political feature, this act required coordination and planning at a substate level of program operation. Substate organizations, later called Areawide Agencies on Aging (AAAs), under John Martin's stewardship, were chosen or designated by each state. The AAAs received federal funds from the Administration on Aging (AOA) that were passed through the states, for the planning and coordinating activity. Bypassing states was begun in 1964 with the first federal legislation to break significantly with the traditional patterns of intergovernmental social program administration. The Office of Economic Opportunity contracted directly with local program units, at first completely bypassing state authority. Whereas the Older Americans Act did not bypass the states completely, it supported an interim level of program administration not directly related to a traditional unit of governance. /

In the American system of government, sovereign governing powers are given the federal government, state government, and local and county municipal governments. Usually county governments are designated as local program administrators with obligations to report to the state in such cooperative programs as welfare (AFDC), unemployment, and similar program areas. Under the Older Americans Act, however, a new level of governmental administration was introduced into the traditional intergovernmental service delivery structure (see Figure 4-1).

A final unusual feature of this act was the special authority Congress exerted over the structure of the Administration on Aging (AOA). Originally, the Senate wanted a separate administrative agency to give full authority to dealing with older adults. While Congress accepted the compromise that left AOA within the DHEW administrative framework, it insisted that the administrator be appointed by the president with the advice and consent of the Senate. The administrator of AOA reported directly to the secretary of DHEW. The power to administer the Older Americans Act was therefore given to DHEW, even though the administrator of AOA had considerable authority within the DHEW structure. The structure offered opportunities for older people to react to programs at the highest administrative level in DHEW. This arrangement left DHEW as the administrative agency of the Older Americans Act. As time went on, however, DHEW undertook activities that gradually restricted the administrative authority of AOA.

Congress sought to limit the authority of DHEW over AOA by spelling out the authority of AOA in detail rather than leaving authority discretionary with the secretary of DHEW. The Older Americans Act assigned seven functional authorities to AOA: to serve as an information clearinghouse, to provide technical assistance to the secretary of DHEW, to develop research and demonstration plans, to provide federal assistance to states (as discussed before), to publish educational materials, to gather statistics, and to stimulate broader utilization of services to include older

FIGURE 4-1   Patterns of Intergovernmental Program Administration

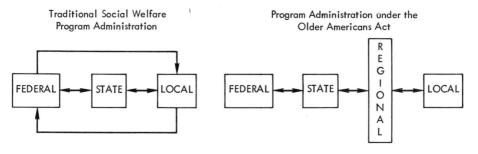

people.[15] AOA also had administrative authority under its mandate to provide federal assistance to states and programs, but this authority was limited by the fact that the only grants authorized were those to states for coordinating and planning at the substate level. The federal legislation spelled out what was required of states in order to be eligible for funding under this grant authority. Thus, as a practical matter, AOA had very little authority over the use of these funds. For example, the administrator of AOA reported to the secretary of DHEW; state plans had to be approved by DHEW rather than by AOA. By specifying the powers of AOA and DHEW, carefully combined new powers produced a new organization, unique among the other administrative structures within DHEW, but with limited power over any aging programs. In other words, AOA had no practical authority to direct the product of any aging programs that might be offered in the typical local community. AOA's independence from DHEW was exclusively dependent on the amount of interest Congress showed in aging programs, and this interest, in turn, was a product of the growing effectiveness of the newly developing voluntary organizations (interest groups) of aging people, like AARP.

RELATIONSHIP OF EARLY AOA EFFORTS
TO EXISTING POLITICAL STRUCTURES

Congress appointed William Bechill the first commissioner of AOA, and John Martin succeeded him in 1969. Bechill was an astute bureaucrat who served in DHEW under Wilbur Cohen, when Cohen was assistant secretary of DHEW and during the time Cohen was acting secretary of DHEW. Bechill was a social worker, with experience with and support from the Senior Citizen Advisory Committee, a large national organization representative of aging groups. His diligent work in DHEW and Cohen's good name and good favor with Congress paved the way for Bechill's appointment. Bechill's main task was getting the agency started, and this he did ably. Bechill related to the aging constituency, and he became a respected figure in the powerful Senate subcommittee on aging.

John Martin, however, set a different tone for the aging program under this act. Martin was a lawyer from Grand Rapids, Michigan. He had served as auditor for Michigan and had been a member of the Michigan Senate. Most significantly, he was a well-known member of the Republican National Committee from 1957 to 1958. Although he had limited experience with older people, he had ideas similar to the president's for reshaping federal-state relations. Martin supported amendments to the Older Americans Act that he felt would chart a new federal role for serving older people. This new federal role was predicated on exploiting the new substate level of program administration as described above. The issue was how to give greater responsibility to states, rather than to local governments, as had been the practice during the 1960s. Since each state was responsible for developing a state

---

[15] *The Older Americans Act of 1965.*

plan that spelled out how Older Americans Act monies would be spent, Martin fore-saw that, by strengthening substate regional administration and the state's control over these regions (AAAs), the authority of local units to provide services to older people could be limited. Thus a new role had to be developed for the AAAs, and Martin provided the strategy and content for realizing that new role.

Martin endorsed a new concept called "area planning," and he supported amendments designed to create a new planning and coordinating form called "area model projects." Since AOA's grant authority over aging programs only covered planning and coordination, giving greater emphasis to AAAs and expanding their authority over localities would be one way to control local programs. There was no requirement in the Older Americans Act that AAAs had to be multijurisdictional units. In fact, Pennsylvania implemented the Older Americans Act by making each of its counties an AAA. Martin used area-wide planning as a way to encourage multi-jurisdictional AAAs. He then initiated demonstration area model projects in which states were offered incentive funds to engage in multijurisdictional planning and service coordination. At first area-wide planning—multijurisdictional planning as it really was—was optional with the states. However, in writing the regulations to implement Title III of the 1969 Amendments to the Older Americans Act, AOA de-veloped strict guidelines for the use of Title III funds that included requirements that states engage in area-wide planning through appropriate area-wide planning organizations. In the words of the regulations, "Following the determination of planning and service areas, for which area plans will be developed, . . . the state shall designate a single public or non-profit private agency or organization as the area agency on aging" (see Figure 4-2).[16]

Since the states had wide options in designating which organizations would undertake area planning and coordinating functions, and since the scope of these functions appeared relatively benign, these regulations prompted very little debate. Furthermore, Martin's administrative initiatives took place during a time of intense discussion about the effectiveness of local government in the face of growing com-plexity of local social problems. Across the nation, states were making it possible for local governments to enter into cooperative planning and, in some cases, cooper-ative program administrative activities with governments in close proximity to each other. These government cooperative activities were undertaken in Councils of Government (COGs) across the country, in which local governments contributed funds to the COG that were used to hire a staff of planners. The COG staff then recommended cooperative projects to the council members (the local governments), and helped them work out details for implementing cooperative projects.

Two related federal initiatives supported the development of Councils of Government across the nation. The first was Bureau of the Budget Circular A-95, is-sued in 1969. To be eligible for federal funds, substate regional review was required of certain federally funded projects as a means to eliminate duplication and over-

---

[16] *Code of Federal Regulations* (Washington, D.C.: U.S. Government Printing Office, 1983), Title 45, Sect. 903.

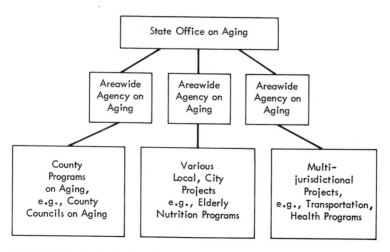

FIGURE 4-2   Service Delivery Structure under Title III Older Americans Act.

lapping services in contiguous local administrative units. The second related federal activity derived from a new title of the Housing Act. Section 707 provided federal funds for substate regional planning projects related to community development. Under Section 707, federal funds were available to support Councils of Government planning staffs. Since most of the A-95 reviews related to projects that were also related to 707 planning, such as waste water treatment, solid waste disposal, transportation, and public safety, and since A-95 review covered projects that raised little local controversy, Councils of Government were promoted as alternative administrative structures to sluggish local governments. By the early 1970s, Councils of Government existed in most states, and since COGs had responsibility for substate, area-wide physical planning and A-95 review authority, most of the states designated the COG as the area-wide aging agency (AAA) as Title III of the Older Americans Act became implemented under the new regulations.

Although linking area-wide aging planning with area-wide physical planning and cooperation seemed logical enough at first, it eventually set in motion a new pattern of federal–state relationships in social program administration. COGs are quasigovernmental bodies in the sense that they are created out of the membership of local governments within a particular geographic region. They have public accountability only through the local officials who appoint themselves to the COG boards and the COG governing committees. COGs, therefore, have limited jurisdiction for most public functions, such as raising funds and administering programs. When controversial issues do arise with respect to a cooperative issue, there is no opportunity for consumer or taxpayer input into the council decision structure. Thus, by design COGs were deliberately insulated from the mainstream of public discussion and debate. In the words of one political analyst,

The individual taxpayer who feels the need to provide the Council with his own views on some matter which appears on its agenda cannot be certain that he can do so effectively by conferring with the elected official of just one of what might be more than a hundred constituent units. By the same token, the citizen who feels the need to react against an action or decision of a Council of Governments cannot and should not hold a locally elected official responsible.[17]

Furthermore, COGs do not have one set structure or some set range of issues of concern. Rather, COGs are responsible for planning on the broadest multijurisdictional scale. If anything, COGs have become weighed down by lack of specificity of task and function. Characteristic of a traditional planning approach, COGs quickly became instruments of information-gathering. According to the American Assembly's analysis of this movement, the potential of the COG to improve local administrative effectiveness was limited. The American Assembly noted the COG is evaluated by its opponents as "a toothless tiger or—even worse—a protector of the inadequate status quo. It seems clear that a COG can be anything from an Elks Lodge to the beginning of a new metropolitan government."[18]

THE CHANGING CONTEXT OF POLITICAL ACCOUNTABILITY

The Older Americans Act created a whole new political environment for older people. The act did not provide services; rather it provided a structure in which older people and their advocates could compete for existing resources. Unlike the political activity of the Townsend movement, which focused attention on Congress, contemporary political struggles are focused at the substate and local level. Also unlike the political activities of the Townsend period, which were organized around identifiable interests, such as pensions, contemporary political struggles differ from one locality to the next. As the arena of political activity for older people has become smaller, older people have been more effective in getting better resources, but their political influence on national policy issues has become more fragmented and less effective.

The contemporary political activity of older people often focuses around a local organization, such as a Council on Aging, which will provide a focal point for a variety of political activities to insure that local resources are available for older people. Because the AAA has planning authority for several local jurisdictions, there is considerable competition among local aging organizations within the planning region. In this way, the AAA encourages political sophistication among older peo-

---

[17]The American Assembly, *Making Local Government Work* (Boston: Little Brown & Co., 1967).

[18]Alan K. Campbell, *The States and the Urban Crisis* (Englewood Cliffs, N.J.: Prentice-Hall, 1970, p. 67.

ple, but only with respect to the political contests that are resolvable within the jurisdiction of the AAA. In this way the AAAs have changed the context of political accountability. Instead of congressional accountability to local and national aging constituencies, AAAs are the first line of accountability for the aging constituency. As weak political organizations, AAAs and their sponsoring organizations, usually COGs politically-weak also, lacked political authority. During a time when older people were growing numerically and becoming politically active in established governmental structures, the development of regional planning units outside the existing political structures changed the context of aging politics. In other words, the institution of substate, regional planning and coordination within politically impotent structures fragmented and misdirected the growing politicization in the field of aging.

It is unfair to suggest this depoliticizing movement deliberately was designed to weaken the effectiveness of older people. Much of the discussion of the Older Americans Act and its subsequent amendments focuses on those efforts to improve services for older people. In this respect, focusing political activities at the local level has indeed maximized provision of resources for older people which no amount of national political activity could have produced. Thus the shift in political accountability is a two-edged sword.

Yet even the potential for achieving better social services for older people has been handicapped by the existing AAA structure. COGs might have been ready to meet the social planning functions required of the newly mandated area-wide aging agency, but they were in no position to administer social programs. Yet COGs were in place, and COG staff welcomed the challenge presented by the new program emphasis of the Older Americans Act, if for no other reason than the availability of funds to fortify the fiscal base of the COG movement. There is considerable research and opinion that the social planning or coordinating activity mandated to AAAs is not an effective strategy to improve services. Robert Hudson's analysis of the expectations of Title III provides one such criticism of the planning and coordinating strategy. According to Hudson, "the notion that there are untapped resources lying around out there merely for the asking is untenable." Hudson points out that most coordinating efforts in the past have served to preserve vested interests, under the guise of eliminating duplicated services. Hudson sees "nothing about the area agencies which gives one reason to think they will be less subject toward these pressures."[19]

Of the many problems AAAs encountered within a COG structure, none has been more difficult than finding personnel to carry out the planning and coordinating mandates. By 1969, most of the people who worked in the field of aging were gerontologists. While gerontologists were knowledgeable about the problems of older people, they had little experience or training in planning or coordinating serv-

[19] Robert Hudson, "Rational Planning and Organizational Imperatives: Prospects for Area Planning in Aging," *Annals of the American Academy of Political and Social Science,* 415 (September, 1974), 54.

ices for older people. On the other hand, physical planners who staffed most COGs knew little about the complexities of social problems, less about the intrigues of social program administration, and even less about older people. Upon close analysis, uniting area-wide planning in aging with COGs did not appear a wise choice. The area-wide COG movement might well provide new forms of federal–state relations, but its potential for fragmenting unified political activity has become its greatest liability.

THE POLITICAL CONSEQUENCES OF THE AAA

In order to improve the planning and coordinating capability of the AAAs, the Administration on Aging gradually gave COGs greater powers over decision making in those areas of the Older Americans Act that could be put under their jurisdiction. Before the mid-1970s, AAAs operated in the following manner: Almost all the services available to older people were provided under legislative authority other than the Older Americans Act. For example, in-home services, such as helping keep the house clean and helping fix meals, were available to older people through Departments of Social Services, under provisions of the Social Security Act. The area-wide aging planner, in the course of planning and coordinating the variety of services available to older people, would note in the "area plan" how much in-home services was needed. Then the area-wide planner would go to the Department of Social Services and try to convince the department to provide more in-home services to older people. This was a job in salesmanship, which required skills in problem analysis, resource mobilization, and community development. Obviously, the Department of Social Services had other constituent groups to serve. Giving more services to older people might result in taking some services away from children, for example, unless the county commissioners could be convinced to provide new money. "Coordinating" services for older people was tough work for area-wide planners, and preliminary analysis of this work suggested that funds spent for planning and coordinating did not convert into more services for older people.

As problems with area-wide planning grew, AOA tried to strengthen AAAs. The AAAs had the effect of creating a desirable new form of federal–state relations as federal funds were used to create and maintain substate regional structures. As the Older Americans Act was modified to make area-wide planning a requirement, rather than an option, additional funds were provided to states for expanding the scope of AAAs. The 1973 amendments to the Older Americans Act permitted AAAs to provide social services directly, when the state agency judged that such provision of service "is necessary to assure an adequate supply of such service." Included as services that AAAs could provide were information, referral, and transportation. Now AAAs were in direct competition with other local service providers, and no longer needed to "coordinate" with respect to these services. These new authorities of the AAAs were strengthened when the Administration on Aging made resources available to help establish a National Association of Area Agencies on Aging (N4A). This organization, although legally a private organization, grew to become a close partner with AOA in promoting legislation that would preserve and strengthen the AAA structure under Title III of the Older Americans Act.

The AAAs continue to present an unusual pattern of intergovernmental social program administration. In a time when regional planning and COGs generally have become less attractive governmental instruments, AAAs have become key links in the aging network. Yet AAAs lack an independent political authority. AAAs have no citizen constituency among older people to elect them, nor are they created by local governments as are the COGs. AAAs have become much more administrative units than organizations effective at planning and coordinating local service resources. AAAs appear to be equally uncertain about the significance of providing services through these unique social organizations. According to Hudson, "No amount of central direction from federal and state agencies can generate resources which are controlled by different actors at different levels."[20] Thus the development of the most unique feature of the Older Americans Act—coordinating and planning at the substate, regional level—has become little more than another effort to develop a new structure through which the administrative bureaucracy at the state and federal levels can manipulate local community resources and frustrate the development of a national aging constituency.

THE SECOND AND THIRD WHITE HOUSE CONFERENCES ON AGING

Gilbert Steiner has objected to the White House Conferences for Children for the failure of these conferences to develop either a national program or a national constituency for children. Steiner argues that White House conferences are useless exercises that have little impact on future policy directions: "The truth is that the 1970 children's conference had little consequential impact on either Congress or the White House, or anyone else. The limits of public responsibility for children, and how to discharge that responsibility, are no more clear after the conference than they were before."[21]

This is not an adequate conclusion to draw about the White House Conferences on Aging (WHCOA). The second conference was held in 1971 and the third in 1981. These two conferences represent the only national forum presently available for expression of the growing political potential of older people. Particularly the 1981 conference helped mold a coalition of older people and related interest groups, with clear focus on national policy objectives. Even the socially conservative Senator Barry Goldwater (Arizona) conceded the growing political significance of older

[20] Robert Hudson, op. cit., 56.

[21] Gilbert Y. Steiner, *The Children's Cause* (Washington, D.C.: The Brookings Institution, 1976), 130.

people as an outcome of the second WHCOA. Endorsing the second WHCOA, Goldwater recognized that "unlike the young ones [older citizens] enjoy the right to vote. In fact, the participation of the older people in the voting process is greater than the national average."[22]

Planning and developing the 1971 WHCOA was more elaborate than that for 1961. States easily fell into the pattern of local and state meetings in which a wide variety of policies were discussed and program changes were proposed. Area-wide planning coordination under the AAAs was just beginning, and the AAAs played an important part in planning and conducting thousands of local meetings with high levels of active participation by older adults. The Administration on Aging took major responsibility for providing materials to be used for programming these state and local meetings. Widespread participation and high interest in a variety of policy issues produced thousands of policy statements that were summarized into fourteen major areas for deliberation by the delegates. At the conclusion of the 1971 WHCOA over 700 recommendations were made to improve the lives of older people. Some of the recommendations required state actions to implement them; some recommendations required actions by the AOA; other recommendations required congressional action. Congress, particularly the Senate, praised the efforts of AOA in developing the 1971 WHCOA and its recommendations. It referred to the report of the WHCOA as a national policy statement on aging, and quickly began to develop legislation to implement recommendations.

On November 30, 1971, Congress legislated a new Title to the Older Americans Act—the Elderly Nutrition Program. This was a program designed to feed older people a free lunch. It was a product of the WHCOA deliberations. This program was expensive, but provided an important cornerstone for further development of an aging constituency. Perhaps because of its possible high cost, President Nixon vetoed the initial appropriation of funds for the program. Subsequently AOA appointed a post-WHCOA board that was designed to review and act as watchdog for the recommendations from the conference. The review of this board was pessimistic in light of the range of expectations contained in the WHCOA recommendations. But if AOA and the President did not appreciate the political potential of older people by this time, Congress certainly did. In 1973, Congress reapproved the Elderly Nutrition Project, with large appropriations that the President could not impound. It also authorized the creation of the Federal Council on the Aged, which was given broad investigative power over programs administered by AOA. This council was required to report to the president, AOA, and the Congress. Thus with the special Senate Subcommittee on Aging and the Federal Council, Congress had established considerable control over aging policy development and program administration. While John Martin wanted more authority to develop area-wide planning, Congress was quite willing to expand the Act in any direction, and when AOA made its requests in 1973, Congress lavished its financial abundance on it. The

[22] Barry Goldwater, op. cit., 158.

products of the 1981 WHCOA are not as demonstrable, although Social Security has been blessed by the president and Congress and its immediate future is no longer in question. The remaining recommendations are still being reviewed for their legislative significance.

INTEREST GROUPS AND ALPHABET SOUP

No political theory of aging would be complete without examination of the interest groups that have developed to advocate for older people. Along with the growing political authority of older people themselves, these groups played an important part in the activities that led to the expansion of programs for older people during the 1960s and 1970s. Built on the prototype of the Townsend movement, those interest groups seek political access by virtue of their large numbers of persons who would be affected directly by programs designed to assist older people.

Many years ago, David Truman, an outstanding analyst of the American system of government, observed that different interests had different access to political decision-making, based upon the characteristics of the groups that represented those interests. For example, monied interests have limited access to the legislative process, but these groups have gained access in the most influential legislative structures. Banking has access in the House Commerce and Banking Committees, and chambers of commerce have access in the Ways and Means Committee and Senate Finance Committee. Civil rights groups have obtained access through courts, while professional groups have obtained access through the administrative bureaucracy. Groups with broad-based membership do not obtain access to specific legislative structures. Rather, the influence of these groups is felt along a wide spectrum of access points.

Like labor groups, which have the capacity to speak to all legislators in their home districts, groups reflecting the interests of older people had widespread access to centers of political decision making during the 1960s and 1970s. Although the Senate developed a special structure to deal with the issues of older people, the real power of the aging interest groups matured as the groups expanded their membership bases, and like the Townsend Clubs that preceded them, the interest groups of the aged of the 1960s and 1970s were strong because they could talk to legislators at home, and legislators, in turn, opened the doors to these new legislative advocates.

The National Council of Senior Citizens √

Interest groups composed of older persons are the most politically active of the special interest groups, and the major ones warrant some extended discussion of their base of membership, their interests, and their activities. One of the most politically sensitive groups is the National Council of Senior Citizens (NCSC). To understand the significance of this group, one has to recall the struggle for health care for older people. Aimé Forand (D-RI) introduced the widely publicized, almost legislated Health Insurance Bill in the House of Representatives in 1957. This bill, often referred to as the "Forand Bill," had the strong support of the AFL-CIO, which under the leadership of Nelson Cruikshank, head of AFL-CIO Social Security Department, had actively supported earlier proposals to develop a publicly supported hospital insurance program. It was a long-overdue idea; planners of the original Social Security Act (1935) had also considered a health insurance proposal. The insurance bill introduced by Forand proved to be a central event around which many interest groups, including the AFL-CIO, could converge.[23] Out of this effort the National Council of Senior Citizens was born.

The ups and downs of the Forand Bill and medical insurance continued into and beyond the 1961 White House Conference on Aging. Forand attended the 1961 conference, and he entered a discussion with union leaders about developing an organization of senior persons to support medical insurance. According to Richard Harris, Cruikshank opposed this sort of organizing activity, but Charles Odell of the United Auto Workers and James O'Brien of United Steel Workers agreed to put up a small fund from their unions to start an organization, and Forand agreed to be the chairman.[24] The beginnings of this organization also derived from another politically visible older people's group, Senior Citizens for Kennedy, organized with its base in New York City in 1959. The interest that many older citizens had shown in medical insurance legislation was galvanized into support for Kennedy as he campaigned on a program to support medical insurance.

President John F. Kennedy's support of older people, particularly in his 1963 Message to Congress on the needs of older people, derived from this group of older persons who developed an active and effective arm of his presidential campaign. The connection with Forand and later support from NCSC only sweetened this association for Kennedy. President Johnson and the Democratic 89th Congress welcomed the 1,400 members of NCSC who watched as Congress acted on Medicare proposals in 1965.

The National Council of Senior Citizens now boasts more than three million members, although dues-paying membership is considerably less. Most members of NCSC and of the national board are retired union members or union officials. Nelson Cruikshank himself became president of NCSC in 1972, and he remains active with the national board. The close union ties of NCSC have assisted this organization in gaining access to the congressional legislative process. It is not particularly effective or visible in the activities of AOA, but its close ties with organized labor permit NCSC to offer a number of important membership benefits beyond association with an interest group, such as travel plans, discounts on drugs, and legal services, to mention a few. Sympathetic unions contribute to the operating costs of NCSC, which keeps dues and membership service costs quite low.

[23] James L. Sundquist, *Politics and Policy* (Washington, D.C.: The Brookings Institution, 1968), 287-321.

[24] Annals of the American Academy of Political and Social Science, *Studies on Aging*, 423 (November, 1976), 112-134.

The National Retired Teachers Association
and the American Association of Retired Persons

The largest membership organization of older people developed from two different organizations that were originally concerned with insurance benefits for retired adults. The National Retired Teachers Association and the American Association of Retired Persons (NRTA-AARP) is the oldest, still active, and effective voluntary membership interest group. These organizations, which began with a strong orientation to member services, have become much more active in attempts to achieve policy objectives that will benefit older people. Dr. Ethel Andrus, a well-known California educator, was a very active member of the National Education Association. In 1947, she founded the National Retired Teachers Association out of her concern for improving the well-being of retired educators. Her original idea was to provide member benefits, mostly insurance programs, to educators who retired. The growth of membership in NRTA until the mid-1950s, when Dr. Andrus became associated with a New York insurance agent, Leonard Davis, was slow. Davis had been instrumental in developing an insurance program for retired teachers in New York State. Andrus and Davis developed an agreement by which a private insurance program, similar to that developed in New York, could be available to members of NRTA. Davis himself provided $50,000 to underwrite the program, which proved immediately successful. NRTA memberships soared.

The NRTA insurance benefits proved attractive to retired noneducators as well, so Andrus and Davis founded a parallel organization for them in 1958—the American Association of Retired Persons (AARP). Although this new group had its own legal structure, the two groups cooperated very closely, particularly in fiscal matters. The membership potential for AARP was quickly realized. The combined NRTA-AARP membership in 1959 was 15,000. Today it is over seven million people, making it one of the largest voluntary-membership organizations in the country. Membership is attracted to NRTA-AARP because of its membership benefits—insurance, travel, pharmacy discounts, and vocational and retirement training services. Although NRTA-AARP is an effective, active advocate for social legislation, its close association with the insurance industry requires some restraint in NRTA-AARP political activity. For example, during the debates over Medicare, the organization proposed an insurance bill advocated by Dr. Andrus that would have developed national health insurance for older people through a private trusteeship operated by private industry. NRTA-AARP was criticized for trying to line its own nest.

The NRTA-AARP is potentially as powerful an interest group as NCSC. While ties with organized labor account for NCSC's political effectiveness, the large membership and financial resources of NRTA-AARP account for its effectiveness. It maintains a team of six to ten congressional lobbyists. Financial resources of NRTA-AARP are difficult to pinpoint, but Henry Pratt estimated that membership alone accounted for over $3 million annually ten years ago. Pratt also estimated that at that time memberships accounted for only about 50 percent of annual revenues.

At least 40 percent of NRTA-AARP's annual income came from the insurance programs, and the rest from travel fees and advertising.[25] Recently, the original insurance underwriter, the Colonial Penn Insurance Company, was challenged by rival companies for its high underwriter's fees. While NRTA-AARP does not project an aggressive lobbying image, its political power is most noticed among Washington policy makers. When President Reagan announced proposals to reduce social security in 1981, NRTA-AARP was quick to voice its firm opposition to such changes, and the flood of mail to Congress, principally from NRTA-AARP members, led quickly to an overwhelming Senate endorsement for Social Security.

The National Association for Retired Federal Employees

The National Association for Retired Federal Employees (NARFE) was founded in 1921 shortly after Congress enacted legislation to give pension benefits to federal employees. Since that time, NARFE has continued to develop as a force to protect the retirement benefits of federal employees. The political strength of this organization derives not so much from a large number of members nor its financial resources. Both are modest. The strength of NARFE comes from the character of its membership—present and retired federal employees. These people have direct access to national decision-making processes, and while NARFE has not taken an active role in issues beyond those of immediate concern to its membership, it has had important influence on the issues it has engaged with. For example, NARFE was not active with the development of the Older Americans Act, Medicare, or any of the White House Conferences. But when Congress proposed to roll together government pensions and social security, and tighten provisions for "double dipping" with social security, NARFE came out of the closets. In 1977 and 1979, Congress tried to cut social security costs by requesting federal employees to pay social security taxes, thereby insuring security in both funds. But NARFE beat the efforts back, preserving special retirement privileges for its members.

The National Council on the Aging

The National Council on the Aging (NCOA) was founded in 1950. Unlike some of the other groups whose members are largely older adults, NCOA's membership is composed of individuals and organizations directly or indirectly serving older people. Six constituency units make up the NCOA: the National Institute of Senior Centers (NISC), the National Institute on Work and Retirement, the National Institute of Adult Day Care (NIAD), the National Institute of Senior Housing (NISH), the National Center on Rural Aging (NCRA), and National Voluntary Organizations for Independent Living (NVOILA).

The oldest constituency unit is NISC, which was organized in 1960 and comprises the largest membership in NCOA. NISC members of NCOA elect a delegate

[25] Ibid., 234–246.

body of one representative from each state plus ten at-large delegates. Through the delegate body of NISC, issues of importance to the senior center field are identified, discussed, and researched, and appropriate measures designed for handling. The scope of concerns includes legislative and policy matters, promotion of good professional practice, visibility of senior centers, research, and technical assistance to centers at the local level. Senior center standards and guidelines for practice were developed, and NISC is currently working on a certification process and/or accreditation of senior center administrators.

The National Institute on Work and Retirement has developed with an advisory committee structure steering the efforts into research and publication of a journal. A major thrust of this unit is advocacy for older adults in the workplace, especially in regard to mandatory retirement abolishment. The National Institute of Adult Day Care operates with a delegate body elected on the basis of the ten federal regions. A major emphasis is the development of national standards for adult day care. The National Institute of Senior Housing is an outgrowth of a nonprofit Housing Corporation sponsored by NCOA. Organizational structure of this constituency unit is in the formative stage, with some type of delegate council likely to emerge. NISH provides consultation on housing design for older adults, provides assistance to local developers interested in building residential housing for older adults, advocates for housing options to be available, and watchdog legislation. The National Center on Rural Aging, led by a delegate council of regional representatives, develops policy related to the needs and interests of rural older adults, provides technical assistance and consultation to programs at all administrative levels, and serves as a clearinghouse for information on the rural elderly.

The National Voluntary Organizations for Independent Living was formed after the White House Conference of 1971. Any national, civic, or professional organization is invited to join the efforts to promote measures aimed at maximizing the capabilities of older adults to remain in their own homes by assuring the availability of supports the older adult may need to do so. More than two hundred national organizations, including associations representing nurses, dentists, optometrists, and religious groups, are listed and associated with NVOILA. A major purpose of NVOILA is not only to involve organizations at the national level, but to funnel voluntary services of members of these organizations to the programs at the local level.

NCOA operates a number of programs including some funded by the Federal Administration on Aging for research and training, and by the Arts and Humanities Program, which aims to stimulate and assist local efforts to enrich older adults' lives. It also conducted the widely acclaimed social attitude survey in 1974 and repeated in 1980 with the assistance of Louis Harris. Thus NCOA is a diversified organization that acts as an umbrella for a variety of individual and group interests that reflect regional and national concerns. It is the most diverse of any of the organizations that serve older people. Consequently, it is able to encompass a wide variety of issues with a wide variety of activities and techniques. It is perhaps one of the most politically influential of all the groups that serve older people. NCOA recently convened the first National Assembly on Aging. This Assembly called together one hundred key leaders in the field of aging to make recommendations on policy that would improve the lives of older people.

POLITICAL THEORY OF AGING

Compared with public policies designed to serve children, minorities, and other special groups, public policies that serve older people are highly politicized. The size of the older adult population and the degree of political efficacy among older people at the polls and through interest groups provide the foundation for the politics of aging policy. The long-standing political tradition among older adults, dating to the Townsend movement, lends a certain credibility to the relationship between politics and policy with respect to older people that is lacking among other groups. In other words, there is greater public acceptance that legislation favorable to older people is a result of the political influence of older people. Somewhat in contrast with policy affecting older people, legislation relevant to other groups must meet some specific social expectations, such as social need. Policy for older people spans a wide range of social and economic conditions for eligibility.

Figure 4-3 depicts a paradigm of the policy process suggested years ago by David Easton and applied here to the development of aging policy. This paradigm is helpful in understanding the influence of older people in the policy-making process. A brief definition of the elements of this paradigm is followed by a current example as reflected by the 1981 White House Conference on Aging.

Public Issues

It is significant to the policy-making process who defines what issues. Fundamental differences exist in policy products when policy decision makers, or professional persons, or consumers, define the issues. When policy decision makers, such as legislators and administrators, define the issues they do so with some consideration for the outcomes they would like to realize. These outcomes may not always be consistent with the best interests of the consumers, in this case, older people. For example, congressmen considering the need for higher social security benefits might be more concerned about tax rates than benefits for older people. Administrators, anticipating new program requests, might suggest program alternatives that would promote the agency rather than the best interests of older persons.

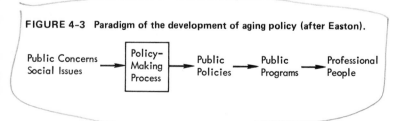

FIGURE 4-3   Paradigm of the development of aging policy (after Easton).

Public Concerns
Social Issues → Policy-Making Process → Public Policies → Public Programs → Professional People

A major characteristic of aging policy has been the extent to which older persons themselves have defined the problems for which policies have been developed.

The Policy-Making Process

Much has been said and written about a public policy-making process. It is important to note here that legislatures, administrations, the courts, and executives, as well as leaders of influential private organizations, usually through interest groups, are all involved in a complex network that somehow creates public policy. This process is uneven, built small piece by piece over a long period. Because of their age and experience, older people are more likely to be among the actors in the institutions involved in the policy-making process.

Public Policies

Public policies either may be general statements of a public philosophy or ideology, or they may be clearly defined public laws, court decisions, or actions by the president, governor, or important administrative officials. Because of the complexity of the policy-making process, public policies always represent compromise. They must reflect central philosophical and national tendencies if they are to be useful statements about courses of action to be undertaken.

Public Programs

Public programs are the products of the public policies. The Older Americans Act is a policy that also spells out programs that need to be put into place in order to realize the objectives of the policy. Developing rules and regulations is the part of the policy-making process that gives final definition to the programs. As can be seen from the significance of issuing the regulations governing Title III in 1970, programs can be changed significantly by regulations, and the translation of policies into useful programs is by no means an automatic process. It should also be obvious that older people are likely to play an important part in shaping programs and carrying them out.

Professional People

Professional people are those who work with the people whom the public policies and programs were designed to serve. Professional people use skills that are developed during the course of professional training. Professional people bring these skills to program recipients, in this case older people, within the context of prescribed programs. In this view, understanding about the programs, the policies that formed them, and the public problems that generated them is every bit as important to the professional person as the specific helping skills that the profession provides.

Professional people who work with older adults are a special group. As mentioned at the outset of this text, neither gerontology nor geriatrics constitutes a unique profession. Both are specialized fields that depend upon people from a wide variety of professions to apply their talents in the study of and service to older people. In other words, existing professions, such as nursing, social work, medicine, dentistry, law, and others provide the basic education and skills of most professionals. These basic professional skills are then applied in a specific context or with specific groups of people.

This text is designed for professional people who plan to concentrate their professional efforts on helping older people. The context for this work is the framework described in Figure 4-3. Suppose, for example, a well-trained nurse and social worker come to the conclusion that what would be most helpful for a particular older person is a plan that would support the older person outside of the nursing home. All of the counseling and all of the nursing care for this person would be ineffective if these professionals did not know which programs would be available. If some programs were restricted by policy from providing certain services, this information would be essential to make the professional help effective. For example, Medicare cannot pay for nonmedical in-home services. Thus the professional person who works with older adults must understand the policies that govern the programs they use in the helping environment, and they must also understand the dynamics that shape these policies and programs.

CONCLUSION

The politics of aging provides some explanation about the development of the policies and programs that serve older people. The politics of aging shows how older people have been effective in attempts to improve the quality of their lives. Together with the social approaches to understanding older adulthood, and the economic issues of growing older, the politics of aging provide perspective on the problems of older people, on the ways these problems are defined, and on the individuals and groups who experience the problems. In at least a limited way, the social, economic, and political understandings of aging give some insight into the processes of policy making for older people.

The example of the third White House Conference on Aging illustrates several crucial factors in the maturation of policy to serve older people. The conference itself was a platform for the development of policy for older people. It was made possible by Congress, which remained interested in its success. Older people were closely involved with the development and implementation of the conference. The groups representing older people were unusually effective. They kept conference planning moving; they helped focus the conference agenda, and when the conference looked as though it would deteriorate from the purpose that had originally been generated, they provided leadership and options for resolving the disputes that limited the conference's effectiveness. This last function was in the best tradition of the role of voluntary associations in America and continued to preserve the heritage of open assembly and debate.

Not to be overlooked was the role that older people themselves played. Older people were leaders in many of these activities. Because many had served in government, they had rich experience as leaders of social policy making. Older people knew how to do things. They were able to mobilize resources from the larger society that contributed to a useful and productive White House Conference. The recommendations that this conference generated will be the subject of debate in the coming years. Almost all of the six hundred recommendations addressed current programs designed to assist older people with a view to how these programs could be improved. The core of these current programs will be discussed in subsequent chapters of this book.

The way Americans view older people, and the reasons they view them as they do, are an important part of understanding how problems are defined and why certain political activities are more acceptable and effective than others in shaping policy. For example, the economic plight of older people might be characterized as exploitation of older people, or it might be characterized as the struggle of older people to maintain their own independence and dignity. Either characterization may generate sufficient concern and excite a policy development process into action. The activity of the policy process and the policy and programmatic outcomes may be strikingly different, depending upon how the problem is characterized.

Such different perspectives on problems and what should be done about them derive from those things Americans believe to be true. If one believes strongly that older people are exploited, this influences how the problem and its solution are framed. Thus ideology plays a significant but often overlooked role in serving older people. Ideology is often acknowledged but seldom discussed, on the grounds that it is too complex and perhaps of limited practical value for practitioners. The exact opposite, however, may be true. The next chapter discusses the significance of ideology for professional assistance to older people.

CHAPTER FIVE

IDEOLOGIES AND BELIEFS

Americans cherish strong beliefs about one another and the society in which Americans live. Such beliefs are reflected clearly in everyday responses to each other. Views for and against a particular public event, perhaps an election or a new domestic program, are often debated with great agitation, and the beliefs that generate most spirited debates are quickly visible. For example, strongly held positions were debated when the Reagan administration proposed reductions in social security benefits. Many advocates of reductions *believed* that federal expenditures were too high and that the social responsibility of the government should be reduced. Those who opposed the reductions *believed* that older people had a right to live in dignity and that the government had an obligation to act in ways to promote human dignity.

Words like "government responsibility," "personal rights," "individual dignity," "social obligations," and "personal freedom" abound in conversations about personal and social responses to growing older and older adulthood. The previous section of this text discussed a number of economic, social, and political theories about growing older in America. Despite the fact that many of these are founded in scientific proofs, students may still study these chapters with a certain amount of disbelief. In other words, beliefs about human and social phenomena may be much more persuasive explanations for those phenomena than all the scientific information that may be available. Beliefs are powerful tools of understanding that often influence behavior much more strongly than other forms of knowledge.

For example, considerable factual knowledge exists to demonstrate that age itself does not cause older people to seek less active, more socially isolated lives. Moreover, evidence from observing older persons' activities shows increased sociability and activity among the large majority of older people upon retirement, and recent studies suggest that active older people are more healthy and live longer. Despite this evidence, most Americans believe that older adults prefer to be by themselves and that they are too frail to continue life at a fast pace.

The economic, social, and political theories discussed in the first chapters provide some explanation of older adulthood, but not all the explanation. The beliefs that Americans hold about older adulthood must also be explained in order to understand older adulthood and how to help older persons. Understanding these beliefs is just as important as understanding the theories about older adulthood, because beliefs influence professional activities in two ways. First, the beliefs influence the ways that each professional person is likely to behave in attempts to assist the older adult. Second, the beliefs influence the kinds of programs that are developed, and those that helping professionals use in the helping situation. For example, beliefs influence what kind of social security system will be developed, and social security benefits are one set of helping resources available.

These next chapters, therefore, are designed to acquaint professional people with the belief systems that influence American personal and social behavior. There are three major contexts in which ideology has great significance for shaping professional helping activities.

The first context is the influence of ideology on the behavior of the professional person who is in direct contact with the older person. In this context, what the professional person believes to be true about an older person, or the aging process, will influence what the professional does. While all professional persons operate under ethical codes, which prescribe professional behavior, it is impossible to escape the conclusion that variation in professional behavior exists and that this variation is a result of ideology.

The development of public policy provides a second context in which ideology influences responses to older people. Public policy sets the conditions under which social resources will be mobilized and how they will be used. The influence of ideology in this context may be harder to document, but no less significant than in the individual professional situation. Large-scale public policies rise and fall on ideology. The Social Security Act of 1935 is clearly a product of a change in ideology. This monumental legislation reflects a different belief about people and what causes poverty.

The administration of social programs defines a third context in which ideology influences responses to older people. Although public policies set forth the ideological framework for social programs, the programs themselves may be provided within different ideological perspectives. Nowhere is this more apparent than with respect to the social security retirement program. Much of the disagreements about social security as presented in the previous chapter are a result of ideological differences among administrators of the program. Those who believe that social security should be closely related to the person's work history (a belief deriving from a capitalist ideology) administered the program one way. Those who believe social security should be a program to insure income on retirement regardless of work history (a belief deriving from liberalism) attempt to administer the program in another way.

Professional persons must work within all three contexts. They must work as individual professionals, and they must also work within the scope of existing public policy consistent with existing programs. Thus, understanding and dealing with ideological issues is more important for the professional person than is generally realized. The first task is to understand which ideologies are the strongest ones in American society and to unscramble the ways these ideologies operate. This is the task set forth in Chapter 5. The next task is to identify the programs that these ideologies have generated and under what ideological constraints they are made available to older people. This is the task of Chapters 6 and 7.

INTRODUCTION

Americans reflect heterogeneity and high conflict over lifestyles and values. Any melting pot boils, and it boils over from time to time, but older adults are the epitome of the melting pot metaphor. Older adults remain distinguishably Irish, Polish, German, Jewish, black, white, and more; they also carry a specific American identity with their ethnic and national orientations. It is no wonder older people defy all efforts to generalize about them. Thus, a complex mixture of beliefs held by and about older Americans direct different life courses.

Belief systems are called ideologies. An ideology is a collection of ideas that is believed to be the truth. Whether what is believed is really true is not as important as the fact that people believe the ideas are true. Usually belief systems, or ideologies, are partly truth, partly myth, and partly what people wish were true. Each ideology is a collection of beliefs, and when these beliefs fit together in a systemized way that seems to "make sense," they become ideologies. Ideologies that generate untruths often are accepted as untruths but are not replaced because the more accurate beliefs do not fit together into the belief system as it presently exists. These untruths are often called myths. There are many myths about older people: that they are crabby, or that they do not like children, or that they are too old to work.

Occasionally a new belief, either factual or traditional, will emerge, and occasionally this belief will seem so powerful, so "sensible," that it challenges the entire belief system. Then it is possible to observe the development of a new or different ideology or, more likely, a change in the old ideology. For example, an early belief within liberal ideology placed high value on the noninterference of the federal government in domestic affairs. But the assertion of social justice as a powerful American belief, played out in the civil rights movement of the 1960s, forced a reevaluation of liberal ideology. Now liberal ideology embraces the belief that the federal government must play a strong role in advancing racial and social justice.

Liberal ideology has changed. The change appeared modest at first, but over a prolonged time period liberalism has shifted noticeably.

Ideologies are the substance of popular reactions to older people in the same way that ideologies provide the substance for reactions to a whole spectrum of social conditions. For example, Americans, including older people, are fiercely independent. This belief in personal independence is a product of a liberal ideology, and it directly affects a range of reactions and behaviors from and about older people. In some cases it is impossible to get older people to accept social security payments, even though the older person might be terribly deprived. Why? Or why do so many people believe that at some age older people reach their prime, and at another age they become burdens to society? Or what explains the persistent belief that in America, things are constantly getting better? All these beliefs directly affect the treatment of older people. In order to understand these responses to older people and older adulthood itself, it is important to explore fundamental American ideologies; where they came from, and where they are likely to lead.

Despite the vast variety of American beliefs and the profound complexity of American ideologies, three belief systems, or ideologies, have provided a base for shaping contemporary American thought: capitalism, positivism, and liberalism. These ideologies have roots deeper than the American experience, and they have been re-formed and modified as America has grown and changed. Therefore, some of the elements of these ideologies are the same, and some are different than they used to be, and all three ideologies promote myths and half truths about older people. The purpose of Chapter 5 is to examine these three ideologies for their impact on how professional people help older people.

Table 5-1 provides a summary of these ideologies, the major beliefs that comprise each of them, and the attitudes toward older people that these belief sys-

TABLE 5-1   Ideologies and Impact on Older Adults

IDEOLOGY	MAJOR BELIEFS	ATTITUDES TOWARD OLDER PEOPLE
Capitalism	Work is the measure of value	Older people are inferior because they do not work
	Individual responsibility	Older people should take care of themselves
		Personal value is based on previous work history
Liberalism	Individual freedom	Limited government involvement in helping older people
	Equality	Self-help is the best help
	Community	Individual dignity
Positivism	Survival of fittest	Government assistance disrupts "normal" process
	Science solves problems	Leave older people alone
	Things are getting better	

tems generate. The attitudes toward older people may be positive or negative ones, depending upon how those attitudes are implemented and in what circumstances they are applied. For example, positivism generates an attitude that older people ought to be left alone. This can be a positive attitude if it assures privacy for the older person, but it can have a negative effect if an older person is sick and dying.

In order to understand how these attitudes about older people came about, and whether these attitudes are likely to be used in a negative or a positive way, the central elements of each ideology must be examined.

CAPITALISM

Capitalism appears to be the simplest of America's ideologies. At first glance, capitalism appears to provide a clear and compelling argument for personal success: make money. It also seems to provide the basis for understanding a serious problem associated with growing older: social discrimination based on changing economic class. The differences in quality of life between the rich and the poor have been discussed. Americans are familiar with capitalism as an economic theory, but capitalism is more than economics. Capitalism is ideology as well, and it is the ideology of capitalism, not its economics, that is discussed in this section. Capitalism is much more than a formula for economic success. As an ideology, its roots have their source in the religious upheaval and revolution of the sixteenth century; yet only recently has the ideology of capitalism been identified and discussed.

Capitalism as ideology is a controversial idea. The ideology of capitalism was first identified by the German social scientist Max Weber. Much of Weber's thinking is presented in *The Protestant Ethic and the Spirit of Capitalism,* which was first published in 1904 (though not available in English until 1930). Consequently other explanations for the American capitalist experience, particularly its economic emphasis, had been widely reported and accepted long before Weber's observations were available.

Weber's examination of capitalism begins by questioning the contemporary economic character of capitalist behavior. He asks why a modern version of capitalism did not develop earlier in history if capitalism is explained only as economic behavior. Weber asks if capitalism is a product of an acquisitive instinct, why did not the Oriental traders, or explorers like Cortes, develop a capitalist system? If capitalism is a product of a highly developed economic society, why did some of the richest empires of civilization dissipate their resources on luxury and war? Weber argues that capitalism is not an orgy of materialism. It is a particular blend of personal conduct and a system of human relationships and social ethics that had their origins in the religious teachings of Protestantism. In Weber's view, capitalism is a complex belief system in which its economic character plays a minor role.

Weber says Benjamin Franklin exemplifies the belief system behind capitalism:

He that idly loses five shillings' worth of time loses five shillings, and might as prudently throw five shillings into the sea. . . .

The sound of your hammer at five in the morning or eight at night heard by a creditor, makes him easy six months longer. . . .
A penny saved is a penny earned. . . .
A stitch in time saves nine. . . .

These maxims preached by Franklin are not friendly conversation, says Weber. "Truly what is here preached is not simply a means of making one's way in the world, but a peculiar ethic. The infraction of its rules is not treated as foolishness, but as forgetfulness of duty."[1] Capitalism is not a theory of how persons make and maintain wealth, nor is capitalism "unscrupulousness in the pursuit of self interests by the making of money."[2] Capitalism, says Weber, forges the Calvinist idea of a "calling" with a puritan emphasis upon personal conduct.

Wealth for the capitalist is not personal wealth, but the product of doing one's duty to God. According to Calvin, Weber argued, man was God's trustee over earthly treasures, and to answer one's calling, man was required to protect and make purposeful God's gifts. The capitalist was bound by duty to follow his pecuniary abilities as were laborers bound "to their work as to a life purpose willed by God."[3]

The idea of man's duty to his possessions to which he subordinates himself as an obedient steward . . . bears chilling weight on his life . . . the greater the possession the heavier . . . the feeling of responsibility . . . for holding them unblemished for the Glory of God and increasing them by restless effort.[4]

Thus, capitalism emerged as a product of ethical behavior, strengthened by its purposeful and rational character. At the center of this belief system was work. Work governed all ordered conduct, and anything such as "impulsive enjoyment of life [which led] away both from work as in a calling or religion, was as such the enemy."[5] Thus the founding Americans, in particular, were provided with a strict code of personal behavior that assisted the achievement of external and, consequently, temporal goods. Blessed with rich natural resources, a completely unstructured economic system, and a liberal political ideology that stressed personal freedom and *laissez-faire,* the ethic of Protestantism found fertile ground in America and generated America's economic masterpiece, capitalism.

This is not to say that today's capitalists are all Protestant ministers, nor that the ethical origins of capitalism have prevented contemporary use of capitalism for purely personal gain. The ethical fervor of today's economic system is decidedly less than when America experienced her great industrial revolution. The outstanding capitalists who energized the American system in the late nineteenth century were

---

[1] Max Weber, *The Protestant Ethic and the Spirit of Capitalism,* trans. Talcott Parsons (New York: Charles Scribner & Sons, 1958), 51.
[2] Weber, 181.
[3] Weber, 177.
[4] Weber, 170.
[5] Weber, 167.

not particularly happy with their wealth. Many lived humbly, surrounded by vast stores of wealth, and ostentatious displays of wealth attracted social criticism. The philanthropic movement that flourished during this period was not so much an act of personal charity but clearly one of social responsibility.[6] But by the twentieth century, "wealth and material have gained an increasing and finally an inexorable power over the lives of men as at no period in history," Weber observed.[7] Thus, the processes, or the ideas that generated capitalism, once begun, could continue without the support of capitalism's ethical foundations. In other words, a person like Andrew Mellon could create a particular capitalist structure, which others, not driven by the ethic of capitalism, could use for personal gain. Thus, America's capitalistic system has demonstrated the capacity to stand alone, independent of an ethical system, and explained only as a system of economics.

The Continuing Ideology of Capitalism

If capitalism today is understood best for its economic functions, a capitalist ideology remains deeply ingrained in the American experience. Work is the most significant legacy that this capitalist ideology has given American society. Work has become the measure of the society and the individual. Not only do Americans measure material success in terms of productivity from work, but individuals are evaluated by the type and amount of work in which they engage. "He worked hard; he deserves it," is frequently heard in conversation among older people. Along with income, occupation has become the most significant measure of social status. Moreover, the entire American welfare system has been constructed with some related reference to work. Everyone is expected to work. For those who cannot work, because of age or disability, there are need-based welfare programs. Other welfare programs exist exclusively for those who do work. If there is any distinctively American ethic it would be likely to be the "work ethic." In other words, work is believed to reflect morally right behavior in America.

Not only has work become the most significant consequence of the capitalist ideology, but social order also remains a highly valued belief. Not only did work govern conduct, but the conduct was ordered. On the one hand the capitalist ideology presumed that everyone had some place in the order of things—there was something for everyone to do. On the basis of the notion of a "calling," every person was valued for what that person did, as long as it was done well. The capitalist was just as valued for being a good money-maker as the humble laborer was valued for being a good shoemaker. Status was assigned on the basis of how well the job was done, not on which job one was doing. At first glance this notion of social order in capitalism appears similar to the idea of the classless society Karl Marx envisioned as the product of capitalism's demise.

[6] Robert Bremner, *American Philanthropy* (Chicago: University of Chicago Press, 1966), 89–104.

[7] Weber, 181.

Contrary to a classless society, however, the type of social order envisioned by early capitalism supported stability over classlessness. The capitalist social order was one in which everyone stayed in their places. In other words, early capitalism actually intensified class distinctions. As capitalism began to discard its Protestant and religious underpinnings, and as wealth and occupation became desirable ends, class lines became more pronounced. A scramble began for personal achievement and social advancement, usually through hard work, but often by other means. In order to insure that there were enough laborers to undertake menial tasks, efforts were often undertaken to institutionalize the existing social order. Unions were brutally attacked by capitalists, and those who sought greater class equality were persecuted as un-American. But opportunity abounded in America, mitigating many of capitalism's more oppressive features.

Richard Cloward and Frances Fox Piven attack capitalism's emphasis on social order.[8] They claim that through exercise of political and economic power, capitalism as we know it acts to repress certain classes while providing opportunity for exploitation by other classes. Thus Cloward and Piven find support for the Marxist critique of capitalism, even though the explanation for capitalism's existence, as provided by Weber, suggests a different conclusion. Most simply stated, Weber expected that classical capitalism would certainly serve the public good. Marx, on the other hand, and subsequently Cloward and Piven, understand capitalism as a system that exploits the public good. On balance both views are likely to be partly true, since both have their origin in capitalism's early emphasis on an "ordered" society. Depending on the type of order, capitalism may serve or exploit those whom it serves. The distinction in views must be made, however, since there is confusion today about capitalism on this point of social order.

The two most enduring beliefs of a capitalist ideology are the virtue of work and the value of social order. These two beliefs often operate interchangeably and virtually unnoticed. We speak of working one's way to the top, giving great respect to persons who work their way up. Americans also value success, defined by money and occupation, when it is a product of hard and diligent work. These beliefs remain highly visible and acknowledged as an explanation for the success of the American experience.

LIBERALISM

Liberalism in some form pervades the whole conduct of America. Political philosophies, intellectual traditions, social programs, government policies, and even cultural expressions are influenced and discussed with reference to liberalism. As a belief system, liberalism may not be as systematic as other ideologies, but it is certainly the most far-reaching in its attempt to bring widespread and diverse beliefs under a

[8]Richard Cloward and Frances Fox Piven, *Regulating the Poor* (New York: Vintage Books, 1960).

single ideological banner. Thus, if liberalism fails to represent a consistent point of view, as critics complain, it provides breadth under which many may take shelter.

Liberalism is perhaps the most confusing, least understood, and most criticized American public ideology, yet it ranks with capitalism as a generator of beliefs that have had a profound impact on the development of American public policy. Most of this confusion stems from confusing liberal ideology with liberal political philosophy. Liberal ideology is based on individualism and a belief in limited government; present liberal political views, on the other hand, support collectivity and an expanded role of government as regulator and distributor. This difference between liberalism as ideology and liberalism as political philosophy has prompted great debates about the relevance of liberal ideology.

Liberalism, as ideology, is different today than when the thirteen colonies declared their independence from England; at that time, no distinctions existed between liberal ideas and liberal politics. The liberal ideology expressed in the Declaration of Independence reflected the eighteenth-century synthesis in liberal political ideology; the roots of liberalism as expressed in the early experience of America have a much earlier origin. In order to appreciate public reactions toward older people reflecting liberal thought, it is important to examine the development of liberal ideology in three periods: at its beginning, during America's formative years, and presently.

Liberalism's intellectual roots emerged from the Renaissance (circa A.D. 1300), as people began to express an interest in "rights." This idea of personal rights presented a sharp contrast to prevailing philosophy that insisted that citizens had obligations to God and the king (the state). The new interest in human rights awakened a rudimentary form of individualism that recognized the moral worth of each person and his uniqueness as a human being.[9] This new idea of rights developed as the Reformation destroyed the belief that an intermediary was necessary between God and man. The Reformation proclaimed that each individual was responsible for his own relationship with God. This new responsibility emphasized individual autonomy over personal responsibility to the authority that would deny human autonomy. Early liberalism thus emphasized individual freedom as its primary goal—freedom from capricious authority and freedom to develop one's full human and spiritual potential.

This early form of individualism existed for reasons different from those that support individualism today. Americans have become so accustomed to the notions of individualism and personal rights that they do not think about the fundamental reasons that support those ideas. Four hundred years ago individualism was so revolutionary an idea that its existence had to be explained and justified. The first supporting argument for individualism derived directly from Christianity, which asserted that all men were *equal* in the eyes of God. Since men had a common Father, they

---

[9] The gender orientation in this and subsequent sentences is intentional. The rudimentary concepts of rights applied only to men. John Locke (*Two Treatises of Government*) was the first political philosopher to suggest that women might have limited rights as well as men.

were spiritual brothers. Thus a community of equals was presumed to exist. Both the notion of community and equality were fundamental to establishing early liberalism.

A second supporting argument of early liberalism also derived from Christianity. Not only were men equal in the eyes of God, but they were *valuable* as well. For the first time men had a relationship with authority in which they were valued for their own existence as opposed to being valued for what they could produce. More significant perhaps, this value, or absolute moral worth, brought with it responsibility for each to live a moral life. God was concerned about each person. Each person had his own relationship to God for which he, alone, was responsible. When man became valued, he preserved a personal relationship with God. Thus, men were responsible for leading a proper life in order to maintain this relationship with God.

Equality, community, and personal moral responsibility were justifications for early individualism, which then, as now, so pervades liberal ideology. And, as it does today, this rudimentary form of liberalism conflicted with the established authority of the state. Individualism was at the center of controversy with authority. If each person is equal, and if each behaves in an individual way, what orders this behavior in the life of the community? There were two issues here. The first was the behavior of the individual as an individual. The second was the behavior of the individual as a member of the brotherhood, the collective society, or more significantly, the state. Each person could behave as he or she wished at the individual level, but behavior in the collective society required some restrictions on individual behavior. When the two issues were joined, liberalism as we know it today was born.

Just as early capitalism was not a personal philosophy for accumulating wealth, so early liberalism was not unbridled pursuit of individual freedom. Individuals existed in the community, not separate from it, and consequently freedom under liberalism required what might be called social responsibility today. In other words, freedom for the liberal required responsibility to others since, in the community, for each individual to have freedom, then all individuals must respect some authority. Invariably, under such conditions some freedoms would be restricted. The intellectual and practical questions raised by the joining of individual and community are adequately asked by political philosopher John Hallowell.

> How can the notion of individual autonomy be reconciled with the necessity for political authority? How can individuals conceived as having absolute and *equal* rights submit to political authority without denying the absoluteness or equality of their claims?[10]

The problem of freedom in the community has been and remains the stumbling block of contemporary liberalism. Restrictions on freedom in an organized community frustrated the development of capitalism in the seventeenth century and

---

[10] John Hallowell, *Main Currents of Modern Political Thought* (New York: Holt, Rinehart & Winston, 1950), 88 (emphasis added, to identify that the equality issue has taken on new significance in contemporary statements of liberalism).

the realization of a truly "free market." The same restrictions on personal freedom under liberalism threatened the realization of economic and social "laissez-faire." Most people recognized quickly that freedom without authority to limit freedom was, in fact, no freedom at all. For what the liberal truly sought was not license to do whatever one wanted, but freedom from specific injustices, something later called liberty. In other words, what liberals sought was freedom within a *just* community. This was the issue of liberalism facing those who formed the American system of governance.

Thus arose the problem of defining what kind of authority would govern the community. What kind of authority could men submit to and still be free? Some would go so far as to say, as did Hobbes and Locke, that only by submitting to the authority of community could a person be truly free. Others saw submission to any authority as a loss of freedom. The answer began to emerge from the intellectual revolutions in seventeenth-century England and France. The social contract became the cornerstone of political authority that could define that law which would set restrictions on individualism without restricting liberty. In its simplest form, the social contract is an agreement among members of the community:

> Each puts his person and all his power in common under the supreme direction of the general will, and, in our corporate capacity, we receive each member as an indivisible part of the whole.[11]

Whereas Rousseau might have written about the social contract and its binding *general will,* it was John Locke who identified the social contract and the necessity of "the rule of law" that binds the social community. Locke assumed that, by nature, all men were "free, equal, and independent" (a classic expression of liberalism), and that men could remain so only when political authority existed with the consent of the governed. This rule of government by consent produced new forms of law. Rather than law made by kings, this new form of law was discovered from natural truths. It was objective, impartial, and reasonable law, which would be discovered in much the same way as the laws of nature could be discovered—by examining certain presumably evident truths. In the now famous words of Voltaire, "Freedom consists in being independent from every thing but law."

Liberalism at the Beginning of the American Experience

By 1776, liberalism had already gone through its first transformation. From an unbridled assertion of individuality, liberalism was now defined as freedom within the political community that sets limits on individual autonomy. The foundation of the political community rested on the consent of the members of the political community to exchange some autonomy for protection against injustice. Thus liberty, rather than individual freedom, became the central element of the modern politi-

---

[11] Jean Jacques Rousseau, *The Social Contract and Discourses* (London: Everyman's Library, 1938), para. 5.

cal community. This liberty was preserved by law that was objective, reasonable, and discernible from the basic agreements of the social contract. The assumptions underlying eighteenth-century liberalism remained the same: individual autonomy, equality of all, freedom to realize one's full human potential, and the need for a social community in which these assumptions could be realized.

The Declaration of Independence has been called the best statement of eighteenth-century liberalism that exists. A few excerpts should demonstrate this contention.

> We hold these truths to be self-evident, that all men are created equal, that they are endowed by their Creator with certain inalienable Rights . . . Governments are instituted among men, deriving their just powers from the consent of the governed. . . .
> A Prince, whose character is thus marked by every act which may define a Tyrant, is unfit to be the ruler of a free people. . . .
> And for the support of this Declaration, with a firm reliance on the protection of Divine Providence, we mutually pledge to each other our lives, our fortunes, and our sacred Honor.

The amazing clarity of eighteenth-century liberalism expressed in the Declaration of Independence remains fundamental for an identification of American democracy. Yet contemporary developments have led to questions about the continuing influence of liberalism as a guiding ideology. Perhaps most controversial is the assertion of rights within the present-day American political community. The liberal ideology asserts inalienable rights as a fundamental quality of the nature of man. Some rights' advocates argue that rights, and consequently freedoms, derive from social responsibility that is a requirement of the social contract. Although a liberal ideology embraces both natural rights and socially determined rights, once a principle of rights is established, it is difficult for the liberal ideology to harmonize the varied debates that a belief in rights precipitates. Does a person have a right to property, for example, regardless of the way it might be utilized? What happens when inalienable rights collide? If they are inalienable, how can one right be more important than another? Are some rights more important than others, and if so, how are these decisions reached? A liberal ideology fails to answer these difficult questions.

Liberalism in the Contemporary Political Community

The rights dilemmas have sparked a number of debates about liberalism. In 1776 there was much greater homogeneity of thought about what constituted rights. Thomas Jefferson, for example, was able to list ten rights, which seemed to capture the essence of the rights debate of that day. Such agreement would be impossible to achieve today. At a time when the view of rights is expanding, American society is becoming more complex. The original thirteen colonies that formed the first United States did not constitute the complex network of interdependence reflected by the present association of fifty states. Moreover, public pressure has increased for a form of government that will promote desirable social objectives, rather than a government of limited scope designed to protect liberty. In such a climate, each expansion of government to promote some social objective, places restrictions on some personal rights. Thus, there has developed severe criticism of government that presumably espouses liberalism as its underlying ideology while promoting debatable social objectives.

In his depressing critique of liberalism, Michael Novak calls America the Nordic jungle rather than the melting pot.[12] Novak argues that divergent groups do not assimilate, but hold on to their distinctive ways of viewing life. Thus, rather than some sort of general American view of what constitutes the social good, there are an increasing variety of views that do not blend very well. Novak rejects a liberal ideology as incapable of supporting collective social goals. In a similar vein, Jeffrey Galper shows that the pursuit of rights makes it impossible to achieve desirable social objectives at the same time.[13]

This same observation has been discussed by a number of political scientists who have studied the increasing fragmentation of American society reflected in the growing number of interest groups. Since eighteenth-century liberalism depended upon agreement between the governed and the governing, the existence of varied interest groups, always in disagreement rather than forging an alliance, undermines liberal ideology. The most scathing attack on liberal ideology has been made by Theodore Lowi, Yale University political philosopher. According to Lowi, contemporary American liberalism frustrates government from planning or acting with respect to the many public problems facing it. Although John Madison foresaw the possibility of deadlocked government,[14] the context of government today requires large-scale responses to common problems, which interest-group liberalism has made impossible. According to Lowi, governmental institutions have lost the sense of popular respect and control, new structures of privilege have been created, and conservative rather than progressive government has been created as a result of contemporary liberal ideology.[15]

Yet with all these criticisms, liberalism has transformed individual rights from vague yearnings into legal guarantees. Liberalism has made possible heightened forms of self-expression and creativity that have benefited immeasurably the whole American society. In this respect, liberalism has humanized the American experience. Whether liberalism is sufficient to achieve a perspective of a whole society in the face of rapidly expanding individualism remains unclear. Embracing the national government, as the ideal of Voltaire's "rule of law" suggests, is no longer an adequate liberal political response. But despite the disaffection with classic American liberalism, liberalism as ideology continues to shape public responses to older people in profound ways.

[12] Michael Novak, *The Rise of the Unmeltable Ethics* (New York: Macmillan, 1972), 8–24.

[13] Jeffrey Galper, *The Politics of Social Services* (Englewood Cliffs, N.J.: Prentice-Hall, 1975).

[14] *The Federalist,* no. 10.

[15] Theodore Lowi, *The End of Liberalism* (New York: W. W. Norton, 1969), 86.

POSITIVISM

Whereas capitalism may be the best known American ideology and liberalism the most influential, positivism has become almost unknown as ideology in contemporary American thought. Of the three ideologies discussed here, positivism, although unfamiliar by name, influenced early American behavior in direct ways more than either capitalism or liberalism. For example, most Americans agree that a planned approach to a task is the best way to go about it. Positivism is the foundation belief system that underlies that preference. Americans are confident that technology and the accompanying "scientific method" will solve the most difficult problems. This view has its origin in positivism as well.

Positivism is a much younger belief system than either capitalism or liberalism. Positivism is an outgrowth of the great intellectual prestige that the natural sciences achieved during the seventeenth and eighteenth centuries. Indeed, the capacity of the physical sciences to explain the world and to make it more prosperous appeared superior to explanations offered by theology. When Galileo asserted Copernican theory that the sun, not the earth, was the center of the universe, science and religion polarized the world into two groups: the believers and the discoverers. The tension was not so much a consequence of any difference in conclusions, since Galileo recanted, as it was a difference in the way the conclusions were reached. Theological truths were revealed to men by God, but scientific truths were discovered by men without God's assistance.

"As the man of the Middle Ages turned to theology for salvation," observes John Hallowell, "the nineteenth-century man turned to science for an understanding and solution of social problems. . . . Positivism is an attempt to transfer to the study of social and human phenomena the methods and concepts of the natural sciences in the belief that human phenomena, like physical phenomena, obey certain laws of nature which can be inductively discovered by the empirical examination of successive events."[16] Positivism, however, is more than applying the laws of the natural sciences to the social and human world. Positivism carries with it a particular view of human events. Just as the physical scientists demonstrated that by rigorous application of the laws of nature, a more prosperous and physically comfortable world was possible, so the new social scientist believed that the application of these scientific principles would improve the social world as well. Thus these social scientists adopted a "positive" view of the social world, namely, that a better world could be produced when guided by the scientifiç principles of scientific discovery.

Auguste Comte established the foundation for modern sociology. Comte systematically applied what was known in the natural sciences to the social world. In his extensive work on "positive philosophy," Comte claimed to have discovered the "law of three stages" to explain the history of human thought. The third and final stage Comte called the *positive* stage, to which the other stages of history had

[16] Hallowell, 289-92.

been evolving and in which science prescribed perfect order and harmony. Comte called for a new science of society that would lead all other sciences in discovering and perfecting this ultimate society. Comte's theory and his commitment to a scientific study of society was the subject of extensive exploration by John Stuart Mill. Gradually scholars reached consensus that human society was evolving to its logical and perfect state.

Somewhat independent of Comte's ideas of social development, positivism received what seemed unequivocal endorsement from the work of Charles Darwin. Although a theory of biological evolution originated with his grandfather, Charles Darwin provided evidence in his *Origin of Species* that natural selection is a product of a struggle for existence. The fittest survive the struggle, and by this process of natural selection the world evolves into a better one, as stronger traits are passed to the next generation. This work of Darwin was synthesized with Comte's social theories by Herbert Spencer. Spencer likened society to the biological organism, drawing what Hallowell calls "fantastic comparisons between biological organisms and societies."[17] For Spencer, biological laws governed the evolution of society of which Comte spoke.

For Spencer, and his disciples John Fiske, William Graham Sumner, and Lester Ward, a few of the early American sociologists, government should not interfere in this natural process of social evolution. Every kind of interference with the normal or natural affairs of citizens would disrupt and delay the evolution of the perfectly balanced society. Government was necessary only to insure that people experience both the good and evil effects of their own natures. In short, government should not regulate individual behavior since such regulation would disrupt the natural laws.

Richard Hofstadter, revered American historian, emphasizes the central position of William Graham Sumner in the development of contemporary American thought. "His sociology bridged the gap between the economic ethic set in motion by the Reformation and the [prevailing] thought of the nineteenth century, for it assumed that the industrious, temperate and frugal man of the Protestant ideal was the equivalent of the 'strong' or the 'fittest' in the struggle for existence."[18] American sociology, therefore, joined ideas of scientific progress with individualism and the Protestant ethic within the boundaries that came to be known as "social Darwinism." The elitist orientation of these views is ably demonstrated by Hofstadter.

> Sumner concluded that these principles of social evolution negated the traditional ideology of equality and natural rights. In the evolutionary perspective, equality was ridiculous; and no one knew so well as those who went to [the] school [of] nature that there are no natural rights in the jungle.... In the cold light of evolutionary realism, the eighteenth century idea that men were equal in a state of nature was the opposite of the truth. Masses of men

[17] Hallowell, 307.

[18] Richard Hofstadter, *Social Darwinism in American Thought* (Boston: Beacon Press, 1965), 51.

starting out under conditions of equality could never be anything but hopeless savages.[19]

The influence of positivist beliefs extends far beyond their application in sociology. According to Hofstadter, America had developed in such a way that positivism appeared to answer many of the most pressing social problems. "With its rapid expansion, its exploitation methods, and its peremptory rejection of failure, post-bellum America was like a vast human laboratory of the Darwinian struggle for existence and survival of the fittest."[20] Positivism lent chilling evidence to support notions that disease, ignorance, and poverty were not only inherited, but also that social progress could not be made by supporting those who demonstrated such biological or social inferiority.

Moreover, the positivists believed that science could solve pressing social problems. Belief in science is positivism's most enduring legacy. This is a science based upon reason, a science that can induce conclusions from repeated observations. It is a science presumed to rest on certain immutable laws that themselves can be discovered. It is a science that discovers ways in which social objects regularly behave. Faith supports capitalism's and liberalism's belief systems. Freedom, equality, and success as a result of hard work and personal responsibility cannot be established by the scientific method of discovery. Science, by contrast, is established through reason, and consequently the positivist belief system assumes that reason and faith are distinct and that reason is more valuable.

Positivism is not lacking in human values as much as the whole positivist approach rejects all values in its search for truth. Today's empirical social scientists are not uncaring. Rather their efforts are directed toward those facts that detract from the human condition in the desire to improve society. Social advances made possible by the natural and social sciences are indeed indisputable evidence of the validity of positivism's claims. Yet there remains an uneasy truce between society and its scientists. Positivism cannot offer the answer to the ultimate nature of a good society, nor can it assume that its scientific discoveries will be used to promote that good society.

THE IMPACT OF IDEOLOGIES FOR OLDER PEOPLE

The foregoing discussion provides some measure of the impact of ideology in the lives of Americans. As presented in Table 5-1, each ideology emphasizes certain beliefs that have particular relevance for those who work with older people. Work as a measure of value and individual responsibility are products of capitalism. Liberalism promotes individual freedom, equality, and community. Positivism generates beliefs in survival of the fittest, science, and a view that through an application of

---

[19] Hofstadter, 59.
[20] Hofstadter, 16.

science, the world is getting better. These beliefs, in turn, generate attitudes held about older people and about the ways America responds to the challenges of the older adult population.

The low opinion of older people finds easy explanation from the foregoing examination of positivism. To the extent that beliefs in survival of the fittest prevail, negative attitudes toward older people are easily supported. For example, it is not unusual for persons to refer to older people as an increasing burden on society. Particularly when an older person is ill, discussions about the value of sustaining life often revolve around such questions as the person's overall fitness to survive for any period of time and whether the "quality of life" for the older person will be sufficient to encourage life-sustaining efforts.

The primary belief system supporting the death-with-dignity movement and, to some extent triage, derives from a positivist belief in survival of the fittest. Although both these movements are more comprehensive in their ideologies, a survival-of-the-fittest belief often dominates those beliefs that would support letting people make up their own minds. Thus, it would be very easy for the death-with-dignity and triage movements to support subtle forms of genocide if ever they become devoid of other belief systems that place high value on life and personal dignity.

Positivism contributes another set of attitudes toward older adults through its belief in science. Although science has indeed contributed to lengthening life and improving the quality of life for many older people, a biomedical approach to understanding and assisting older people appears so compelling that other understandings about older adulthood seem irrelevant. For example, there is an immediate reaction to take an older person to a hospital, perhaps for an operation, to *cure* a particular problem, rather than examining whether the older person might live just as comfortably, and perhaps more satisfactorily, if the older person could be *cared for* instead. Many of the theories that explain aging are based upon the scientific approach, often overlooking humanistic theories.

The recent movement to provide in-home *care* services, as alternatives to institutional care, or risky cure of problems associated with aging, provides a current example of efforts to move beyond traditional beliefs in science. Often the caretakers are friends or family. Often the care is more comfortable than scientific. Beyond cost-effectiveness, care of older people offers important ideological advantages to them as well. Triage certainly promotes the care approach to older people with all its comforting advantages.

Liberalism and capitalism also have influenced older people and the America in which they live. To the extent that Americans believe that work is a measure of human value, older people who no longer work are often held in low esteem, particularly by younger persons who are still employed. Consequently retirement has been a strenuous experience for older people. Clinically, retirement brings depression that accompanies loss of job, useful activity, and job-related prestige. Fortunately, American society has begun to develop acceptance of retirement from work largely as a result of liberalism's belief in individualism. Many retirement activities provide socially valued alternatives to work. Yet the Harris surveys still indicate that older people, particularly those who were successful in their jobs before retirement, prefer work. This preference derives from a capitalist ideology that emphasizes work so strongly.

With respect to capitalism and the value of work, social security is an ingenious program based on the value of work, which carries the value of work into retirement. Social security is available *because* an older adult has worked, and the value of social security is related (although somewhat loosely) to the value of work. Thus, the debate over future social security purposes is ideologically related to providing work-related value to older people, even after they retire. To the extent that older people, and others, believe they have *earned* their social security, and that those retirement benefits are a right based on their previous labor, loss of esteem in retirement is greatly reduced.

Capitalism also promotes belief in personal responsibility for current circumstances. This belief has often fostered the attitude toward older people that they get what they deserve. Such a belief in personal responsibility can be liberating as well as debilitating for older people. The belief in hard work to achieve personal success, the pull-yourself-up-by-your-bootstraps attitudes generated by personal responsibility, and the attitude that things can be different when seen through to their conclusions, are often liberating attitudes for older people. Frequently, older people who have had relatively unattractive lives before retirement found that by taking personal responsibility for their own postretirement lives they could realize many objectives that, years before, seemed like fantasy.

Liberalism, too, adds to an understanding of older adults. The belief in equality has fostered many positive attitudes toward them, particularly among older adults. For example, there is a growing recognition that older people should have the same resources and the same opportunities in life as any other group. The belief in equality challenges stereotyping attitudes and promotes attitudes of equal treatment regardless of age. Such attitudes have contributed both to legislation banning age discrimination in employment and, recently, to legislation eliminating mandatory retirement ages. Among older people themselves, equality seems to be more easily realized than among groups within the society as a whole.

Individual freedom, too, is a belief that has generated many attitudes toward and from older people. In fact, older people are the most fiercely independent of any people, at any age. Perhaps the belief in freedom, combined with many years of personal freedom, makes individualism a highly valued belief among older people. The attitudes that develop from freedom go far beyond the freedom claimed by each older adult. Family attitudes have reflected personal freedom as older people consistently live lives more free of family commitments than ever before. As financial security in older adulthood has increased, older people are free of the psychological burden of depending on their children. Older people, therefore, have potential for realizing the independence they seem to desire.

The belief in community and impartial government is part of the liberal ideology that appears to have fostered and supported much of the political activity among older people. The strong sense of patriotism among older people derives partly from the fact that during their lifetimes they built the schools and churches, fought the wars that preserved American values, created the financial infrastructure for this successful nation, and raised their children to protect and promote their contributions. This sense of community among older people reflects a contract between them and the government they have created and preserved. In many ways, this sense of patriotism represents the ideal of Jeffersonian democracy and the liberalism reflected in the Declaration of Independence.

The strong belief in community among older people has not found expression in the elimination of ethnic and racial divisions in American society. America, as melting pot, has not materialized, but the belief in one community is sufficiently strong to propel older people to seek, collectively, public solutions for their problems. The outpouring of unity among delegates to the 1981 White House Conference on Aging provided a stunning demonstration of the commitment to community among older people. The personal and collective politics of growing older in America is explained in part by the belief in community so deeply imbedded in the liberal ideology.

IDEOLOGY, VALUES, ETHICS, AND THE PROFESSIONAL PERSON

Examination of ideology and discussion of beliefs may provide some explanation for current attitudes toward and among older people. The foregoing discussions may also seem confusing. Some beliefs seem to generate attitudes and activities that appear good for older people. Others seem to put older people at risk. Some beliefs seem to have a direct bearing on the lives of older people, such as the belief in work, while other beliefs have less influence or have influence only when mediated by other beliefs. This discussion does not suggest which beliefs *ought* to be maximized in order to assist older people in living more satisfying lives, and this situation often makes such discussions seem confusing.

In order to think about which ideologies and which beliefs best serve older people, it is necessary to understand something about values. Values are simply the means for ordering priorities. Some ideas are valued; others are not; some are valued more than others; some ideas are more valued by different groups of people. Ideologies do not suggest which beliefs are valuable and which are not. In fact, to the extent that there are multiple ideologies, the task of choosing the *best* beliefs to promote desirable consequences for older people becomes quite confusing. For example, liberalism promotes a belief in personal freedom, but the ideology does not suggest which freedoms to exercise. Since the exercise of some freedoms may restrict the ability to exercise others, choices over freedoms must be made. The choice to exercise one's freedom to live in a housing complex, complete with a full range of recreational and social amenities may limit one's freedom to live a private life.

Thus, values are applied to the belief system as a means to maximize one set of beliefs over another. For example, the capitalist ideology supports strong belief in work; liberalism supports a belief in individualism; positivism supports strong beliefs in the scientific method. Suppose an older person is debating the choice of whether to retire or not. Capitalism may urge the older person to continue to work. Liberalism may urge the person toward more personal freedom, making retirement attractive. Positivism may confound the choice by making available medical evidence of health problems the person is likely to encounter in later life, some more or less likely due to employment status.

Similar complexities confront the professional helper. An older person hospitalized for a stroke is stable enough to leave the hospital. A professional person must help develop a plan for the older adult. The doctor *believes* that the person will probably need continuing care since the person is only partially self-maintaining. The doctor suggests an intermediate-care home. The doctor's belief is based on medical-scientific knowledge. The older person, fiercely independent, does not want to go to an institution. The children have their own families and do not think it wise to bring the older person into their own homes. On the other hand, the children *believe* if they all work hard and pull together they can provide the kind of care for the older adult to maintain care in that person's own home. Their belief is based on all their proven economic ability. The professional person is forced to sift through all the facts that support all three belief systems and in reaching a conclusion, the professional person inevitably sets priorities, and consequently identifies values, or sets of values, that the professional person seeks to maximize through the professional plan of action.

Guidance for these types of value choices comes from ethics. Ethics are morally right behaviors in their simplest explanation, and although there are many ethical decisions that professional persons make, not all these decisions are accompanied by soul-searching. In fact, many of the decisions professional persons make are rather spontaneous. The general ease of ethical decisions is due to the existence of ethical systems that inform everyday actions. Religion provides an ethical system. In Christianity the Sermon on the Mount and the Golden Rule provide the framework of an ethical system. Professions have ethical systems as one of their outstanding characteristics. Social work has a Code of Ethics to which all social workers subscribe. Physicians take the Hippocratic Oath, lawyers have a Canon of Professional Ethics, and nurses subscribe to the Code of Nursing Practice. The code of social work ethics is specifically discussed in Chapter 11.

In each of these professional codes, the right behavior for the professional person is clearly set forth. Within that code it is possible to discern where each profession places greatest value with respect to the many belief systems each professional is likely to encounter. In social work, for example, greatest value is placed on dignity and worth of the *individual.* Therefore, beliefs in individualism are maximized as part of a social worker's ethical system. In the example above, the social worker, if asked for a conclusion, would and *should* support the choice of the older adult, all other things being equal.

In actual practice, the process of helping older people is not as straightforward as the discussion about values and ethics may suggest. Any professional person must work within the constraints of available resources. These resources, generally called programs and policies, are also derived from a selective application of belief systems and reflect values as a result of public choices, as contrasted with the private choices of the professional person, usually through some political process. Thus the professional person is constrained by the need to work within the context of the resources. The professional person also applies skills and technologies in the professional helping process. These skills and technologies, while reflecting ideology, allow the helping person flexibility in the helping situation. In most professions, actions do not always come down to value choices, since application of different skills and technologies within the structure of available resources may affect outcomes as much as emphasis of a particular belief system.

In concluding this discussion, it is important to repeat an earlier statement about ideologies. The responses to dealing with the circumstances of growing older depend upon what people believe to be true about themselves, the society in which they live, and the persons around them. The way professional persons respond to older people depends upon beliefs held about them. America embraces three belief systems, each of which generates a range of attitudes about older people and among older people.

These belief systems, capitalism, liberalism, and positivism, provide the intellectual context in which professional assistance is given. If it is believed that old people are a product of the process of natural selection, and if that belief is highly valued, older people will be treated much differently than if the belief in personal freedom is highly valued. The distinction that results from different beliefs exists not only in the professional helping situation but also in the process of developing the policies and programs that determine the helping context. These policies and programs are the subject of the next two chapters.

CHAPTER SIX

PROGRAMS
FOR OLDER PEOPLE:
Income, Health,
and Social Services

The Great Depression has become the watershed event in American social policy. The striking economic and political changes thrust upon the American people forced Americans to change many of their attitudes and beliefs. New beliefs, in turn, opened the way for the development of new social programs. Before the depression prevailing attitudes harshly identified the unemployed as shiftless and lazy. Wholesale unemployment in those years, however, brought a new reality into focus. Similar to the 1980-83 recession, many otherwise solid citizens suddenly found themselves without jobs. Before the Great Depression, those who accepted welfare support were believed to be inferior in mind and body, but economic circumstances of the Great Depression indiscriminately forced close family and friends into public jobs and onto welfare.

Unlike the 1980-83 recession, when unemployment offices were jammed with persons filing new unemployment claims, there was no unemployment insurance during the Great Depression. There was no safety net of welfare programs in 1929 and 1930. Attitudes toward government before the Great Depression were classic in their liberal orientation: Government is best that governs least. The Great Depression forced Americans to change their traditional liberal views about government. Only government, and only the federal government, had the capacity and authority to protect Americans from economic calamity. With the growing political capacity among older people, these changes in attitude were converted into a new era in which the federal government found constitutional authority "to provide for the general welfare." The Social Security Act, legislated in 1935, was the first and most durable commitment to provide welfare programs by the federal government. Almost fifty years later, the Social Security Act remains the mainstay of public programs designed to assist older people. Public programs supported under the Social Security Act, the Older Americans Act, the Housing Act, and the Health Services Act represent tangible responses America has made to the issues raised by the social, economic, and political aspects of aging. Through these programs, Americans collectively have set public goals and agreed to taxes to support public spending to achieve these goals. Thus the practitioner should understand what these programs are designed to provide, the extent to which the programs achieve these expectations, and what other programs may be necessary to compensate for concerns about growing older that these programs do not address.

The rich array of public programs are the means by which professional persons assist older adults. The skills professional persons apply in implementing these programs are discussed in the final section of this book. The programs themselves, however, are an integral part of serving older people. It might be helpful to think of a carpenter going to work with a variety of tools, then using his or her special skills with the tools to do the particular job that is required. Just as the carpenter must understand what the saw or hammer can and cannot do, so professional persons must understand the programs with which they work. Just as a carpenter manages the tools skillfully in completing the specific task, so professional persons must develop skill in bringing the programs together with the older person who will benefit from them.

PROGRAMS UNDER THE SOCIAL SECURITY ACT

Because the Social Security Act provides the greatest amount of assistance to the largest number of older people, it is important that professional persons understand what attitudes are behind this legislation. To achieve this understanding, a small bit of public welfare political history is necessary.[1] Briefly, before the Great Depression the states assumed the burden of providing resources to older people, as carefully discussed in Chapter 4. In 1854, President Pierce vetoed legislation proposed by Dorothea Dix that would have given only a modest welfare role to the federal government. Pierce proclaimed that welfare was the business of the states and of no concern to the Federal government.[2]

Practical barriers, as well as ideological objection, handicapped federal public welfare activity fifty years ago. First, the Federal government had very little money

---

[1] America's welfare history is carefully and clearly provided by June Axinn and Herman Levin, *Public Welfare: America's Response to Need* (New York: Dodd, Mead, 1980).

[2] In addition to Axinn and Levin, see Andrew Dobelstein, *Politics, Economics and Public Welfare* (Englewood Cliffs, N.J.: Prentice-Hall, 1980).

before 1913, the year the Sixteenth Amendment to the Constitution was ratified. This amendment allowed the federal government to levy and collect an income tax. During the nation's first 125 years, the federal government financed its modest operations largely through the sale of public lands. The present structure of public programs is even more amazing when one realizes that adequate financing for large-scale public programs has existed only for seventy years.

Limited federal financial resources were complicated by an absence of a national constituency to advocate for welfare programs. In other words, there was no clear or organized nationwide consensus that the federal government should become involved in welfare matters; nor was there any consensus about what type of welfare matters should be addressed even if the federal government were to become involved. The effort of Dorothea Dix never developed a national following, and furthermore Dix's efforts were primarily directed at the states instead of the federal government.

Two events joined to develop a national constituency for welfare. The social reform movement was the first event, diffuse as it was. Essentially the reformers dedicated themselves to rid municipalities of political corruption. Fraud—by welfare administrators, not welfare recipients—was a frequent target of these reform efforts. Mary Richmond, considered by many to be the founder of contemporary social work, crusaded against welfare abuse in Baltimore and Philadelphia. Social reformers sought assistance from government, usually state government, in their reform efforts. These reform efforts succeeded in convincing President Theodore Roosevelt he should call the first White House Conference on Children in 1909. In 1912, as a result of this conference, Congress created the U.S. Children's Bureau. Thus an attitude gradually developed that the federal government should intervene when welfare problems required large-scale answers.

These reformers were also women for the most part, but they were women who did not have the legal right to vote until 1920, when the Nineteenth Amendment to the Constitution was ratified. It is not possible to detail the struggle for the right to vote here. In many ways it was similar to the effort to ratify the Equal Rights Amendment. Ratification took a long time, and it took meticulous and disciplined political organization in all states and most local communities. Thus, for the first time in American history there emerged a national coalition concerned with social issues. This women's coalition, it might be called, was composed of the "reformers" and the "right-to-voters," and because they were women, they infused this coalition with public concern over things women traditionally worried about—children and families, including elders.

Thus through the concerted effort of this coalition, President Warren G. Harding, hardly an advocate for federal government initiative, reversed his long-standing opposition and supported a bill to provide federal funds to establish maternal health programs. This maternity bill, known also as the Sheppard-Towner Act, was the first substantive federal public welfare legislation. It was passed in 1921, renewed in 1926, and ended in 1928.[3] Though short-lived, the Maternity Act

---

[3] Joseph Chappatis, "Federal Social Welfare Progressivism in the 1920s," *Social Service Review* 46 (June 1972), 118–37.

marked the political maturity of a national welfare coalition, at a time when federal monies were available to fund public programs.

Once a national coalition existed and the funds were available, the ideological changes in the responsibility of government, forced by the Great Depression, established the climate in which federal response to older people could be developed. Whereas the women's coalition promoted a national concern about children, the Townsend movement promoted a similar concern for older people. Thus, the public arena was established for considering permanent welfare legislation, finally realized in the Social Security Act.

Attitudes Underlying the Social Security Act

The Great Depression signaled the need for federal action to reduce hardship and suffering from economic calamity. The election of President Franklin D. Roosevelt introduced the forthcoming federal response to human hardship caused by this economic disaster. President Roosevelt acted swiftly to establish legislative authority for a range of relief programs designed to meet the emergency. They did not need much political support beyond Roosevelt's personal commitment to respond to the existing crisis. But as the harshness of the depression began to abate, there was growing interest from the women's coalition and Townsend movement for permanent programs designed to meet the needs of children, families, and older adults.

Thus, on June 29, 1934, President Roosevelt created the Committee on Economic Security. The Congress had been considering legislation that would require states to guarantee unemployment insurance, and legislation to pay one-third of state cost for old age pensions. Roosevelt was not enthusiastic about such legislation, preferring, instead, the more comprehensive approach contained in the idea that the federal government should develop some structure to insure against similar personal tragedy in the future. Thus Roosevelt charged the Committee to "study problems relating to the economic security of individuals" and "report to the President not later than December 1, 1934 its recommendations which . . . will promote greater economic security."[4]

Roosevelt sought no sweeping innovations in welfare policy and programs. Instead he proposed to develop programs based upon "lessons and experiences . . . available from States, . . . industries, and from many nations of the civilized world." Roosevelt was also "looking for a sound means which I can recommend to provide at once security against several of the great disturbing factors in life—especially those which relate to unemployment and old age."[5] Roosevelt's own philosophy about the role of the federal government was equally cautious. The federal government was the last resource to be brought into play only after states and localities had done all they could to resolve personal economic problems. Speaking about federal funding for the Federal Emergency Relief Administration, Roosevelt said:

[4] Office of the President, Executive Order 6757, 1434 (1 December 1934).

[5] U.S. Congress, 73rd, 2nd H.R. Document 397, as quoted in Edward Witte, *The Development of the Social Security Act* (Madison: University of Wisconsin Press, 1963), 5.

The principle which I have on many occasions explained is that the first obligation is on the locality, if it's absolutely clear that the locality has done its utmost but that more must be done, then the State must do its utmost. Only then can the federal government add its contribution to those of locality and the State.[6]

Although President Roosevelt and his staff were reluctant to promote far reaching new welfare initiatives, they were faced with the necessities of the depression and the public pressure of the Townsend movement. Thus an intellectual compromise was reached about the permanent programs that would be created under the Economic Security Act. First, insurance-type programs would be the mainstay of federal involvement; and second, the welfare-type programs that would be required, would be operated jointly by the federal government and the states. A division between insurance-type and welfare-type programs would reduce the cost of government programs. Benefits under insurance programs would be provided from funds collected from future beneficiaries and kept in government trust until needed. Furthermore, it was assumed that, as more and more people earned better coverage under the insurance programs, the welfare programs would decrease in importance, further decreasing the need for federal financial support.

The original Social Security Act contained two financial support programs for older people: an insurance program, social security, and a welfare program, old-age assistance. Social security benefits were to be based upon contributions to the social security system, as discussed in Chapter 3, and Aid for the Aged benefits upon financial need. The federal government was required to administer social security, but Aid for the Aged was administered cooperatively by the federal government and the states. Since there was such intense political pressure by older people during the formative years of social security, these two programs were placed at the beginning of the legislation. Old-age assistance was Title I and social security was Title II. Thus from the outset, two categories of financial assistance were available to older people—one for the poor and the other for those who were not. Social security was provided both for the retiree and survivors, children and spouses of persons who were covered. It was called Old Age and Survivors Insurance (OASI).

Administration of old-age assistance was shared with the states. Partly from political motivations, and partly from practical considerations, payments to older people under this program were established by the states. States were able to keep these payments somewhat on a par with state living standards, while at the same time maintaining control over who would be eligible for these payments. Although the federal government would have preferred to set national standards for old-age assistance, Congress opposed efforts that appeared to override state authority. Instead, Congress agreed to let states control the payments as long as they were of amounts sufficient to meet "standards of health and decency" without saying what constituted those standards.[7] These ideological differences extended to program

---

[6] Quoted in Richard Leach and Andrew Dobelstein, "The Federal Role in Public Welfare Today," *Forensic Quarterly* 47, no. 2 (May 1972), 69–84.

[7] Andrew Dobelstein, "In Quest of a Fair Welfare System," *Journal of Social Welfare* 2, no. 2 (Spring/Fall 1975), 32–33.

financing. Social security was financed by a tax on employers and employees. The constitutionality of this tax was upheld in 1937. The old-age assistance program was financed by the categorical grant-in-aid that had been established with the Maternity Act program. This left states free to choose whether they wanted to have the program, and the level of support they wanted. Thus separate financial issues affected each program. Although states were more or less forced to participate in OAA, they still had options about the level of participation.

In 1950, the social security program (Title II) was modified so that workers who were covered in the program could collect social security benefits if they had become disabled and consequently unable to work. An additional payroll tax was added and a new trust fund was set up. The name of the program was changed to Old Age Survivors and Disability Insurance program (OASDI). As discussed in Chapter 4, medical coverage for older people was added to the Social Security Act in 1965 as Medicare, Title XVIII of the act. A separate payroll tax was established to support Medicare, and a separate trust fund was established to secure employer and employee contributions. The name of the program was changed again to Old Age Survivors Disability and Hospital Insurance program (OASDHI).

A companion medical assistance program that greatly benefits older people was added to social security also in 1965. Medicaid, added as Title XIX of the act, provides medical assistance to all needy persons. In 1972, Congress modified the original Aid for the Aged program by combining it with aid for the blind and disabled. This new program was called Supplemental Security Income (SSI) and incorporated under Title XVI of the act. Finally, in 1974 Congress created a social services program as Title XX of the Social Security Act. It is from this social services program that many important programs are offered to older people.

The titles of the Social Security Act that have greatest significance for older people are summarized in Table 6-1. It is important to stress again the ideological differences between the insurance and assistance programs. Insurance programs are those that are available to older people only if they made contributions to the programs during their working years. Consequently, older people are eligible for these programs without regard to other income sources they may have. Since older people are entitled to these programs because they contributed to them, the insurance programs are often called "entitlement programs." The assistance programs on the other hand are available to older people who are financially needy. These programs help support poor older people, and since these programs provide financial support calculated on the basis of how much each older person may need to reach a certain living level, these programs are often called need-tested programs.

Table 6-1 also summarizes the type of benefits each program provides. Social security (retirement), disability insurance, and supplemental security income all provide cash to the older person. Medicare, Medicaid, and social services provide products, or benefits in-kind in the form of medical care and social services respectively. The programs also differ with respect to whether the federal government or the states administer the programs. In general, need-tested programs are administered by states, because need is a condition that varies greatly from state to state. On the other hand, the entitlement programs have no reason to be concerned about

TABLE 6-1 Summary of Social Security Programs

PROGRAM	KIND OF PROGRAM	TYPE OF BENEFITS	ADMINISTRATOR OF PROGRAM
Title I Old Age Assistance (1935–1972)	Assistance (Need-tested)	Cash	State Government (Now rescinded)
Title II Social Security Retirement (1935)	Insurance (Entitlement)	Cash	Federal Government (Social Security Administration)
Disability (1950)	Insurance (Entitlement)	Cash	Federal Government (Social Security Administration)
Title XVI Supplemental Security Income (Former OAA)	Assistance (Need-tested)	Cash	Federal Government (Social Security Administration)
Title XVIII Medicare (1965)	Insurance (Entitlement)	In-kind	Federal Government (Social Security Administration)
Title XIX Medicaid (1965)	Assistance (Need-tested)	In-kind	State Government
Title XX Social Services (1974)	Assistance (Need-tested)	In-kind	State Government

economic variation, and consequently they can be administered centrally, by the federal government.

Program Characteristics

The above summary of the Social Security Act provides the framework for a more careful examination of the characteristics of six programs identified in Table 6-1. Since professional people are called upon to use these programs in serving a wide variety of older persons, and since these programs are provided from different ideological perspectives, there are considerable differences among the programs as to who is appropriate to receive them. The following discussion should help professional persons understand exactly which programs are right for which people.

Social security insurance is available to older people under a variety of circumstances. Currently there are over thirty-five different criteria by which people might become eligible for social security. In total there are close to thirty-six million social security beneficiaries.[8] This means 15.4 percent of the civilian population receive

---

[8]For purposes of consistency, all data presented in this chapter are drawn from 1980 Census Data as displayed in *Statistical Abstracts of the United States,* 102nd ed. (Washington, 1981), unless otherwise noted.

TABLE 6-2   Social Security Beneficiaries: Major Types of Beneficiary Status and Average Monthly Payment, 1980

BENEFICIARIES		AMERICAN MONTHLY PAYMENT (IN DOLLARS)
Retired workers	19,583,000	$341.00
Disabled workers	2,861,000	371.00
Wives and husbands	3,480,000	164.00
No. Children	4,610,000	—
Widowed mothers	563,000	246.00
Widows and widowers	4,415,000	308.00
Parents	15,000	276.00
Special beneficiaries	93,000	105.00
Total Beneficiaries	35,620,000	

Source: *Statistical Abstracts of the United States* (1982), Table 535.

social security benefits although people age sixty-five and older comprise 11.2 percent of the population. Therefore, while older retired persons are the primary recipients of social security, other persons are covered by social security as well. Table 6-2 summarizes the major categories of social security beneficiaries and the average monthly payments they receive. Though it is impossible to overemphasize the significant income maintenance impact of social security, it is also important to stress that social security does not account for all retirement income, nor was it expected to do so. President Roosevelt's vision for social security was that it would provide one of three sources for income protection, in retirement.

[I]t seems necessary to adopt three principles [for old age security: ... old age pension for those [unable] to build up their own pensions. ... compulsory annuities which will in time establish a self-supporting system for those now young and for future generations. ... [and] voluntary contributory annuities by which individual initiative can increase the amounts received in old age.

Roosevelt also warned that social security "does not offer anyone either individually or collectively an easy life—nor was it intended to do so."[9]

In 1974, Congress passed the Pension Reform Act, which set standards for protecting workers' retirement benefits in company-related pensions. Among other provisions, this act required firms to assure worker benefits after five years on the job regardless of the financial future of the firm (vesting). The act also permitted certain geographical relocations without loss of benefits. In 1981, Congress approved legislation to permit individuals to establish tax-deferred individual retirement savings accounts in order to stimulate personal savings for retirement. (These developments were discussed in detail in Chapter 3.) As a result of a surge of pro-

[9] Quoted in Dobelstein, *Politics, Economics and Public Welfare,* 81.

grams developed over the years, retirees have a number of options for income protection in retirement years. (The actual source of income for older people has been summarized in Chapter 3.)

Despite the varietal forms and sometimes limited purposes for social security, it provides an important source of income for almost 98 percent of all Americans over age sixty-five. Therefore, any professional person working with older people should be sure that the older person receives social security benefits, unless there is a clear reason why those benefits are not available. Application for benefits is made at the local Social Security Administration office. The offices, located in most larger cities, handle inquiries and claims for benefits. Since every person has an individual social security account, benefits for each person will be different.

In general, benefits for retirees are determined in two steps. First the person's average monthly earnings are calculated for the appropriate periods for which social security taxes were paid. Once the average earnings are established, a primary insurance amount (PIA) is established for each individual by applying the following formula: 146 percent of the first $110, plus 53 percent of the next $290, plus 50 percent of the next $150, through a progression of a total of eight steps, increases in the Consumer Price Index are applied to the formula, so that if the CPI increased by 10 percent, the first step in determining the PIA would be 161 percent of the first $110. Suppose a retiree has average monthly earnings of $500.00; that retiree's PIA would be $364.30 per month. Each time the benefits were increased, the increase would be added to the PIA, so it is possible for a retiree to receive a monthly benefit much larger than the PIA, depending upon the number of benefit increases the retiree experienced.

The formulas for calculating benefits have been changed from time to time since 1935, contributing further to the variation in social security payments. The formula provides a higher percentage of the average monthly earnings in the early steps of its application. This is why low earners have higher percentages of their preretirement income replaced by social security than do higher earners. This is one reason why social security has taken on redistributive elements, as discussed in Chapter 3. In any event, the professional person must know under what circumstances social security is available to older people, but there is no way the professional person, or even the beneficiary, for that matter, can accurately determine the amount of monthly benefit. This must be done by staff at the Social Security Administration, from the individual's payroll records. There is no preestablished maximum or minimum social security benefit.

Supplemental Security Income (SSI) was created by Congress in 1972 by combining the Old Age Assistance program (Title I) with Aid for the Disabled and Aid for the Blind. Thus, in principle, SSI operates for older people in the same way as Old Age Assistance did. Since it was presumed that, gradually, fewer and fewer older people would need income support because they would be covered by social security, the number of older people receiving SSI is small. In 1980, 1,808,000 older people received SSI. This represents 7 percent of the older adult population.

TABLE 6-3   An Example of Monthly Income for an Older Person Who Receives Both Social Security and SSI

PROGRAM	FUNDS AVAILABLE	TOTAL FUNDS AVAILABLE
Federal minimum SSI benefit	$267	
State supplement (optional with states; amounts vary)	50	
Total SSI benefit available		$317
Social security benefit (low earner, based on a PIA of $200)	$226	
Allowable $20 "pass-through"	−20	
Total social security benefit available as a financial resource		$206
Amount of "unmet need"		$111
Social security benefit		226
Total monthly income available to older person		$337

SSI is a means-tested program; eligibility is based on an applicant's financial status, not on work history. In other words, SSI is a program to support low-income older people. Even though only slightly less than two million older adults get SSI benefits, the existence of SSI raises several questions. If social security covers about 98 percent of older adults, this would mean that only about 510,000 older people would need SSI. Instead there are more than three-and-a-half times as many older people on SSI. The reason, of course, is that in many cases the social security payment is below the minimum SSI payment, because social security is computed on the basis of work history, not on the basis of need. In fact, as many as 70 percent of the SSI recipients are also receiving social security at the same time. The average social security payment for persons also receiving SSI was $198.56 in 1980.[10]

The overlap between SSI and social security (illustrated in Table 6-3) raises additional policy questions about these two programs. SSI is administered by the federal government's Social Security Administration, which sets a national minimum benefit payment. For a single person, this amount currently is $267. All states have the option of supplementing this basic payment if they choose, and some states are required to do so. About half the states supplement, but the amount of the supplement varies from state to state. If the social security benefit is less than the SSI benefit, the older person is classified as financially needy, and the difference be-

[10]U.S. Department of Health and Human Services, Office of Research Statistics, *Program and Demographic Characteristics of Supplemental Income Beneficiaries* (Washington: Government Printing Office, May 1981).

tween the two amounts, plus a $20 social security "pass-through," is paid to the individual in the form of an SSI benefit. The individual in this case would get two checks: one for $226 from social security and one for $111 from SSI.

Suppose, however, that the individual never worked and consequently had no social security benefit. In this case, the older person would receive a check from SSI for $317. Compared to the older person who worked, it seems unfair that the non-worker would get almost as much in postretirement income as the person who worked. Looked at another way, because social security benefits are viewed as financial resources they are "taxed" at 100 percent in determining eligibility for SSI. Examined in yet another way, social security funds are being used to supplement funds raised by general revenue taxes, since the full social security benefit is used to offset both what the federal government and the state would have to contribute to income maintenance if the social security program did not exist.

The overlap between social security and SSI creates questions of fairness in income-maintenance efforts for older people. Is it fair that someone who works for a marginal income will get almost no credit in retirement for his or her many social security contributions? Is it fair that marginal earners and persons who have never worked will get about the same income benefits in retirement? Is it fair that monies taken from workers and placed in trust can be used to defray income support costs that are raised by more progressive taxes levied on the entire population? These questions add to the controversy about social security, as discussed in Chapter 3. Some suggestions for dealing with these issues will be offered in the concluding chapter.

Practical considerations about SSI remain for the professional person who serves older people. A professional worker should know the amount of SSI payment in his or her state, and if the social security payment is about the same or less than the state benefit amount, the older person should be encouraged to seek additional financial support from SSI. The professional person should be aware that the local social security office should be contacted with these questions since the benefits for social security and SSI will always vary from person to person. Additional benefits may be available to the older person as a result of being an SSI recipient. For example, the older person would be accepted for Medicaid and might be eligible automatically for some Title XX services. Even though the SSI supplement may be only a few dollars, it is worth examining eligibility for many older people who have marginal income.

Medicare is medical insurance for older people who qualify. To qualify, older people must be eligible for social security, and they must join the program by paying a monthly premium. Medicare coverage does not come automatically once an older person starts receiving social security checks. Medicare is very similar to private sector health insurance. There are two parts: Part A covers hospital-related costs. Part B covers a number of non-hospital medical costs. There are limitations on services and deductions from the monthly benefit check for both Part A and Part B. The major difference between Medicare and private sector medical insurance is the difference between the small monthly premium paid by the older person, and the true cost of the insurance, which is made up by the federal government from the medical insurance trust fund.

Presently about 21,730,000 older people are covered by Medicare, representing 85 percent of the older population and about 92 percent of older, eligible social security recipients.[11] The amount of medical costs paid by Medicare is amazing. In 1979, $16.9 billion was paid in Medicare reimbursement for medical services. Almost 40 percent of the people covered by Medicare, 8,676,000, were admitted to hospitals in 1980 at the staggering cost of $22.8 billion, for an average $2,626 of hospital charges for each admission.[12] In contrast Medicare paid only $172 per claim for home health care services. Reimbursements per claim in a private nursing facility were $573.

The bill for nonhospital-related medical costs (Part B) was equally sobering. A total of $120.1 billion was billed to Medicare in 1979. Physicians billed 77 percent of this total, at an average cost of $75 per bill. Hospital outpatient departments billed 12 percent, at an average cost of $49 per bill. Home health billed Medicare for .7 percent, at an average cost of $144. Miscellaneous bills accounted for the remaining 10 percent. Only 77.4 percent of physician costs and 55 percent of outpatient hospital costs were reimbursed. By these standards, the cost of medical care for older people is truly alarming. Whether all the services are necessary, and whether or not the costs adequately reflect realistic medical costs, without medical insurance, older people could never begin to afford the medical care they are presently receiving.

The professional person who works with older people should appreciate how expensive medical care can be and should be sure that all elderly social security recipients are also members of Medicare. Many older people will still belong to private health insurance plans, which may be quite costly for older people. The professional person should review the benefits of these private plans against Medicare benefits. More likely than not, Medicare will offer equivalent or superior benefits. Frequently private plans will pay benefits *only* after Medicare has been exhausted, so that the small amount of liability assumed by the private carrier may not justify its cost.

In reviewing medical costs, it is also important for the professional person to keep in mind that home health services are less costly than hospitalization or skilled nursing care. Although home health services are more costly than physician charges or out-patient services, the amount of service given in the home is more comprehensive than that given in the doctor's office or clinic. Furthermore, services in the home can contribute to preventive health practices. The professional person would

---

[11] The data describing Medicare and Medicaid programs, as reported in *Statistical Abstracts*, are derived from separate data bases: Current Population Reports (U.S. Census) and Social Security Administration. Different data are reported for some categories, making the comparisons described in these sections difficult at times (see, for example, Tables 546 and 547 in *Statistical Abstracts*).

[12] The difference between total Medicare expenditures and hospital and other medical charges is paid by the individual older person.

do well to evaluate the use of home-based medical services whenever the option exists. A further discussion of home-based services appears in the next part of this book.

Medicaid is a medical cost reimbursement program run by states with federal funds for everyone who is medically needy. Medicaid, therefore, is available for children, families, and adults, as well as older adults, whose medical expenses outstrip their financial ability. Because many older people have modest incomes and have heavy medical expenses, they are likely to be medically needy and eligible for Medicaid in addition to Medicare, even though they may not be eligible for other need-tested programs. About 3,288,000 older people receive Medicaid assistance. The full range of overlap of Medicaid and Medicare is unclear since each state determines the financial and medical eligibility for Medicaid. About 34 percent of the older adult population who receive Medicaid are below the poverty level while about 10 percent are above the poverty level.

Most of the Medicaid payments to older people are used to reimburse hospitals, nursing homes, intermediate care homes, and group homes for the prolonged care of older people. Recent studies done by the General Accounting Office substantiate that in many circumstances care in their own homes could substitute for institutionalized care. Not only would the costs be more reasonable, but the care itself would be more personalized and more desirable.[13] Yet, the rules for Medicaid reimbursement do not permit routine reimbursement for in-home services since most of these services are not identified as medical services.

Medicaid, like Medicare, provides funds to reimburse health care providers. In other words, approved health care providers—doctors, nurses, and in some cases social workers—provide approved services, such as diagnosis and treatments in the form of various therapies. Federal and state governments have laws which determine who can be reimbursed, the kinds of services that are reimbursable, and the amounts of reimbursement. Persons who need medical care but have no resources to pay for it must present to the provider some sort of verification that the provider will be reimbursed for the services. This verification is often in the form of a sticker that the provider attaches to the bill, when it is presented for payment.

There are many issues and problems associated with the Medicaid program, especially as it is provided for older people. Most of these issues are related to the whole area of health and medical care generally, and they will be discussed in that context later in this book. Much of the criticism of Medicaid has been addressed in the context of a lack of adequate funding, but while this is true, there are more fundamental concerns that need further evaluation. As far as the professional worker is concerned, there should be an understanding of Medicaid as a medical care resource for older people. Since Medicaid is based on medical need, a good number (over 10 percent) of older people who are not poor are eligible for this resource.

---

[13]Comptroller General of the United States, *Entering a Nursing Home—Costly Implications for Medicaid and the Elderly: A Report to Congress* (Washington: Government Printing Office, November 1979).

This is because medical expenses are subtracted from established income levels before financial eligibility is determined. For example, suppose the income eligibility level for Medicare was $250 per month. Suppose that a person had $400 per month in income but also had medical care bills of $200 per month. The medical costs would be subtracted and the adjusted income would be $200, making the person eligible for Medicaid.

For the professional person, then, it is important to consider carefully *all* resources and *all* expenses of the older adult to determine whether Medicaid resources are available. Since local (county) departments of social services usually administer Medicaid, it would be well to check with an eligibility worker in the local agency to see if a particular older adult would qualify for a particular medical service.

Social Services are the latest set of programs under the Social Security Act that are available for older people. Social services translate into many and varied programs for older people—day care, chore services, group therapy, or just about any kind of service that might be imagined—as long as the state, which runs this program, approves the service. Thus, in theory, many forms of assistance could be provided to older people through publicly-funded social services. Most of the in-home services are provided in this manner. Unfortunately there is no way to know just what the impact of publicly-funded social services has been on the lives of older people because the Department of Health and Human Services has ceased to collect information on the amounts and types of service that states provide under this program. To understand why this is so and to understand the way social services may be used for older people, it is necessary to take a short detour into the politics of social service policy.

When the Social Security Act was passed in 1935, most people thought that giving money to people who needed it would be straightforward. This was not what happened. In the first place, those who were responsible for deciding who was needy had to make an investigation, and in so doing they became familiar with the needy person in a broad context of family and social relationships. In the second place, those who made the decision about who was eligible for help also provided assistance beyond financial help, often directed toward the elimination of financial need itself. Suppose Mrs. Jones came for aid because she had no job. In the course of determining eligibility, the worker found out that Mrs. Jones was an excellent seamstress. The worker approved Mrs. Jones for financial aid, but she also told Mrs. Jones about Mrs. Smith, who was looking for someone to help in her dressmaking business. Mrs. Jones visited Mrs. Smith, who hired her. Thus, in all of the need-based programs there existed this informal and rudimentary kind of social service. Hospital arrangements were made, child care was arranged—examples are endless.

As the profession of social work took on greater definition in America, particularly after World War II, these rudimentary social service activities increased to the point where public welfare workers were actively seeking ways to expand the use of social work skills to reduce or prevent applications for public aid. This was all well and good, except there was no way to pay for these activities. The federal government, at first, contributed to the welfare payments while the cost of administrative activities associated with this work was borne by the states. Later the federal government agreed to share in some of the administrative costs, but it was hard to justify these helping efforts as the usual type of administrative activities. Furthermore, social workers argued that if they had more time to help people, instead of only giving out money, they could prevent economic dependency or at least mitigate some of its effects if it could not be prevented. For example, perhaps an old person had no pension, could not work, was not eligible for social security, and needed Old Age Assistance. If this economic need could not be prevented, the social worker could help the older person find a comfortable and affordable home, and so forth.

Several studies done during the later 1950s seemed to confirm that social services were useful, should be continued, and should be adequately funded. Thus, in 1962, Congress modified the Social Security Act to make it possible, specifically, to provide social services rather than "administrative services," as they had developed, and in 1964 Congress appropriated funds to carry out this program change. Then, however, social workers began to complain that because they had to spend their time deciding who was eligible for aid, as well as doing a variety of service tasks, they were not able to give as much help as they might if relieved of eligibility responsibility. In 1969, the Social Rehabilitation Service (of DHEW) ordered states to separate social service activities from eligibility determining functions, and in 1972 Congress underwrote this administrative decision through appropriate legislation.

Then, just when things seemed to be going well for social service advocates, a strange series of events occurred. It started when states began to use the new social service money and authority as a means to underwrite a wide variety of social programs that they had operated without federal support in previous years. Many states used the social service money to support mental health programs. California went so far as to put forward a plan to underwrite its whole corrections system with federal social service money. While states were ingeniously creating new ways to spend the new social service dollars, DHEW Secretary Robert Finch ordered regional offices to deny funding to states that proposed to use social service money for social services that were not approved by DHEW. Immediately a storm of protest developed over these proposed regulations, and over 750,000 letters of objection flooded DHEW.

While the staff at DHEW was laboring to respond to the avalanche of mail, the Congress, already frustrated over the Nixon administration's impounding of housing money and threats to eliminate the Office of Economic Opportunity, opened public hearings on the controversial regulations proposed by DHEW. The situation quickly turned to a stalemate. The Nixon administration refused to withdraw the regulations. Congress, subsequently, passed a law that prohibited DHEW from finalizing its regulations for a year. Thus for a year, at least, things remained as they were. States were free to do whatever they wanted with federal social services money.

As the year drew to a close, however, Congress was no closer to a solution of the problem of social services. Under the threat that DHEW would finalize its regulations and take social service funds away from the states, Congress hastily enacted Title XX to the Social Security Act as one of its last pieces of business in 1974. Known as the Social Service Amendments, this legislation set a ceiling on federal spending for social services, and it divided federal funds for these purposes among the states, based on a strict population formula. However, the legislation specifically forbade the secretary of DHEW from deciding what constituted social services. As long as the service met one of five general goals and as long as the states said it was a social service, as far as Congress was concerned, it was a social service. Period.

States, by and large, did no better at defining social services. Faced with mounting pressures from varied interest groups for more funds for specific social programs, many states passed to the counties the difficult problem of deciding just what kinds of things would be considered social services. If counties were not completely free to determine their own social services, they were limited only by pressure groups advocating for special programs for their constituencies. Women's groups wanted more day-care services and funding for shelters for abused women. Senior citizens wanted in-home services. Some groups wanted adolescent counseling programs. Others wanted recreation activities. In the final analysis each county sorted out priorities, often on the basis of who spoke loudest and longest, and these choices were passed to the state, which in turn included each locality's laundry list in its social service plan. Faced with the impossible task of trying to account for the endless variety of social services, DHEW abandoned all efforts to provide reports on social service activity in the states. So while DHEW still required states to collect social service information, it no longer required that states submit it. Thus, there is very little information about how many older people are helped by public social services or what kind of help they get.

In many ways, social services as created by Title XX represent a dramatic policy victory for social work. After years of struggling to have the act of providing social services separated from the act of determining whether people were eligible for public aid, Title XX provided, for the first time, an independent funding base for social work activity. Unfortunately for the general public, the social work profession assumed that social workers would learn what services to provide and how to provide them; and in the mistaken notion that social service, by definition, was something social workers did, little direction has been given to systematic efforts to maximize the use of these resources by focusing social services on the problems of the most people. Thus efforts to provide social services for in-home care for older people, for example, have become less professional decisions than political ones.

The helping professional should know that social services exist, that social services have great potential to assist older people, but that there is very little pattern as to how they are provided to older adults. For all practical purposes, eligibility for social services is based on income. However, the income guidelines range quite widely from state to state and from service to service. Federal law requires that at least half of the state's social services must be provided to the poor, so that within that context, states have wide variation in how they determine eligibility. It is also possible for states to establish "group eligibility" for social services, and in some states older people are eligible for Title XX services by virtue of being older. In the final analysis who is eligible, what services are available, and what must be done to get those services is the responsibility of the local Department of Social Services, and the professional worker would do well to consult with this local agency about the specific services that might be available for older people.

THE OLDER AMERICANS ACT

Unlike the Social Security Act, the Older Americans Act is not a policy instrument designed to transfer funds or resources to older people. Instead, the Older Americans Act provides a national legislative authority for combining and organizing a variety of public resources for older people. Chapter 4 examined the political and structural context of the Older Americans Act. That discussion identified the Older Americans Act with contemporary liberal philosophy as evident during the 1960s. With the growth of Great Society programs that provided income support, housing, food, jobs, self-help, and medical care with the full support and assistance of the federal government, the Older Americans Act sought to provide governmental authority for coordinating the abundant resources in order to make them more effective for older people. That the federal government should provide resources for such coordinating activities represented considerable ideological development beyond the philosophy that supported the Social Security Act. The Older Americans Act stated that federal funds would be used to excite, stimulate, and encourage the development and refinement of efforts to get greater shares of the social welfare "pie" for older people.

The philosophy of the Older Americans Act was sharply confronted by the Nixon administration, which correctly assessed the political potential older people possessed for realigning national welfare spending priorities. In a controversial and contestable article in *Parade,* a Sunday supplement magazine, DHEW Secretary Robert Finch challenged the direction of public policy development as embodied in the Older Americans Act, claiming that there were many times as many children in the United States as older people. "But federal benefits and services of all kinds in 1970 will average about $1,750 per aged person and only $190 per young person."[14] *The Wall Street Journal* quoted similar remarks that caused many congressional supporters of the Older Americans Act to defend vociferously what Senator Harrison Williams (N.J.) called "federal acting on behalf of the elderly."[15]

As discussed in Chapter 4, the heart of the Older Americans Act, and of the philosophical debate over the act, was Title III. By 1969, four years after passage of the act, the emphasis on the Title III philosophy was beginning to be felt. John Martin, Commissioner of the Administration on Aging, reported:

[14]*Parade,* June 15, 1969.
[15]*Congressional Record* 115, pt. 12, June 12, 1969.

Through this act, the Administration on Aging was created as a focal point of the Federal Government's concern for the needs and problems of older citizens. In addition, as a direct result of this act, states and communities throughout the Nation have created state and local agencies on aging to fulfill a similar role at other levels of government.[16]

Martin and other supporters of the act recommended "expansion of the Title III program to strengthen the State agencies on aging and [provide] . . . flexibility to the decisions of the State agencies on aging."[17] Martin boasted that 1,000 new community projects were established by 1969 as a result of Title III.

The Older Americans Act is subtitled "An act to provide assistance in the development of new or improved programs to help older persons through grants to the states for community planning and services and for training. . . ." The title of the act sets forth ten objectives, the final one being that older Americans are entitled to "freedom, independence, and the free exercise of individual initiative in planning and managing their own lives." The absence of legislative authority to provide services to older people is reflected further in Title II of the act, which establishes the Administration on Aging. The act specifies seventeen functions for the Administration on Aging, but designates only one direct service responsibility. The remaining sixteen functions involve various supportive services: coordination and planning, research and demonstration, training, and evaluation.

Title III of the act, the most comprehensive, has the greatest importance for practitioners. This title provides funds for grants to states and community programs on aging. Title IV authorizes training, research, and demonstration projects. Although Title IV gives the AOAs considerable latitude in the use of education, training, and demonstration funds, AOA efforts to improve career education, or to define the field of serving older people through research and demonstration, have been very disappointing, compared with education, training, and research activities implemented under the Social Security Act. In general, grants provided to educational institutions have lacked any level of consistency that would help provide professional or career education for people who wanted to work with older adults. For example, nursing students who wanted to work with older people would find no educational support from Title IV. Title V defines the Community Service Employment program, also important for this discussion. Title VI of the act specifies special programs for Indian tribes.

Title III: State and Community Aging Programs

The purpose of Title III is clearly stated: "to encourage and assist state and local agencies concentrate resources in order to . . . foster the development of comprehensive and coordinated service systems to serve older individuals. . . ."

[16] John B. Martin, "Testimony," *Amending the Older Americans Act of 1965,* Hearing before the Senate Subcommittee on Aging (Washington: Government Printing Office, 1969), 63.

[17] Martin, 63.

The purpose of Title III is clear; implementing this purpose has created a complex network of different programs throughout the nation.

The *Area-wide Agency on Aging (AAA)* is the crucial program structure under Title III. As explained in Chapter 4, the AAA differs significantly in structure and function from previous social welfare organizations. Each state is required to divide itself into distinct planning and service areas in which the details of the Title III purposes will be carried out. These planning and service areas may be a geographical or politically defined region, a general purpose local government, a subsection of the state, or in some cases, the entire state itself. The organizational designation for an AAA may be a public organization, or a private nonprofit organization. Thus even though each state must designate an AAA in the state, each AAA will be differerent from place to place.

The AAA's main purpose is to develop for its service area an area plan that is submitted to the state. These area plans generally tell how the services available to older people in each area will be prepared and presented. In practice, the work of the area-wide planner is to make some judgments about which agencies and organizations within the area will receive funds for the services that are funded under the Act. The planner must take into account the extent to which the resources and services, *overall,* will be improved for older people by choosing one local organization as opposed to another, as the recipient of the funds provided by Title III.

Certain services can be funded with AOA money; an example is transportation or nutrition services. The transportation must be provided to facilitate access to nutrition services. Nutrition services must be provided in a congregate setting and must include nutrition education. A number of agencies in an area may seek transportation funds for older people. Social service departments may try to get funds to transport older people to social services. Health departments may want transportation funds to bring older people to clinic appointments. Both recreation departments and senior centers may seek transportation funds to bring older people to activities, and at the same time senior centers may also seek nutrition service funds. After considering all the alternatives, the area planner might choose to assign both transportation and nutrition funds to the senior center since this decision might maximize the use of services for older people better than other possible decisions.

The *area plan,* then, must take into account all the agencies and organizations that serve older people in each community. The plan must show how the funds would be divided among selected organizations in such a way as to get the most value for older people for the money. Suppose, for example, the recreation department in Jonesville proposed to use transportation funds to pick up older people and take them first to an activity program, then to the senior center for nutrition services. This might be an appealing suggestion by which the transportation funds could buy more services for older people in Jonesville. In Midville, however, the recreation department may have very few programs for older people. The area planner might use transportation funds differently in that community.

Without being uncharitable, Title III represents the "carrot-and-stick" approach to social welfare program development. It offers the lure of financial re-sources to local service agencies if these agencies will refine their programs so as to provide better and more effective services for older people. The Midville recreation department might be offered the chance for transportation resources if they develop a program similar to Jonesville, for example. Thus, there is an assumption in Title III that service money can be used to stimulate competition among local organizations to do more and better things with and for older people.

Perhaps the professional person can understand why it is difficult to discern any exact pattern of services for older people as a result of the Older American's Act. Each planning area in the United States will have a different pattern of services because within each area are a variety of local communities, each with different social agencies and each with different social resources. The professional person needs to know that there is an AAA that knows the service pattern for each community. Thus, the professional person should be in touch with the AAA to determine what services are available to older people as specified in the area plan. On the basis of that information, the professional person will have some better idea of what assistance would be available under what circumstances. The combination of social services and programs for older people in any community is often called the *aging network.*

Specific *social services* are provided through the Older Americans Acts, even though the exact form of the service may vary from place to place. Some of these services are available to meet discrete objectives, others meet general objectives. Services to meet discrete objectives are allowed to be funded: health education, training, "welfare," information, recreation, homemakers, counseling, referral, and transportation. Despite the fact that the names of these services are very clear, the elements that constitute the actual service are very different from place to place. Usually area planners decide which sets of activities qualify as services under the OAA. For example, are innoculations against influenza and discussions about body care both health services? If they are, which service most likely achieves the objective of a health service? The degree of interpretation of services varies so widely, that, once again, the professional person is likely to find no exact pattern as to social services available under the Older Americans Act.

There are also services with general objectives. Services to encourage older people to use other services and services to help older people obtain adequate housing are some of these general services that can be provided, ranging all the way to crime prevention services and victim assistance programs. There are fourteen of these possible general services, including "any other service . . . necessary for the welfare of older individuals." As a result of such vagaries, each community and each social service agency competes vigorously for the funds available from the Older Americans Act. In many cases, this competition contributes to better services for older people. In other cases, however, the decisions are based on political expediency, since there are no established standards that would guide decision making.

Senior Centers may also be funded under Title III-B. Money is available to renovate facilities, construct new facilities, and staff facilities, if approved in the area plan. Just exactly what constitutes a senior center is not clear in the legislation. The National Council on Senior Centers has established elaborate criteria for senior center development. These standards are frequently used as guidelines for determining whether a center for older people qualifies for these funds. In the simplest form, a senior center is a focal point of activity and services for older people. Ideally, all the services approved under Title III area plans should be available through a local senior center. Most local communities have a senior center, and professionals should know where it is located and what resources it makes available to older people. A detailed discussion of how the professional works in and with senior centers is provided in Chapter 10.

Nutrition services are now provided under Title III. Originally, nutrition services were provided under a separate title. Nutrition services now are subject to the same state plan requirements and regional planning activities as outlined earlier. In this way, nutrition services are supposed to be more integral to all efforts to help older people. Ideally, nutrition services ought to be provided in the senior center, and nutrition services should become the center of activity at the senior center.

Most simply, nutrition services consist of three distinct activities rolled into one: (1) a hot meal (usually lunch) served in a group environment; (2) nutrition education, aimed at instructing older people about good eating habits; and (3) a program designed to help older people learn about other resources in the community that would contribute to a satisfactory life. The meal is available without charge, although older persons are encouraged to make a contribution to defray some of the expenses. The meal must meet nutritional standards as established by the National Academy of Sciences. Although some of these meals may be delivered to older people who are unable to leave their homes, most of the meals must be provided in a friendly and inviting group environment.

There are a lot of misunderstandings about this program. Since it is available without charge, it is a non-means-tested program, and it is an in-kind program. The purpose of the program is to use the meal as an inducement to get older people out of their homes and into some healthy social interaction with others. Therefore nutrition services are available to anyone age sixty or older, and to spouses of such persons, even if the spouses are not sixty years old. As one might expect, this is a very expensive program. The number of people served, and the cost in 1981 was over 410,000 daily, at a cost of $350 million. Even so, there are many people who might like to participate in the program if more funds were available.

There are related expenses to this program. Particularly in rural areas, transportation to a central group site may involve personal expense much greater than the value of the meal. Furthermore, older people may not be able to drive long distances, so that transportation usually has to be provided at public expense in such situations. There are other expenses required to maintain a setting suitable for such a program. This is why it makes good sense to offer nutrition services along with a senior center program. Although 90 percent of the funds for nutrition services come from the Older Americans Act, 10 percent must be provided by the local project sponsor. Such a complicated program, along with a general misunderstanding of the program's purpose, has made it controversial in many places.

Professional workers should be aware of this resource. Moreover, they should be aware that the greatest value is likely to result from the programs that accompany the provision of the hot meal. In other words, the meal is the means to get older people together so that they have an opportunity to interact with one another and learn about other opportunities available to them to live successfully. Too many nutrition programs consist of a meal and a second- or third-rate program. This defeats the whole purpose of the program, and professional persons should insure that the full range of nutrition services are available at each nutrition site.

Title V: Community Service Employment

Community Service Employment for older people grew out of earlier efforts to engage the skills and talents of older people. Originally legislation established a domestic volunteer program for older people similar to the VISTA program. Many older people volunteered their services; but many older people and professional workers believed that older people should be compensated for employment, particularly when the work was essential to successful program operation. In 1978, therefore, the Older Americans Act was changed to create paying jobs for unemployed low-income persons age fifty-five and older.

Eligible persons may be employed in public or private nonprofit organizations at jobs appropriate for older people to perform and jobs that do not displace regular employees or eliminate regular jobs. This program is administered by the state aging agencies and, subsequently, through the AAAs. Therefore, most of the older people who are served by this program perform jobs in organizations and programs that serve older people. By far, most of the older people served under this program work in senior citizen centers and nutrition projects. In this way, the Community Service Employment program fulfills a dual purpose. Older people are provided with paid employment and many organizations that serve older people are able to hire persons to expand and improve the services they offer to older adults.

Professional persons should realize that funds for this program are limited; there are not many of these jobs available. The program is means-tested, and therefore restricted to low-income persons who must also be unemployed. They may not leave a job and then become eligible for a job funded by this program. Despite these restrictions, the program has been well received. Many older people prefer to work, and many older people need additional income. Programs serving older people are in need of more personnel, and older people usually have tested skills and abilities that can be utilized very quickly.

CONCLUSION

The programs available to older people under the Older Americans Act are summarized in Table 6-4. Together with the programs available to older people under the Social Security Act, they comprise an impressive array of resources and services for older people. The programs generated by these national laws provide a basic frame-

TABLE 6-4   Programs for Older People Available Under the Older Americans Act

PROGRAM	PROGRAM TYPE	PROGRAM BENEFIT	PROGRAM ADMINISTRATION

Title III-A
   Community Planning
   and Coordination
      (1965)
	---	Planning
		Coordination
		Technical assistance
			Area-wide agency
			   on Aging (AAA)

Title III-B
   Social Services
      (1973)
	Not means-tested	In-kind
		(depending on each
		community)
			Local agencies

Senior Centers
   (1978)
	Not means-tested	In-kind	Local
			   senior citizens
			   councils

Title III-C
   Nutrition Services
      (1973)
	Not means-tested	In-kind	Local
			   project
			   sponsor

Title V
   Community Service
   Employment
	Means-tested	In-kind	Local
			   project
			   sponsor

work of income support and social services, touching the lives of almost every older person in this country to one degree or another. There are legitimate criticisms of these programs, which will be explored in detail at the conclusion of this book. Yet, it is important to keep in mind that these programs provide the foundations upon which more complex, more comprehensive, and more intensive programs for older people are constructed. Some perspectives on these more elaborate programs for older people are the subject of the next chapter.

CHAPTER SEVEN

PROGRAMS FOR OLDER PEOPLE:
Housing and Services for Independent Living

Mrs. Wesson arrived at the bank while the tellers were still putting the cash into their drawers. Mr. Franklin, the "all-business" vice-president, was still fixing the door latches, and the vault, where the safe deposit boxes were stored, was not open yet. Those who saw Mrs. Wesson offered smiles. The rest went about opening the bank for a busy day. The customer service representative helped Mrs. Wesson get settled in a room with her safe deposit box. Almost half an hour later, Mrs. Wesson asked the customer service representative, Mrs. Satterwhite, for help. Mrs. Wesson's eyes appeared tear-stained, and her voice quivered as she asked for help. The bank had assisted the Wessons in establishing their trust fund and had provided legal assistance in the management of Mr. Wesson's resources after his death.

Assuming Mrs. Wesson was having a difficult moment, Mrs. Satterwhite helped her collect the papers and put them back into the box, and making sure she had all the coupons she needed, helped return the box to the vault. When Mrs. Wesson sat down at Mrs. Satterwhite's desk, her cheeks were tear-stained. She blurted out that she had to move and did not know what she was going to do. She felt lost, confused, and helpless. As she talked, she began to cry openly.

Mrs. Wesson had been notified on the previous day that the city had acquired options on all the land on her side of the street to improve and enlarge the city park. She was offered $15,000 for her property, or they could go to court, but in any event the city expected her to vacate her property within six weeks. Mrs. Wesson had called her attorney, who suggested they try to get $20,000 for the property, but he suspected that the final settlement would probably be close to $15,000, and it might not be worth the anguish and legal costs to try to get more.

It was not the money, however, that had so distressed Mrs. Wesson. She had no idea what to do or how to do it. To move, at her age, after thirty years in the neighborhood, was unthinkable, and there was no place close by that could be purchased for $15,000 or $20,000. She had called her friends, who said they would be on the lookout for something near them. She called her children, who lived out of town, and they agreed to contact some real estate firms to see what could be found, but none of these offers of assistance satisfied the wave of fear and uncertainty sweeping over Mrs. Wesson.

Mrs. Satterwhite was a bit overwhelmed herself with Mrs. Wesson's anxiety, and she was very uncomfortable that Mrs. Wesson who, sitting across the desk from her, seemed to be "falling apart." A sensitive young woman, Mrs. Satterwhite felt she would like to help, but she did not know what to do. So, she excused herself and went to Mr. Franklin's desk to ask his advice. After listening a few minutes and reassuring Mrs. Wesson by a few quick glances in her direction, Mr. Franklin asked Mrs. Wesson to join him in one of the closed offices at the rear of the bank.

After listening to Mrs. Wesson's story again, Mr. Franklin told her that he could help her get a plan started, and while she was still in the office, Mr. Franklin first called the Public Housing Authority and made an appointment for Mrs. Wesson to talk with a relocation counselor that afternoon. Next, he called the mental health center and made an appointment for Mrs. Wesson for the next morning. Finally, he called the senior center, talked with the outreach worker, and told her what temporary arrangements he had made for Mrs. Wesson. He also told the outreach worker he would be bringing Mrs. Wesson by shortly so that together they could complete the plan he had put in motion.

Mrs. Wesson was visibly relieved. She and Mr. Franklin agreed that she need not redeem all the coupons she had clipped and that she had enough money in her checking account for the next couple of weeks; and they went back to the safe deposit box. Mr. Franklin said he would telephone Mrs. Wesson's attorney to discuss establishing power of attorney, if necessary, and to be sure that Mrs. Wesson would have legal representation in the pending house sale. Then he and Mrs. Wesson got into his car and drove to the senior center, where the outreach worker, Mrs. Patterson, was waiting for them.

GETTING THE SERVICES TOGETHER

What might be most amazing about the story above is that more and more commercial establishments offer some form of initial social services as part of their overall service for older people. Banking institutions in particular realize that circumstances such as Mrs. Wesson's are more and more often encountered by banks that serve older people. Banks are undertaking to prepare their managers to deal with personal crises, when necessary, in order to retain what has always been a good business—older clients. Churches, of course, have struggled for many years to insure that pastors and church workers can provide some initial and, on occasion, continuing social service assistance to older people. Airlines provide special services to older travelers. At times there seem to be many resources available to older people, but at other times there seem to be very few.

Locating the resources when they are needed becomes an important factor in providing these special services. While most of the services available to older people come under the authority of the Social Security Act and the Older Americans Act, there are many other services available, some of them from extremely nontraditional sources. Although it would be impossible to identify all the sources of assistance for older people, some of the better-known publicly-funded sources are identified and discussed in this chapter. Nontraditional and unusual services, such as those the bank was able to offer to Mrs. Wesson, are discussed in Chapter 9.

HOUSING PROGRAMS

The Federal Housing Act is older than the Social Security Act. As a postdepression economic recovery program, early versions of the Housing Act emphasized federal stimulus for the construction of private housing, through loans and federally subsidized mortgages. In 1937, a public housing program was added to the Act as a means of creating standard housing for low-income persons. When Urban Renewal and Model City programs were developed in the 1960s, the assisted-housing sections of the Act were modified to extend government construction subsidies to permit the development of moderate-income rental housing (section 235.d3). In 1974, the Housing Act was modified so as to create a rental assistance program for low- and moderate-income persons (section 8), and a new program was created to encourage nonprofit private corporations to develop housing for the elderly and handicapped (section 202). All parts of the Housing Act are important for older people.

Before discussing the specific programs that provide housing resources for older people, it is important to recall that the private residence owned by the older person is the most significant housing resource. In 1979, there were 78,572,000 owner-occupied housing units in the United States.[1] Of those over sixty-five who owned their own homes in 1979, 58 percent had incomes under $10,000. Most older persons have their homes paid for, so they no longer make monthly mortgage payments, and about half of the states have laws that permit older persons to exempt part of their property taxes from state tax payments. The Federal tax laws now permit an exemption from capital gains tax for a person over age fifty-five who sells his or her house, up to $125,000 of capital gain. Thus, as noted in Chapter 3,

---

[1]Unless otherwise noted, all data in this chapter are developed from *Statistical Abstracts of the United States*, 102nd ed. (Washington, 1981).

the private housing owned by older people represents not only a source of shelter, but an important financial resource as well.

Public housing is available to low-income persons. In 1979, there were 25,300,-000 persons, or 11.6 percent of the population, below the poverty level. This number represented 5,320,000 families; or 9.1 percent of all families were below the poverty level. At the same time, there were 3,586,000 people over sixty-five, of whom 15.1 percent were below the official poverty line. Also in 1979, there were 1,254,600 occupied public housing units. Thus about one out of every five families below the poverty line lived in a public housing unit. The elderly occupied 307,300 of these public units. At the conservative estimate of 1.6 older persons per household, about one out of every seven older families lives in public housing. Considering the fact that a greater proportion of older people are poor, a better ratio of older people in public housing might be expected.

On the other hand, considering the number of older people who live in their own homes, the number of older people who are served by public housing is significant. Since 1974, there have been incentives for local housing authorities to expand the number of public housing units available for older people. In general, these units are smaller—usually efficiencies or one-bedroom apartments—and frequently they are constructed with the special needs of older people in mind, including features such as grab bars, raised electrical outlets, and special bathroom fixtures. Ideally, public housing for the elderly will be constructed with centralized activity areas that can provide a variety of on-site services. Some of these services will be provided through senior centers, colocated with the public housing. Some services will be provided by other organizations, such as social service and recreation departments, in space provided by the housing authority.

When a senior center is colocated in a public housing project, a comprehensive array of services is likely to be available to older people, unrivaled by many privately-planned retreat communities. For example, a full range of social and recreational activities might be available, along with health resources, an elderly nutrition program, and special programs—perhaps library services—for the home-based elderly. In some such situations, barbers and hairdressers are available to the participants at modest fees. Because such senior centers would be used by non-public-housing older people as well, a stimulating mixing of people is likely to take place, and new friendships and social support systems are easily developed. Thus, public housing for older people has provided good potential for improving the quality of life for many older adults.

The professional person must understand that public housing is administered by a local housing authority. Because it is for low-income persons, it is means-tested. In general, the rent in public housing may not exceed 25 percent of net family income, and in the case of older people, the rents may be more modestly set. But since government subsidies are available primarily for the construction of the housing units, public housing must generate almost all the maintenance costs by rents. Thus, public housing is not likely to serve the poorest of the poor. Another constraint on the use of public housing for older adults results from apartment size.

Most of the older public housing was constructed with families with children in mind. As a result, there are a limited number of public housing apartments available for older couples and fewer for older single persons. The professional person will find that there are likely to be long waiting lists for public housing for older people.

The above restrictions on public housing suggest that the professional person should plan ahead if it seems that an older person will be eligible for public housing. Even if Mrs. Wesson, whom we met at the beginning of this chapter, were eligible for public housing, the potential for a long waiting list at the local housing authority would probably preclude her finding any assistance there. In general, the older adult should apply at the local housing authority for public housing. Each local housing authority will have somewhat different policies with respect to applications from older adults. However, the local housing authority may be able to provide other housing resources to older people who qualify.

Rental assistance, also called section 8, is another housing program available to older people. In most cases, rental assistance is administered by the local housing authority, too. This program is a means-tested program, but because of its administrative characteristics, it is able to provide housing assistance to persons whose income may be above the poverty level. The program operates on the idea of a "fair market rent" that is established for each community. This figure is computed for rental units of various sizes and types. Then, depending upon the household composition, an amount equal to about 25 percent of net income is established as the household's share of the rent, and the section 8 program pays the difference between that amount and the fair market rent.

For example, suppose Mrs. Wesson found a one-bedroom apartment or house to rent for $275.00 per month. She would report this to the local housing authority at the time, or after she made application to the program. The local housing authority would determine, on the basis of Mrs. Wesson's income, that she was eligible for the program, based upon the following income information: $400 per month social security benefit and $500 per month for interest on stocks and bonds. The local housing authority would inspect the place Mrs. Wesson suggested, and if they found that it met their housing standards it would be approved. Next, they would investigate the fair market rent for such a unit. Suppose the fair market rent was $270.00 per month. Since 25 percent of Mrs. Wesson's income would be $225, Mrs. Wesson would be eligible for a rent supplement between 25 percent of her income and the fair market rent. In this case, Mrs. Wesson's rent would be supplemented by $45.00, which would be sent directly to the landlord. In most cases, the landlord would have to agree with the housing authority to rent the housing at the fair market rent.

Although relatively small in size, the rental assistance program has been a great help to many older people. Not only does it provide another housing resource, but it can be used as a means to rehabilitate housing presently occupied by older people. Suppose an older couple had lived in a small house for many years at a fixed rent. The house has become run down, but because the income of the older couple is low, the owner is unable to raise the rent without forcing the couple out. The landlord, on the other hand, would like to fix up the place, but he does not want the old couple to have to move. Under section 8 the landlord could fix the house and ask for a fair market rent, and the program would pay the difference between what the couple could afford and the new rent. This feature of the section 8 program is the most politically desirable feature of the program. In this way the section 8 program contributes to the overall housing resources.

The professional person should be aware that all housing programs are limited. Therefore, even though a local community might have such a program, there may be no rental units available because the local community has spent its allotment of funds. It is also important to know that the applicant must find his or her own housing, but at the same time, the housing they find may not be approved. It may be too expensive or it may not meet the housing standards. Therefore, a good bit of shopping around may be necessary, and it can be difficult for the older person to do this without some assistance from the professional person. Even though the section 8 program is small, it does a relatively good job of providing housing for older people. In 1982, 1,400,600 rental units were rented under section 8 contracts, and 717,300 of these units were occupied by persons age sixty-two or older. Thus over 50 percent of all section 8 recipients are over age sixty-two.

Housing for the elderly and handicapped (section 202) is a third program operated under the Housing Act that has become an increasingly important resource for older people. Created by the 1974 Housing Act amendments, this program provides congregate housing for older adults (and the handicapped) under the sponsorship of private nonprofit organizations. Under the program, only nonprofit *private* organizations are eligible to apply for federal loans to construct new housing or to substantially rehabilitate older housing in order to make it appropriate for older people or the handicapped. The loans may be as much as 100 percent of the mortgage and be repaid over a fifty-year period. The housing is to be made available to the moderate-income person who may need housing, but who may have too much income to be eligible for public housing.[2]

The program is a modest one. Congress only anticipated that about 65,000 units of housing could be developed under this program in 1980. At present, there are 146,000 housing units available under section 202, compared to the 4,528,000 public housing units occupied by older people. However, 103,000 of these units are supported by section 8 funding. This leaves only 43,000 purely section 202 housing units. There are about five hundred sponsoring organizations that have developed section 202 housing. Most are religious organizations. Most of the units are newly constructed and because so many are sponsored by religious organizations, most of the congregate settings have developed attractive on-site programs to serve the residents. One such project was developed by the Presbyterian Church in a modest-sized town and includes two hundred apartment units, dining facilities, and a full array of medical services and social activities available at the site or at the nearby church.

[2]U.S. Department of Housing and Urban Development, Direct Loan Branch, *Housing the Elderly* (Washington: Government Printing Office, 1983).

As with the other housing resources, the demand for section 202 housing is greater than the current supply, and with the general tightening in federal spending for social programs, no significant expansion in this program is anticipated. Professional persons should know that these resources exist, and should seek them out in local communities. Waiting lists will be common, however. Even though most of these developments are sponsored by religious organizations, applications must be taken without regard to race or religious preference.

The discussion in Chapter 2 suggested the significant contribution of housing to the quality of life for the older person. Not only does the quality of the housing itself—its physical repair and convenience—contribute to a good life, but its location determines the support system that may be available for the older person. The various public programs to improve the quality of housing for older people have not always given adequate emphasis to the environmental aspects. This is particularly true of the congregate housing represented by public housing and housing for the elderly.

Offsetting the advantages of this type of housing are some disadvantages. On the one hand, congregate housing allows for the development of on-site services for older people. On-site services can be available frequently and extensively. Moreover, economies of scale permit housing amenities particularly useful for older adults. On the negative side, congregate housing is age-segregated housing. The housing itself begins to take on an institutionalized character as more environmental amenities are provided internally as a part of the housing operation. Eventually, a cohort develops through a self-selection process, which might foster greater dependence rather than independence. There is evidence to suggest that the longer people live in congregate housing, the more dependent they become on its internally provided services. In his studies of congregate housing, M. Powell Lawton found that congregate residents showed less active use of community resources but had an improved outlook on life, when compared with residents of more traditional housing. This "passive contentment" that Lawton explored was also associated with increased requests for more services the longer tenants lived in congregate housing.[3]

MENTAL HEALTH PROGRAMS

There is so much discussion about mental health programs and mental health services for older people that it is amazing that the mental health infrastructure is so poorly defined in law. There are further ambiguities as to definitions of mental health services, although a number of important professional activities are included

---

[3]M. Powell Lawton, "Applying Research Knowledge to Congregate Housing," in *Congregate Housing for Older People,* eds. Margaret Donahue, Fred Thompson, and William Curren (Washington: Administration on Aging, DHEW pub. no. 77-20284), 97. See also M. Powell Lawton, Ralph Greenbaum, and Adam Liebowitz, "The Lifespan of Housing Environments," *The Gerontologist* 20, no. 1 (1980), 56-64.

under their general category. Two sharp distinctions exist in the programs, however, the hospital, or inpatient services, and the outpatient clinics.

Most mental hospitals are operated by states and, occasionally, counties. There are about 300 state and county mental hospitals and about 190 private mental hospitals in the United States. These hospitals serve about 702,648 persons per year, who experience 1,817,000 patient case "episodes." This constituted 2.9 mental hospital admissions for every 1,000 adults in 1979. Although the exact figures are not available, limited studies of the mental hospital populations indicate that a disproportionate share of admissions are older people, who may or may not be suffering from debilitating mental illnesses. Furthermore, analyses of mental hospital populations suggest that older people comprise a large majority of long-term mental hospitalizations. Often characterized as having chronic conditions, these older people are more likely to lack alternate living arrangements and supporting social resources than they are to have serious mental illness.

Most public mental hospitals have social service staffs who devote most of their energies to developing discharge plans that will insure a physical and social environment that will support living in a noninstitutionalized environment. In many situations, these discharge plans involve continuity of mental health services through a county-based outpatient clinic. With very few exceptions, the public mental hospitals are supported from state funds alone. However, persons who enter these hospitals and who are eligible for Medicare or Medicaid assistance may have the costs of mental hospitalization paid from these funds, providing the hospitals' programs meet the standards set for reimbursement. Thus, there is a federal influence in the management and operation of the hospitals, even though they are essentially funded by the states.

One such federal influence has been the emphasis on "deinstitutionalization." Approved hospitals must have plans to return persons to the community when the medical service offered by the hospital is no longer needed. The emphasis on deinstitutionalization has been greatest among older patients who have been hospitalized for long periods precisely because no reasonable alternative existed for them. Thus, this group of mental hospital patients have frequently been pushed out of hospitals with unrealistic discharge plans. Often these people are eventually sent to nursing homes or intermediate care homes, no more appropriate, but at greater cost.

The professional worker should be aware that states determine public mental hospital admission patterns and practices, and that neither public nor private psychiatric hospitalization is free. Although most public hospitals have a sliding scale for determining fees, and although Medicare or Medicaid will cover some of the hospital costs, additional costs still accrue to the patient. Furthermore, because of the difficulty of developing workable discharge plans, hospitalization should be sought as a last resort. As with other forms of institutional care, efforts to maintain an older person in his or her own home and community are preferred to hospitalization.

Community mental health clinics are preferred to mental hospitals in all but the most severe cases of mental disorganization. The exact number of community mental health centers is very difficult to obtain since there is a wide variety of such clinics. The best-defined mental health clinics are those that are either currently funded with federal support or were established with federal assistance. The Community Mental Health Services Act of 1963 provided federal funding to states to develop local, community-based clinics, and in 1965 federal funds were added to supplement staffing costs. These provisions were incorporated under the Health Services Act, and are now part of the Health Services Block Grant. Thus it is very difficult to give an exact account of their scope. However, in 1977, outpatient community mental health clinics handled about 72 percent of all reported patient care episodes, with publicly-funded programs handling about 26 percent of that amount and private clinics handling the remaining 46 percent.

The number of older adults served in community mental health centers is also difficult to estimate. However, most studies suggest that older people are under-represented among the mental health population. A study by George L. Maddox, for example, suggests that the rate of service to older people through these centers may be as low as 4 percent.[4] A recent survey of mental health services in North Carolina revealed that 0.8 percent of the population of group homes was composed of adults aged sixty years and older, and 8 percent of the individuals served by mental health centers was over the age of fifty-one years.[5] Thus Maddox's estimate seems reasonable. Because there is such a wide variation in the type of mental health clinics, there is bound to be wide variation in the participation rates of older people. Some clinics are even undertaking efforts to develop social service programs for older people in order to serve this population better.

The poor utilization rates among older people are particularly disappointing when it is realized that many of the physical diseases and illnesses associated with growing older carry with them psychiatric symptoms and emotional consequences. Heart disease, cancer, and particularly strokes (cerebrovascular disease) are often accompanied by mental problems such as increased irritability, periods of anxiety and depression, and occasional emotional outbursts. Alzheimer's disease, in particular, a leading disabling condition among older people, carries with it equally emotionally disabling conditions for both the older person and family and friends. As discussed in Chapter 2, however, the exact etiology of symptoms of mental incapacity may not be a consequence of growing older. Thus the professional person must take great care not to equate growing older with an increased need for mental health services.

The professional person should be aware of the wide variety of mental health programs and services that may be available in any community. Such awareness usually takes careful study because of the variety of mental health resources in any community. Furthermore, the professional person should be aware that many established mental health clinics will not be adequately equipped to deal with the

---

[4] George L. Maddox, "The Patient and His Family," in *The Hidden Patient: Knowledge and Action in Long-Term Care,* ed. Sylvia Sherwood (New York: Spectrum Publications, 1975), 87–113.

[5] Maurice Witaker to Waylon Bissette, North Carolina Department of Human Resources, Leher, February 1983; copy in the author's files.

special problems older people may present. However, the greater the extent to which community mental health clinics can be used instead of mental hospitals, the better off the older person will be.

NURSING HOMES, INTERMEDIATE-CARE FACILITIES, AND REST HOMES

Even though it is difficult to summarize these programs, they must be mentioned since they are so widely used and so much discussion surrounds their use. Nursing homes, intermediate-care facilities, and rest homes differ with respect to the level and intensity of medical care provided at the facility. The nursing home, by definition, must have twenty-four-hour nursing care available for the facility. The intermediate-care facility must have nursing and medical care available to it. The rest home need provide no medical care.

There are close to 20,000 nursing homes in the United States, including profit and nonprofit facilities. Since older people are frequent users of hospitals, and since they stay longer than any other group of users, nursing homes have been viewed as alternatives to prolonged hospitalization. When conditions warrant, nursing homes are preferred to hospitalization because nursing-home care is less expensive.

A problem developed, however, since public support was available from Medicare and Medicaid for institutional care, such as nursing-home care, but not available for home-based alternatives, as discussed in the previous chapter. As Medicare and Medicaid expenditures escalated, it became evident that nursing-home care, and to a lesser extent, intermediate-care homes, were absorbing disproportionate amounts of these funds. By 1978, 41 percent of Medicaid funds were spent on nursing-home care. In a similar vein, 48 percent of all nursing-home residents depended upon Medicaid as the primary way to pay their nursing-home bill. Considering the fact that less than 5 percent of all older adults receive nursing-home care and less than 2 percent of all Medicare recipients receive nursing-home care, serious questions were raised about funding nursing homes as opposed to funding other sources of care for older people.

Greater awareness of increasing nursing-home-care costs led Congress to explore whether, because of the availability of Medicaid funding, nursing homes were being used appropriately. Congress asked the General Accounting Office (GAO) to explore these questions, and in November 1979, the GAO issued a report of its study.[6] This report reexamined considerable existing data on care of older people and pulled together a number of studies on the subject into a comprehensive and biting report of nursing-home care. The report raised the ire of the nursing-home industry and contributed to current congressional efforts to restrict escalating medical costs. The report concluded that Medicaid had become the chief support of

---

[6] Comptroller General of the United States, *Entering a Nursing Home—Costly Implications for Medicaid and the Elderly* (Washington: General Accounting Office, 1979).

nursing-home care for the chronically impaired elderly, but that many of the older adults in nursing homes "could have remained in their own homes or communities if long-term health and social services were available to them." The GAO study reported that the earlier survey of elderly persons found only 11 percent of the elderly population to be extremely or very greatly impaired, and that the rest of the older adult population would be able to achieve limited improvements in personal activity levels with some form of community assistance.[7]

The GAO also found that 91 percent of nursing-home residents had a relative, that 56 percent of these relatives were children, that 63 percent of the relatives visited the nursing-home occupant at least weekly, and that 70 percent of the relatives lived within twenty-five miles of the nursing home. Furthermore, 30 percent of the reasons for admissions to nursing homes were because the family was unable to care for the older person at home, rather than for medical reasons.[8] These conclusions suggest a much different picture of the nursing-home resident. Instead of the usual portrayal, nursing-home patients are not isolated from their larger families, and in many cases they could easily be at home if resources were available to help families care for them.

As discussed in Chapter 6, the GAO reported that Medicaid eligibility creates financial incentives to use nursing homes rather than community resources. The GAO concluded that Medicaid's procedures for assessing the need for nursing-home care were not adequate to prevent otherwise avoidable institutionalization. The GAO recommended that Congress establish "mandatory comprehensive needs assessments for all individuals applying to nursing homes whose care would be reimbursed by Medicaid or Medicare."[9] In the wake of this report, many states have established procedures for comprehensive screening of all potential nursing-home patients by multidisciplinary teams of doctors, nurses, social workers, recreation therapists, and physical therapists.

The most important recommendation of the GAO study for the professional person might be its finding that a personal or family crisis may precipitate admission to a nursing home. At such critical junctions, professional persons are not adequately prepared to explore alternatives with the family and assist the family in developing an alternate plan.

> Community long-term options may never be considered because the professional who assists the elderly and their families in arranging long-term care—social service department caseworkers, hospital discharge planners, and physicians—are [sic] often unaware of, or too busy to explain alternatives to institutionalization. Assembling the appropriate package of services can take

---

[7]Comptroller General, 17; see also Comptroller General, General Accounting Office, *The Well-Being of Older People in Cleveland, Ohio* (HRD-77-70, 19 April 1977).

[8]Comptroller General, *Entering a Nursing Home*, 49–52. See also National Center for Health Statistics, *The National Nursing Home Survey: 1977 Summary for the United States* (Washington: Government Printing Office, 1978).

[9]Comptroller General, *Older People in Cleveland*, 162.

TABLE 7-1 Major Federal Programs Funding Community Services for the Elderly

FEDERAL FUNDING SOURCE	SERVICE NEEDS OF THE CHRONICALLY IMPAIRED ELDERLY
Medicaid (Title XIX of the Social Security Act)	Medical services Home nursing services Home health aide
Medicare (Title XVIII of the Social Security Act)	Homemaker services Personal care Chore home-repair services
Social Services (Title XX of the Social Security Act)	Home-delivered meals Shopping assistance Transportation
Supplemental Security Income (Title XVI of the Social Security Act)	Adult daycare Housing assistance Congregate housing domicilia homes adult foster
Administration on Aging	care Respite care Congregate meals
Veterans Administration	Day-hospital services Social recreational services
Housing and Urban Development	Legal and financial counseling Mental health services Information and referral

Source: Comptroller General, *Report to the Congress,* p. 74.

several hours or several days, depending upon the completion of the individual's problems and the types of services available.[10]

There is little doubt that arranging alternatives to institutional care can be a complex and frustrating undertaking. Table 7-1 provides some perspective on that complexity. Yet the evidence strongly supports the view that successful professional practice will emphasize the development of case management that will provide care for older people in their own homes and communities. Despite the fact that a relatively small number of older people are affected, professional persons should be aware that alternatives to institutional care not only save money, but are preferred by older people and contribute to a higher quality of life in older adulthood. Discussion in the next chapters should provide guidance to professional persons about how such tasks may be accomplished.

Little can be added to the above discussion with specific reference to intermediate-care facilities or so-called "rest homes." Although there are no discrete data on these social resources, a number of studies suggest that the problem of maintaining standards in these facilities is a crucial one. Because intermediate-care facilities are subject to different regulations than nursing homes, the overall quality of these facilities may vary widely from place to place. In some instances intermediate care

[10]Comptroller General, *Older People in Cleveland,* 67.

is likely to be of questionable quality. In other cases, older people may be receiving more care than they need. The Congressional Budget Office states, "It is possible to assume conservatively that . . . 20 to 40 percent of ICF residents are receiving unnecessarily high levels of care."[11] Rest homes have no standards for care attached to them, and in many cases they are the least likely places for older people to find rest.

The professional worker should evaluate the need for nursing care, intermediate care, and rest homes with respect to the total needs of older people. This takes a knowledge of the resources available and skill at assessing what older people need in order to live as independently as possible. These assessment skills are elaborated in Chapter 8.

FOOD STAMPS

Food stamps are an important means by which older people supplement their food budgets. In 1980, the federal government spent $8.685 billion in food stamps, of which about 7 percent, or $600 million, went to older people. Food stamp eligibility is based upon family size and the amount of family income. The average monthly food stamp benefit was $34.35 in 1980. Since about 15 percent of all older people are below the poverty line, one would expect that food stamp expenditures for older people would be about twice as much as the current level of food stamp spending for them.

As pointed out in Chapter 3, the amount of disposable income available to older people requires close budgeting. Certainly an additional $35 a month for food would be most welcome. Yet older people are reluctant to apply for food stamps and other public benefits, for reasons discussed in Chapter 2. Furthermore, many older people do not know about food stamps or how they might determine whether they are eligible for them or not. Professional persons can do older people a great service by helping them establish eligibility for food stamps.

Food stamps are administered by the U.S. Department of Agriculture. They have been in existence for many years, but in 1964 they were reestablished so as to phase out the old commodity food distribution program. Since then there has been a lot of unhappiness with the program, because of claims of fraud and abuse. Since the Department of Agriculture does not have local administrative offices, in most cases food stamp certification and distribution is done through the local Departments of Social Service.

In general, food stamps are awarded on the basis of household size. The maximum allowable income for a one-person household for food stamp eligibility is $390 per month net and $507 per month gross. For a two-person household amounts would be $519 and $674 respectively. The amount of the food stamps would be determined based upon the income for the household. Food stamp eligi-

[11] Congressional Budget Office, *Long-Term Care for the Elderly and Disabled* (Washington: Government Printing Office, 1977), 74.

bility also requires that a person cook his or her own meals. Efforts to exempt older people from this rule by permitting them to spend stamps in restaurants, for example, have been unsuccessful. Food stamps are spent in the grocery store for food products just like cash.

DAY CARE AND RELATED SOCIAL SERVICES

Day care for older people is a relatively new idea. There is no national program to support such services, nor is there much consensus on exactly what these services should provide. The idea is based upon the successful experiences of providing day services, or what had been called half-way houses, for persons who had mental health problems but did not need to be hospitalized. Because a number of families could not provide care to older members during work hours, a number of organizations began to offer day care as an alternative to institutional care.

In some cases, it is possible to receive Medicaid reimbursement for day-care services when the services meet medical standards and when they are presented as a form of treatment. In other circumstances, individuals must pay the costs of day care. As more emphasis is placed on developing community alternatives to institutional care, day care will probably become more available to older people.

The quality of such day-care services should be carefully considered by professional persons. Particularly in programs that do not receive Medicaid support and therefore are not subject to state regulations, the quality may be such that more harm than good could be done to older people.

There are a number of related social services that might be available to older people. In most cases these services will vary from place to place. They most likely will be supported with Title XX funds, administered by the Department of Social Service and conducted by the local Senior Citizens Council or through the senior center. Some services that professional workers might look for include: home health services, chore services, homemaker services, companionship services, and telephone or personal reassurance.

The National Council on the Aging has developed standards for home health agencies that attempt to provide home health care. Agencies that meet these standards must have trained personnel and approved procedures for a number of personal health care tasks, such as bathing, administering medicines, and changing dressings. Chore services assist householders with tasks beyond their ability such as cleaning and minor household repair. Homemaker services focus on cooking, cleaning, and related homemaker tasks. Companionship and reassurance involve periodic checks on older people to make sure things are "all right." With any of these services, the professional worker should inquire as to the standards under which the services are given. Think, for example, how much trouble could be caused by dishonest persons who might come into older persons' homes as potential helpers. Some supervision and certification of these helpers should be in place before these services are provided to older people.

THE ROLE OF VOLUNTARY ORGANIZATIONS AND AGENCIES

The important activity of voluntary organizations has been mentioned frequently. Once again, it is difficult to categorize these services, because it is the trademark of the private social agency to provide the kind of service it wants to provide. Senior centers, for example, are private agencies. Services at one senior center are likely to be very different from services at another one. Senior centers and some of their special services are discussed in greater detail in the following chapters.

Perhaps the greatest contributors to services to older people among private organizations are the churches. Again, there is no way to estimate the impact of churches on serving older people. Most significantly, churches provide spiritual comfort and renewal to members of the congregations, and, additionally, within and outside the churches' religious programs, churches serve older people in numerous ways. From social activities to provision for housing, to providing volunteer assistance to the thousands of programs serving older people, churches are a significant and important part of the network of services to older adults.

CONCLUSION

A summary of the services to older people discussed in this chapter is presented in Table 7-2. Along with the programs and services discussed in Chapter 6, these services represent a staggering variety of social resources available to older people. Not

TABLE 7-2 Summary of Additional Social Programs

PROGRAM	PROGRAM TYPE	PROGRAM BENEFIT	PROGRAM ADMINISTRATION
Public housing (Housing Act Title II)	Means-tested	In-kind (housing)	Local public housing authority
Rental assistance (Housing Act Section B)	Means-tested	Cash (rental assistance)	Local public housing authority
Elderly and handicapped housing (Sect. 202)	Means-tested (Middle income)	In-kind	Private, non-profit organization
Mental hospital	(Sliding scale for fee service)	In-kind	State mental health departments
Community mental health clinics	(Sliding scale fee for services)	In-kind	Local mental health board
Nursing homes Intermediate-care homes for aged	Fee for service with some public reimbursement	In-kind	Private, for profit, or non-profit public agencies
Supporting social services	Various	In-kind	Local organizations

only do the services reflect great variety, but they represent great depth of coverage as well, as in the case of social security. This is not to say that all is well; nor does this splendid array of services support the recent claims of the White House Conference on Aging, that today's older people are the best off of any cohort of older Americans. Such comparisons must be made with respect to the context of the times in which we live and the persons' own perceptions of their well-being relative to other populations. Yet the services are there, to be used by skillful professional people in efforts to help older people live more satisfying lives.

The vast array of services available to older people is a reflection of the diversity of the older adult population. Older adulthood cannot be adequately understood when viewed as a stage of life, preparatory for death. Older adulthood is a much more dynamic time of life. Its characteristics are not determined as much by age as by the experiences that the cohort carries with it into these later years of life. Thus no set of services, as effective as they may be for one cohort, will be satisfactory to serve the full range of older people's wants and needs.

Understanding the important ideological orientations of Americans gives greater understanding to the complexity of services for older people. More than any other ideology, liberalism has dominated American political and social thought. The unshakable faith and commitment to individualism is an unchallenged product of this liberalist ideology, and combined with similar products of capitalism and positivism, individualism governs much of what we do in America. On the one hand, liberalism has infused older people with the expectation that they can achieve that which meets individual preferences. On the other hand, liberalism has supported the wide range of different services. More than in any other public sector, choice is the hallmark of serving older people.

Mrs. Wesson is an example of exactly this intersection of the cohort theory and individualism. Her problems are unique to the cohort whose earlier lifestyle emphasized a single residential unit and an independent way of life. The lifestyle was interrupted by a social event beyond her control. Much of her depression could be more easily explained by the anxiety over whether her lifestyle could be re-created than by the loss of her house. Similarly, without a full range of options available, persons like Mrs. Wesson would have no choice of reestablishing her independent way of life. The circumstances for another older person might demand an entirely different set of social services and resources.

The cohort characteristics of older adulthood and the strong ideological support for individualism suggest that the variety of services to older people reflected in the development of contemporary service patterns is most appropriate for older Americans. Variety and choice have become the policy foundation of contemporary program development. Nowhere is this better expressed and implemented than in the Older Americans Act itself. Title III, the heart of the Act, does not prescribe set services but rather provides a context in which local communities can develop those services most responsive to each community's older people. Moreover, it provides the flexibility to change those services as new cohorts of older adults seek resources peculiar to their expectations.

When older people comprise a larger share of the nation's political constituency, greater diversity in social programs will be sought, along with greater resources to support those programs. Even such significant and institutionalized programs as social security will be challenged to provide more opportunity for variety and personal choice. Already work and retirement options under social security have opened the program to greater flexibility. The expanded use of the Individual Retirement Account (IRA) will undoubtedly have a great impact on the income distribution aspects of social security as well.

By examining the social programs available to older people, only the final part of the policy program paradigm is left unexplained. The problems of older people in the social and ideological contexts have been discussed and the policies and programs designed to meet them have been specified and summarized. The professional person is the subject for examination in the next part of this text.

CHAPTER EIGHT

THE HELPING PROCESS

Much has been made of the fact that most older adults, almost 95 percent of them, live and participate in community life outside of residential institutional care. This does not mean, however, that noninstitutionalized older people do not need some assistance. While it is certainly necessary to promote a more accurate picture of adults in their later years, those who are presently caricatured as feeble, decrepit, and useless, equal care should be taken not to characterize all older people as completely independent, which would be equally misrepresentative.

Americans believe tenaciously in the desirability of independent living, but achieving, or maintaining this goal poses many problems for older adults. Mr. Jones, for example, lives on a quiet street in a suburb of a middle-sized city. After his wife died, he chose to stay in the home they had shared for forty years. Two years later he had a stroke. After hospitalization and a brief stay in a nursing home, Mr. Jones succeeded in his determination to return to his own home, largely because his daughter-in-law agreed to assume responsibility for a major portion of his care: light housekeeping, food, and nonmedical personal needs. The social worker at the nursing home, functioning as a discharge planner, discussed the situation with Mr. Jones's physician, who agreed that care at home was feasible. No other barriers to the discharge seemed to exist. On written orders from the physician, the social worker arranged for home visits from a nurse and a physical therapist. The daughter-in-law made daily visits to prepare meals and take Mr. Jones shopping and to medical appointments. This workable solution continued until the daughter-in-law's child became ill. Mr. Jones spent two difficult days until the daughter-in-law called the visiting nurse and services were expanded to include a homemaker.

Many aspects of this case could be examined. Was it a helpful service plan as devised by the institution's social worker? What responsibility for follow-up after discharge should be assumed and by whom? We might even ask whether the consequences of changes in the existing situation at the time of discharge had been fully explored with Mr. Jones *and* his daughter-in-law. The point of this example, however, is to illustrate the dangers of oversimplifying our concept of "independent" living. At what point did Mr. Jones become independent rather than dependent? Would it be better to evaluate the case as one of "appropriate interdependence"? If the daily visits had somehow allowed Mr. Jones to be useful to his daughter-in-law in return, the sharing relationship would have been more balanced. And finally, what effect would it have had on the whole situation if Mr. Jones had lived in a high-rise or retirement village at the time of his stroke?

An even harsher case can be offered for rethinking what really constitutes "independence." Does an older person who lives alone, and whose death may not be discovered for several days, qualify as living independently? Can society—and more pointedly, helping professionals—be satisfied with a goal of "independence" that embraces such a possibility?

In the past decade several research projects have produced definite statistics about the large number of older adults who remain "independent." Seven percent of older adults who live in the community are housebound, and another 7 percent can only leave home with difficulty.[1] The prevalence of disability increases from 12 percent of adults aged 65-69 to more than 80 percent of those aged 85 years or older.[2] One recent study of noninstitutionalized older people assessed 1,600 respondents in five areas: social, economic, physical, mental health, and activities of daily living. Results showed that 20 percent of the older population surveyed had no impairment, 21 percent were impaired in one of the five areas, 18 percent in two, 17 percent in three, and 23 percent in four.[3]

From this brief review of the expected impairment levels in the later years, it must be obvious that help is needed in a variety of forms by at least the 40 percent who are impaired in three or four areas, and possibly by the full 80 percent who are impaired in one or more. It is also obvious that a substantial amount of help is already being given, if only because such a large percentage of those with multiple impairments are not institutionalized. The fact is that even though older people may be living independent lives, most older people need and can use professional assistance to improve their lives.

[1] Ethel Shanas, "The Family as a Social Support System in Old Age," *The Gerontologist* 19, no. 2 (1979), 169-74.

[2] A. J. Akhtar et al., "Disability and Dependence in the Elderly at Home," *Age and Aging* 2 (1973), 102.

[3] *The Well-being of Older People in Cleveland, Ohio,* Comptroller General's Report to Congress (Washington: Government Printing Office, April 1977). See Chapter Seven.

Where does this help come from, what are its characteristics, and how do professional workers relate to it? Part 3 describes that face-to-face, direct system of care and caring for older people. It looks at two segments of the helping system—the informal or natural, and the formal or organizational—that are related to health and social needs of older adults. It also examines the processes of helping older people, basic to all professional disciplines. Above all, it becomes quite clear that a more realistic description of the "independence" of many older people is "interdependence"—with helping professionals, friends, and family. Certainly, interdependence is a more realistic goal for professional helpers to consider as they begin the difficult tasks of serving their older adult clients.

The notion that crises in the lives of individuals should be handled within a small sphere of persons surrounding the one involved has been eroded over time. The list of professionals involved in some aspect of human service continues to grow as a result of the recognition that help may require a level of knowledge and skill beyond that held by relatives, neighbors, friends, or any single profession. Society is accepting greater responsibility for the alleviation of human need. The human value system related to independence at any cost is changing. The prevailing necessity for interdependence is gaining recognition. A shift to stating individual and societal goals from achieving and/or maintaining independence to achieving and/or maintaining appropriate interdependence could help to overcome attitudes which promote feelings of impotence and helplessness in the poor, the handicapped, the frail and declining older adults.

The process of helping older persons has taken a variety of approaches over the years. As attention has been focused on the right to individual destiny, conflicts have arisen with implications for those in professional roles and those in need as well as the general public. The models of the civil and women's rights movements of the 1960s and 1970s are finding use in the decade of the 1980s as prolife forces mobilize to protect the unborn and right-to-die proponents advocate for choices to be in the control of the ill and elderly. It seems that the major dilemma is found today in situations where there is a conflict between the interests of discrete groups, for example elderly *vs.* youth, rather than whether or not all individuals have the right to self-determination.

The conflicts permeate throughout the informal and formal systems of help. The loving daughter who must choose between transporting her live-in parent to a club meeting and her son to a cub scout meeting is an over-simplified but apt example of the conflict involving intergenerational priorities. The physician approached by a son asking for medication for his mother who wanders around the house at night, or the social worker making a hospital discharge plan for a patient who wants to and could go home who is told the family prefers a nursing-home placement, point up intergenerational conflicts faced by professionals.

Within older adult groupings conflicts abound. There is the senior center worker faced by a delegation of participants who want "that old coot" barred from the center because he smells, and the county commissioners, facing the prospect of increased taxes in order to maintain services to the elderly poor, who get calls from senior citizens groups (as well as others) urging that taxes not be raised. The obvious frustrations inherent in such conflicts have brought national, state, and local legislative attempts to solve the problems. The issues of age–specific entitlements for benefits and services and intergenerational concerns were included as part of the White House Conference on Aging in 1981. These and other issues have been dealt with in other chapters.

The service system itself presents another conflict for the worker in the helping process. Professionals who work independently, such as physicians or social workers in private practice, are not subject to the possibility of discrepancies between specific agency practices and professional values. Others who are part of the prevailing system of services that operates through agency or organization structure may find that narrow service goals for an agency, or the need for agency efficiency of operation, will provide constraints on the type and amount of help a professional person can offer. Therefore, helping professionals in agencies have an added task to act as a change agent to the skill base deemed necessary for professional performance. In this way workers help to insure that policies within agencies are suited to serve older people.

The helping process functions to assist individuals, groups, or even communities to achieve a goal accepted by those needing or requesting assistance. As such, it relies on the professionals' knowledge of pertinent facts, techniques of intervention, and basic philosophy of the human right to determine what is desired. The professional's role as an enabler builds on the strengths of the patient or client. Too often it is difficult for a busy worker to tolerate the slow development of identifying what those strengths may be. It is much easier to solve a problem and tell the patient or client what to do. It is time-consuming to communicate information to make it possible for the ones receiving assistance to participate fully in making decisions. It is much easier to make those decisions for them.

One executive of a large agency with an in-home service component has built into the training program for aides a section on when *not* to help the patient. Her observation of those who choose to work as aides found a strong need to help others was often translated into "the more I do for my patient, the better worker I am." This basic need of all persons engaged in human services should be recognized and factored out for the positive and negative consequences. The satisfaction of need to help others can be a contributing quality brought by workers to the day-to-day tasks of their profession. However, the point at which that need to "do for" others keeps the patient/client dependent has to be identified and avoided.

INTERVIEWING

Information given and received by the helping person forms the basis for a relationship and assistance. In most instances, this interaction will take the form of an interview. An interview is basically a conversation with one or more purposes. Through the exchange of words, and nonverbal messages in the face-to-face situations, an interview can be categorized as a mutual exploration by two or more parties. Each seeks and receives information. Unlike general conversation, interviews should eliminate subjects that are not pertinent to the purpose for which the parties have come together or that do not help to set the climate of the exchange.[4] This climate should foster a relationship of trust in order that the purpose may be mutually agreed upon and accepted. The purpose of the interview should be such that it can be clearly stated in task-oriented language. Persons involved need to understand one another. The burden of assuring this understanding rests with the professional. Planning can avoid wasting time, misunderstandings, and barriers to future communication. Beginning professionals will need consciously to identify a beginning, middle, and end for each interview. Each must test what will eventually lead to an individual style that is comfortable and uses the unique strengths of the interviewer, as well as being based on effective, proven techniques. In addition, communication techniques cannot be isolated from sincerity, motivation, and self-awareness in listing desirable qualities of interviewers.[5]

Skill in interviewing should never include negative manipulation of the other person; rather, the worker can use questions that help the client/patient to express feelings, or understand attitudes and the situation or problem.[6] Questions that aim to trick the client/patient or are abrupt or accusing are unproductive. The fast-paced interrogation-type questioning is apt to place the client on the defensive and do nothing to establish an ongoing relationship of trust.[7] In those instances where the client/patient is physically unable to be interviewed or is unreliable because of mental impairment, caution should be exercised in the use of other sources. Bias or prejudice, faulty recall, and even knowing misrepresentation may distort the accuracy of information obtained from others as well as clients/patients. Professionals are further challenged to decide how much information is enough. Sometimes lengthy information-gathering is used to compensate for the worker's uncertainty. Time and energy of all those involved is wasted. On the other hand, busy professionals may make quick judgments, based on early impressions, that suggest a certain type or category of case is being presented. Even when new information is offered, the tendency of some helping persons may be to adhere to the original type-based judgment.[8] When sufficient information is secured, workers must be careful to use all of it to avoid preconceptions. One study concludes, "the evidence strongly suggests that helpers tend to focus on negative aspects of clients, and, accordingly, that positive aspects are underrepresented in helpers' preconceptions."[9]

[4]Cal W. Downs, G. Paul Smeyak, and Ernest Martin, *Professional Interviewing* (New York: Harper & Row, 1980), 5-6.

[5]Downs, Smeyak, and Martin, 2.

[6]Naomi Brill, *Working with People: The Helping Process,* 2nd ed. (New York: Longman, 1978), 141-3.

[7]Armando Morales and Bradford W. Sheafor, *Social Work: A Profession of Many Faces,* 3rd ed. (Newton, Mass.: Allyn & Bacon, 1983), 229-31.

[8]Stanley Wetkin, "Cognitive Processes in Clinical Practice," *Social Work Journal of NASW* 27, no. 5 (September 1982), 389-94.

[9]Thomas A. Wells, "Helpers' Perception of Clients," *Psychological Bulletin* 85 (September 1978), 988.

In order to guarantee a posture of "helping" as opposed to "giving orders," many professionals use verbal and nonverbal communication devoid of any emotional tinge. The intent is commendable, but the result often makes for a sterile atmosphere that defies building that relationship which is needed in working "with" as contrasted to working "for" the client/patient. This is particularly pertinent to working with older adults. Workers must be conscious of language. Language used by the person being helped must be understood by the professional, and the professional's language must be understood by the one being assisted. Words, as with knowledge, should be subject to constant analysis. Emotional language is capable of fraud and deceit; neutral language, at best, contributes little to building a feeling of warmth and a shared relationship. Words should be accurate, without prejudice, and should not bring negative excitement into the relationship.

The initial interview should provide a climate that fosters a positive feeling on the part of the client and makes a sharing relationship possible. Establishing a trust through attentive listening, probing questions limited to what can be handled, and awareness of emotional needs of the client are factors that help determine the length of an interview. Length of time for the face-to-face interview may be consciously used to control the relationship so that it may continue. Rarely will workers extend an interview beyond an hour.

The experienced worker will have moved from the necessity to be minutely conscious of every word, every question, every inflection of language, appearance of both patient/client and him or herself to a more assured level that has become automatic and integrative. Much like a driver learning to use the stick shift in an automobile, the process begins with an overconsciousness of each movement and finally becomes incorporated into a smooth operation. Helping professionals' awareness of what is really being presented by the patient/client may lead to communication that is undesirable and defy any hope for a shared relationship. An attitude of "I don't believe a word you are saying" will immediately skew dialogue away from that which mutually searches for factors that will lead to positive solutions to problems. On the other hand, the search for exact and true expression of facts and feelings is important. "Listening with the third ear" has become a motto for professionals. It simply indicates that one must listen for what is behind the words.

ASSESSMENT

After the determination that the helping professional is to be involved, the next steps in the helping process are satisfied by an assessment of need. Even though the problem may seem to have been identified prior to this step, the assessment reaffirms, expands, or may even change the presenting problem area. In the simplest of terms, an assessment brings together information selected to form a basis for decisions about what goals should be set and what methods the helping professional should use. It can help to locate needs that may be obscure. It also sets the stage for a helping relationship to be developed because it makes possible a more complete understanding of factors that should be involved in seeking solutions. It is a process of appraisal of the worth or value of existing conditions for effecting desired solutions. In using the assessment process, the helping professional seeks to identify the uniqueness of the individual, group, or community requiring assistance and the surrounding influences of persons, circumstances, and events in order to further the choice of service and the receivers' effective use of it. Helping professionals are responsible for using every means to assure success for the helping process, but they must be aware that there is no guarantee that that successful termination will, in fact, occur. One means of greater assurance is a careful assessment.

In recognition of the valuable place of judgment or appraisal of need and resources, the assessment process has been formalized in recent years. Efforts to overcome differences produced by subjective judgments have resulted in a variety of assessment instruments designed to assist the professional in standardizing judgments. The planning process for determining need is mandated as a responsibility to the Area Agencies on Aging. "Needs assessment in planning is multi-dimensional. As a first step in both obtaining the resources to alleviate needs and in setting the priorities when needs exceed resources, it is necessary to determine and document the needs that do exist in the population, a process called needs assessment."[10]

DETERMINATION OF INDIVIDUAL NEED

Judgments about what outcomes are possible and the ways in which to achieve those outcomes are necessary not only for target populations of older adults but for individuals seeking assistance or those who are identified as needing assistance. In the review of the normal process of aging, it becomes apparent that the changes that occur are potential producers of stress. The loss or diminution of physical ability, economic level, social contacts, or productivity as measured by society, produces stress that requires coping or problem-solving ability. Problem-solving outcomes can be successful, elusive, or destructive. Older adults, like humans of all ages, learn behavior that includes problem-solving from parents and other family members, friends, teachers, and from life experiences that reward certain actions and punish others. Older adults, unlike those of younger age, face a mistrust of learned behavior as the societal perception of the later years places them in the category of the less able or even incompetent. The older adult's power rests on the ability to make choices and to continue to grow in coping with necessary adjustments. The helping professional must truly believe that whatever tangible assistance is determined to be needed and is received by an older adult, the major goal is always to preserve, enhance, or restore the individual's ability to function as free from assistance as the ability of the individual and the surrounding circumstances will permit. An individual assessment provides the basis for setting that goal as well as the more specific operational steps immediately needed to achieve it.

[10] Leslie S. Lareau, "Needs Assessment of the Elderly: Conclusions and Methodological Approaches," *The Gerontologist* 23, no. 5 (October 1983), 518.

Professional disciplines dictate the primary focus of the helping person's assessment. For example: since the assessment will be used for a service plan, a physical therapist will include more precise attention to mobility and range of motion than would a social worker. A discharge planner in a hospital will need information not only about the present physical condition of the patient but about the projected condition at the time of leaving the hospital and beyond that to the anticipated schedule of recovery. The determination of eligibility for service can be regarded as a form of assessment. Whenever possible, agencies should avoid duplication of information-taking when the eligibility determination is done by one worker and services are provided by another. The obvious saving of time and the concern for the patient/client's presenting problem makes expedient movement to the operational service important. Older adults, like those of any age, find intolerable the time between the request for assistance and the receiving of it.

In light of the move toward formal assessments and the development of forms and questionnaires, helping professionals' first contact with a client/patient may involve a dialogue that does little to establish a sharing relationship. Asking questions and recording answers for any length of time challenges the professional to devise ways of projecting the concern and warmth needed to invite a partnership. For this reason, many professionals reject the formalized questionnaire, or prefer that this information be received by someone else.

Assessment information should go beyond that directly related to the helping professional's discipline. In addition to identifying information, there should be indication of the living arrangement, family supports available, resources patient/client used in the past, and some developmental history. Since the assessment is used to prepare a service plan, many assessment forms incorporate information about the selected available services to be used. When this is done, the assessment becomes a more comprehensive document than when it is used only to identify need. In-home service assessments are also used as the basis for the contract agreement for homemaker/home health aide assignments. Here the need is translated into very specific tasks for the worker and time to complete tasks is calculated.

PLANNING FOR TARGET POPULATIONS

Needs assessment as a planning tool is linked to a national concept of what is absolutely necessary for human existence and what is desirable for a determined minimum in the quality of that life. As a nation, we struggle to determine both. Values differ in geographic areas of the country and even among populations in the same area. In this context, Lareau, in reporting a study of the state of needs assessment, says: "Since needs assessment has no true theoretical foundation, there is no universal agreement on its meaning."[11]

In spite of this difficulty, it is imperative that some method that can be de-

[11]Lareau, 518.

fended is necessary to justify the placement of resources into certain efforts rather than others in order to alleviate adverse conditions. The current emphasis on objectivity is an effort to remove the personal bias and the narrow information base of decision that have prevailed in the past. Federal allocation of funds for services have been made on the basis of need. Legislators use a variety of determinants in order to focus their response for financial appropriations. The public hearings scheduled by Congress are the most visible of these determinants. Legislative committee staff provide other factual information. Notwithstanding the impact of these inputs, the decisions are also influenced by groups lobbying for special interests.

Another arena for determination of need has been the jurisdiction of federated funds such as the United Way, Catholic Charities, and Jewish Federation. As the organization covering the broadest spectrum of givers and receivers, the United Way has struggled to devise a needs-assessment process that will satisfy both large and small contributors. It has not been easy. Demand for private resources to address more of the identified basic needs of people when public resources are being curtailed has resulted in conflicts of priority allocation. Traditional private agencies providing innovative or fringe services are challenged to document that the expenditures are addressing needs. Requests from newly-created agencies for allocation of some of the federated fund dollars use needs assessments as part of the appeal process.

Five types of conclusions or categories are used most commonly in the needs-assessment process that identifies population needs that planning efforts or fund allocation should address. The study by Lareau evaluated 49 documents and identified the following: "(1) description of the population; (2) description of the problems of the target group; (3) description of available services; (4) description of unmet need or of service components needed; and (5) list of service priorities."[12] The study concludes that the quality of existing needs assessment done by planners and/or those allocating resources can be improved. Some rely on informal efforts that cannot be documented; those who make formal reports show a wide range of type of information being used with only a small percentage using all five types of descriptive information or recommendations. Various methods can be used to provide this descriptive information. They include surveys of the target population, census data, testimony of selected service providers, public hearings, and small groups of selected individuals working for consensus on service needs priorities.

One of the most publicized survey instruments for determination of need is the OARS (Older Americans Resources and Services) questionnaire. This multi-dimensional functional assessment was developed at the Duke University Center for the Study of Aging and Human Development. It provides for rating individuals on a six-level scale of function in the following areas: social resources, economic resources, mental health, physical health, performance of activities of daily living. The questionnaire was used in the widely reported Cleveland, Ohio, study that delved extensively into the profile of the population and the existing services to identify the service gaps and needs.

[12] Lareau, 519.

TRUST

Over and over again the point has been made that the helping process builds on a relationship in which trust is an important ingredient. What is trust? Why is it important? How is it achieved? Can it be misused? This section will explore some of the answers to these questions.

Confidence that others with whom an individual interacts are, in fact, who and what they present on the surface is the basis on which a relationship of trust exists and is sustained. A patient/client—whether individual, group, or community—using the professional helper to achieve something the patient/client needs or desires is depending not only on the knowledge the professional has, but on the professional's skill to effect change and on his or her commitment to achieve what the patient/client seeks. Inherent in the relationship between helping professional and patient/client is a perception that the professional has power that the patient/client requires. That power can range from possession of simple information—where to apply for food stamps—to the exercise of guidance in organizing to achieve environmental changes such as getting a traffic light installed at a dangerous corner or passage of an open-housing law. That perceived power invites a relationship of dependency unless the professional consciously focuses on the shared goals and responsibilities of the helping process partnership. Working together to achieve what both agree is necessary or important and the professional's commitment to continue in the relationship until both agree the result—successful or unsuccessful—has been reached is very different from the helping approach that is based on "you'll do fine if you do what I tell you to do." The trust required by the second approach asks for a blind faith in the helping person. It negates any capability of the receiver, leaving only responsibility to carry out instructions. What also occurs is a reinforcement of dependency rather than a building of strength. This picture presents the extreme. In reality, different circumstances may require helping persons to assume much of the responsibility for decisions. If this occurs, it should be the conscious choice of the professional who has weighed all factors that would prohibit a partnership in goal-setting and working toward those goals in a sharing relationship that includes a mutual trust.

So far, the subject of trust has been explored from the perspective of trust in the helping professional. Two other kinds of trust are involved in the helping process: the trust of the professional in the patient/client and the trust of the professional in him or herself. During the assessment phase of the relationship, helping persons are able to evaluate the extent to which clients/patients are presenting a true and clear picture of themselves and the facts pertinent to the service need. Workers should be able to assume that the presence of the older person asking for assistance means that the assistance is desired and the recipient wishes change to occur. Recognizing this trust in the patient/client, however, does not mean that professionals can expect a straight-line progression to an easy solution of problems. Rather, the worker presents an immediate bridge of faith in the patient or client by saying, "I know you are here because you believe we can work together to resolve a problem or need." The *we* is important. It sets the stage for mutual trust. It moves the interaction more quickly through that period when patients or clients are evaluating the professional in order to determine whether they can trust the professional.

Professionals arrive at a trust in themselves through an acceptance of their human qualities, the assurance of a professional ethic on which to base competent practice, and accumulated success over time. A professional helping person can show caring, warmth, and concern in interactions. Probability may be the only basis on which decisions can be made. The helping person who has learned to trust his or her judgment is not afraid to take the risk of uncertainty.

Clients or patients may present difficulties because of their need for immediate reward, inability to control impulses, and lack of understanding of verbal exchange as an action leading to problem resolution. When older adults reach the point where seeking assistance becomes necessary, their tolerance level for interaction that cannot be immediately translated into relief is apt to be low. This low level of tolerance may be found in working with persons of all ages; however, the current generations of older adults are influenced by the prevailing notion that to need, or even worse, to ask for help means that they have what amounts to a sinful weakness. This causes delay in seeking assistance, which exacerbates the low tolerance level. When a patient or client develops a trust in the helping professional, it is easier to encourage new approaches to life and substitute wellness for illness. Trust brings a desire to please and helps to free the patient or client from a reluctance to reveal feelings and ideas.

A KNOWLEDGE BASE

It may seem perfectly obvious that serving older Americans cannot be effective if professionals, or others whose service area includes this age group, operate in isolation from this population. It is less obvious how those serving persons achieve the most desirable method of service delivery, based on working *with* rather than *for* older people.

For all professions engaged in serving older adults, there are diverse and special methods and techniques to be mastered; however, all disciplines do, and should, share a need for some common knowledge and skills. The characteristics of the older population show both similarities and differences. To be sixty-two, for most of those who are sixty-two, is quite different from being eighty-two. Current literature is beginning to identify two age groups within the older population: the young-old, which includes those under age seventy-five; and those over seventy-five who are categorized as the old-old and regarded as the most vulnerable and at-risk for illness and disability. Chronic conditions with resulting impairment affect the activity level, mobility, and needed health care of this old-old age group.

THE PROCESS OF AGING

All professionals serving older adults intervene in response to physical, emotional, and social human needs. Knowledge of the processes of aging, as tracked in these three areas, constitutes a basic core on which professionals build the techniques of their chosen specialty or achieve the maximum benefit of those techniques. For example, the health professional primarily concerned with physiological or psychological pathology, or the social worker providing case management of a service team for a client referred for protective service, or a minister counseling an older person who has become a recluse, will all need to know what the natural or normal process of aging involves.

Popular notions and conceptions, or misconceptions, should be replaced by reality as documented by research and practice. There is a wide variation among those of any age in the later years with respect to physical health, mental and emotional adjustment and coping skills, family patterns, values, life-styles, economic and cultural levels, and expectations of life satisfactions. Despite the importance of recognizing these possible individual differences, some common characterizations can be made. The previously mentioned division of young-old and old-old is one example; another relates to losses experienced by this age group. Loss of paid employment, loss of friends, relatives, spouse, lost or diminished income, sensory changes, and role changes are common enough to warrant categorization and attention to the adjustments required to cope with the changes.

Biological aspects of the aging process include the changes in metabolic, musculoskeletal, cardiovascular, and other systems. Biological considerations affect such basic needs as shelter and nutrition. Manipulation of the environment can make up for the decreased ability of the body to adapt to temperature change. Housing arrangements can be changed or modified to afford the handicapped greater independence in performing daily living tasks. Psychological aspects of aging involve sensation and perception, learning and memory, and personality and intelligence. Decreased perception and diminished taste and smell may influence dietary habits. Poor diet, in turn, may adversely affect physical health or add to mental confusion. The psychological implications of housing are complex. Housing arrangements go beyond the physical structure to include human considerations such as what family and community supports may be available. This broader perspective is covered extensively under the sections on the challenge of living arrangements in earlier chapters.

The changes accompanying the aging process affect even clothing and other basic essentials of daily life. Clothing can compensate for the inefficient heat regulation of the body. Adaptive clothing without buttons and special shoes are examples of items that may permit greater independence for those with physical handicaps. Psychologically, clothes project the self-image of most older persons; and conversely, clothes will affect that self-image.

Biological and psychological aspects of the aging process give clues to environmental factors that could be checked to prevent accidents. When decreased sight, failing hearing, or loss of the sense of smell occur, psychological problems, as well as a restricted daily living pattern, may result. Detecting hearing loss is of special importance to the helping professional, who may be assuming that the older adult is receiving all that is being communicated when, in fact, she is not. Personality changes may be caused by fear of accidents.

The satisfying use of time is a major consideration for many older adults.

Physical condition is one factor in determining what types of activity are possible. Knowledge of the aging process enables professionals not only to be realistic in helping older adults select satisfying use of time, but also to influence, as to both type and design, the kinds of activities offered.

Sociological aspects of the process of aging add another dimension to the professional's basic understanding of what older clients or patients are experiencing. Changing status and role affect relationships within the family. Intergenerational living arrangements may force some older adults to submerge their own desires in the interest of furthering the future of younger family members. On the other hand, problems may arise for those who live alone if there is no available support person. Widowhood as a role change forces social, psychological, and even economic adjustments.

A knowledge base for the helping professional starts with the broad understanding of the biological, psychological, and social characteristics that constitute the profile of older adults. This understanding must include recognition of the wide diversity of individual profiles within the broad age range included in the later years category. The understanding should lead to an ability to relate these characteristics to environmental situations existing within societal patterns of bias, discrimination, and myth. Even further, these characteristics should be constantly evaluated for validity when used as a basis for intervention with specific individuals, groups, or communities.

GETTING IT ALL TOGETHER

One of the basic guidelines for all helping professionals states: "Start where the client or patient is." It sounds so simple. But when examined carefully, and carried out minutely, the process involved can be time-consuming and frustrating unless some framework of prevailing norms for the individual, group, or community are used as a backdrop. Knowledge of the processes of aging provides such a backdrop. Preceding chapters make no attempt to offer in depth the didactic material that should be covered in gaining an understanding of the changes related to the biological, psychological, and social processes of aging. The point of this section is to convince the reader that such knowledge is important.

Mentioned earlier was the need to work *with* rather than *for* the older individual or population and the necessity for knowing the general characteristics of that age group. The next professional isolation barrier that workers should overcome rests with the complex helping system in existence and the many disciplines related to it. That system is complex as a result of the policies and the services developed over the years. These have been dealt with extensively in preceding chapters. Knowledge of these policies and the system based on these policies makes it possible for helping persons to use the intervention techniques of each one's particular discipline to maximum advantage and to bring greater coordination of services into reality. Health and medical information about nutrition, safety, exercise and rehabilitation, and common chronic or multiple conditions unique to the later years of life are important for all professionals. To this list must be added knowledge of differing cultural patterns and lifestyles.

"Class variables such as income, access, adequacy of transportation, and the attitudes of providers, as well as situational variables such as distance from resources, exert a stronger influence on consumer behavior than do more culture-specific differences related to race and ethnicity. The language frequently used by helping professionals when referring to some clients reflects their class and racist biases."[13] The work of Jane Addams in founding Hull House in Chicago was based on knowing the traditions of the people of the community and working with the individuals to achieve their goals.[14] The senior center movement has built on this fundamental principle by emphasizing the partnership of professionals and older adults in the roles of decision-maker, paid and volunteer staff, participants in activities, and recipients of service. The section on the senior center in Chapter 10 examines this service-providing channel.

Skill in interviewing may be the key to efficiency in securing the specific information needed in a particular situation, in developing trust, and in creating the possibility for future productive interactions. Professionals must be satisfied to act on the basis of incomplete evidence but consciously work toward narrowing the margin of error. Communication and interaction with those in the helping relationship is the basis on which professionals build the helping process. Knowledge, as outlined, helps to narrow the margin of error and affords the best possible climate for mutual trust in the interaction. Workers involved in service provision to older adults are careful to avoid the communication process that becomes an information game in which the helper and the receiver manipulate the situation for control.

COMPLEMENTING PROFESSIONAL ACTIVITIES: TEAMWORK

Much of the professional activity in serving older adults takes place within the context of two broad service areas—health and social services. Sometimes a particular professional helper may work into one or the other of two areas regardless of professional training; for example, a social worker may work in a hospital, a public health department, or a nursing home, or a health educator might be organizing community groups. In the first instance, the skills associated with social services are being used in a setting primarily providing health care; in the second instance, a health-related professional may be performing in an untraditional manner for the specific profession of the worker. Some mandates for service and agency staffing

[13] John W. Match, "Reducing Barriers to Utilization of Health Services by Racial and Ethnic Minorities," in *Removing Cultural and Ethnic Barriers to Health Care*, eds., Elizabeth L. Watkins and Audrey E. Johnson (Chapel Hill, N.C.: University of North Carolina, School of Public Health, 1981), 99.

[14] Christopher Lasch, ed., *The Social Thought of Jane Addams* (New York: Bobbs-Merrill, 1965).

patterns recognize that social workers and health professionals can perform some of the same tasks.

For example, agencies providing in-home services are likely to show a staffing pattern that includes nurses and social workers in a team relationship. The first step in the response of a homemaker/home health agency to a request for help in the home for a patient discharged from the hospital is an assessment of need. This determines the type, scope, and length of service needed. A nurse and social worker, functioning as a team, might decide which one or the other would gather the information, usually through a home visit. The two would then confer on the service plan to be offered to the discharged patient. Once the plan was in effect, either the nurse or the social worker would take primary responsibility for the oversight needed. This team relationship has many advantages. It provides coordination of both health and social service perspectives. It also offers a speedier response to requests for service and handling of problems that might arise. The use of professional teams that perform some tasks on an interchangeable basis is efficient and cost-effective. The proximity of professionals working together eliminates a time delay that is part of any referral system where different professionals are needed to complete a service. Recognition of the importance of professional teams is found in the federal Administration on Aging's Standards for Long-Term-Care Geriatric Training Centers. Such plans must include medicine, nursing, and social work professions, but they might also include such professions as physical, occupational, and recreational therapy. The Administration on Aging trend for multiprofessional staffing has guided new organizations as they plan funding of long-term-care projects.

Another way in which changes are occurring in professional services is found in a shift of tasks from one profession to another. Nurse practitioners and physicians' assistants are performing many of the services formerly done only by physicians. Changes in law and federal guidelines for public funding of services have brought other changes. In the past, an older adult whose disability claim had been denied would have found a friend or social worker provided adequate assistance in an appeal to reverse the decision. More recently, clients have found the services of a private lawyer or legal aid attorney necessary. The legal profession is increasingly involved in serving older adults in cases where there may be violation of nursing-home patients' rights, where there is question about the competency of individuals, or where there is controversy over guardianship or involuntary commitment.

THE HELPING PROCESS WITHIN THE AGENCY CONTEXT

Professionals are relying more and more on the use of objective techniques to provide validation of helping methods. The helping processes, in fact, show changes to incorporate objectivity. Financial accountability in relation to achievement of stated goals is built into many service programs, and as greater accountability is required, the goal of agency efficiency may conflict with the professional helping activities.

Funding sources are moving to a determination of the cost of one unit of service, and the amount of reimbursement made for the number of service units delivered. For example, a contract for transportation would specify a one-way trip as the unit of service with payment to be made only for the number of trips documented in service reports. This trend toward efficiency is reinforcing the practice of functionally dividing agency budgets into service areas and the planning practice that calls for goal-setting and objectives that can be measured by quantity within a time limit. Difficulties associated with the unit cost reimbursement practice are encountered by funding sources in determining service definitions and the quality level of service to be supported. The example of the one-way trip may seem simple to handle, but unit-cost variations between rural and urban areas may mean the establishment of a wide spread of cost range. The unit reimbursement practice for information and referral services, for example, is even more complex. The service definition could be as narrow as one contact session, by phone or in person, including multiple contacts with the same person counted as a contact each time. A broader definition might include the distribution of brochures or newsletters, or group presentations.

Both public and private funding sources are pointing to the need for paying only for service delivered. Progress is evident in the attempts to unify the service definitions to be used as a basis for the reimbursements. Quality assurance under the unit reimbursement system is also being addressed. Greater emphasis is being placed on standards and guidelines for acceptable levels of service provision. These will be much slower to establish and incorporate into the contracts for service than the agreed-upon service definitions.

A negative impact of the unit cost reimbursement will be felt by agency administrators responsible for budgeting and cash flow. Salaries of workers or fixed costs such as rent are determined at the outset of a budget year. Receiving the income for services rendered after the service is given will require a source of funds on hand until the reimbursement is received. Changes in anticipated circumstances during the budget year will require a closer, more frequent monitoring of cost and demand a greater flexibility in budget and contract revisions. What effect will this have on the helping process? Direct service professionals will find pressures for increased statistical documentation or, at the very least, focus on awareness of complete records for statistical purposes. Job descriptions may be affected. Each service provider may be held to a narrower scope of activity in order to satisfy the efficiency of operation as required by the funding source. For example, the information and referral function defined as individual contacts could preclude time spent on group information presentations by a service provider. A discharge planner in a hospital might be constrained from including a home visit because of the cost of time involved. The role of the professional as an agent of organizational change may shift as agencies experience less flexibility in discretionary allocation of funds. Private agencies will be challenged to seek undesignated funds to maintain the operations which fall outside or are peripheral to the defined unit services. Public agencies may experience a more difficult time in convincing public officials to support ill-defined services such as socialization and peer interaction, which often are preventive in nature.

Cost of services not only within organizations or agencies, but among those providing similar services has led to emphasis on coordination in order to eliminate duplication. Within the system of services related to the needs of older adults, the multipurpose senior center concept has been singled out as a service delivery mechanism that offers the greatest possibility for bringing together services of agencies that exist in fragments. Through service co-location and/or referral the multipurpose senior center's potential for achieving coordination is unique in the service delivery spectrum. The standards developed by the senior center field, based on a philosophy of responsibility shared between professionals and the older adults being served, support the claim that this mechanism of service delivery could become the major social institution for older adults. The principal influence on the helping process rests with the collaboration and coordination that may occur. Through the teamwork and linkages that must form the framework of the fully-realized multipurpose center, the conflict of agency expediency versus professional ethics can be minimized. Professionals may achieve a flexibility as each exercises the process of helping from whatever perspective or discipline the professional represents.

In basic terms, the helping process is built upon a philosophy of the right to self-determination and preservation of dignity, and a specific ethic for each profession. It also includes:

- Background knowledge of the aging population
- Identification of the problem
- Collection of pertinent information
- Tentative explanations of the problem
- Identification of changes that will result in alleviating the problem
- Selection of the method of intervention appropriate to effect change
- Establishment of necessary agreements among participants
- Evaluation of success or failure
- Adjustments in intervention as indicated through evaluation

SUMMARY

The number and type of professionals serving older Americans has increased as the number of older adults and the health and social services to meet their needs have increased. Specialization exists within both health and social services professions with some overlap of the kinds of tasks performed. Health care and social service provider organizations show a clustering of different professionals working as teams. Whatever the specific discipline of the helping professional, the helping process will build upon some common factors.

Knowledge of the biological, physiological, psychological, and social aspects of the aging process is accepted as the outstanding basic core for all professionals. Those in direct service share the need for skills in making individual need assessments of a variety of types, developing service plans, working with families of older adults, and forming linkages with other professionals. Administrative and planning personnel share a need for skill in community-needs assessment, policy development, budgeting, and working with committees. It is not enough for the helping professional to have knowledge and skill and commitment. These ingredients must be perceived by the patient or client. In addition, the presence of mutual trust in the relationships or interactions is an essential ingredient in the helping process.

The basic helping process described in this chapter is the way the professional person connects the older adult with the kind of resources necessary to achieve agreed-upon goals. Most of this helping takes place in an agency, or some formal organizational setting, but more frequently, professional people are learning to help older people by connecting them with resources in informal settings. The next two chapters describe the informal and formal systems in which help for older people is obtained. The task of the professional person is to put the basic helping process into action within these settings. Let us examine the informal system next.

CHAPTER NINE

THE INFORMAL SYSTEM

At the end of the second day on the job, a social worker in a senior center demanded of the supervisor, "Who on earth is Marge? All I've heard today is 'Marge says . . .'!" The supervisor immediately acknowledged that part of the orientation to the job should have included the fact that Marge, the beauty operator, was a source of information and a key member—though unbudgeted—of the helping team in the agency. The next conference with the new worker dealt not only with how that team, and in particular the beauty operator, functioned within the agency, but also with the many similar informal systems that assist older adults in many ways.

CHARACTERISTICS AND SERVICES

The array of nonprofessionals who provide assistance and support to individuals in times of crisis is often called the "informal support system." It includes family members, both physically close and extended family, who are available to respond to a need for care. It includes friends and neighbors. It also includes a widely diverse group of people whose primary relationship to the person in need is not as a helper with personal problems. The beauty operator, barber, maid, bartender, dressmaker, taxi-driver, fellow worker, or any person who has established a relationship over time that provides reciprocal support, would be a part of the informal system.

In general, the services of the informal system resolve day-to-day problems, or reduce the possibility of full-blown problems, or support existing strengths of the person in need.[1] These services promote a sense of personal meaning and identity, of security and love, of mutual aid and caring, and of role and status.[2] The informal system provides goods and services in a voluntary fashion, usually without payment, as needed by the recipient. Some individuals, like the beauty operator in the example above, may also play a role as coordinator between the person in need and other providers in the informal or formal systems of care.

Informal systems provide several vital kinds of support that formal systems simply cannot supply on a daily basis. Emotional support ranges from remembering birthdays and holidays, through reassurance and encouragement, to friendly chats or visits. Most emotional support comes from good communication—being a confidant, listening, giving opinions and advice, and answering specific questions. Social support often complements emotional support through visiting or telephone calls, including older relatives and friends in activities by specific invitation, and sharing resources of transportation for shopping. Other kinds of service support provided by relatives, friends, or neighbors include minor home repair, yard work, writing letters, reading, housework, cooking, and personal care such as bathing and dressing. Taking care of finances completely, or giving intermittent advice about financial management, can be a major help to many older people.

Informal systems vary in different communities and neighborhoods. Equally important is the variation and uniqueness of the system for each individual in each community or neighborhood and the possibility that, for some, there may be virtually no informal supports available.

At least one researcher has decried as myth the common impression that older adults are often abandoned by their families; her studies document more frequent contact between older people and the family than has generally been reported.[3] But what is not clear is how successful those contacts were in supporting or even in meeting the desires or expectations of the older people involved. Professionals would do well to remember the phrase "alone in a crowd" and not automatically assume that geographic closeness, or even frequent contact with relatives will satisfy an individual's need for support.[4] The extended family, consisting of spouses and their offspring and a surrounding fringe of relatives, may live in close proximity to the older adult but be without close contact. On the other hand, an extended family that is geographically dispersed may be highly interactive. The needs for emotional and social support at times of crisis can often be satisfied even if physical distance discourages frequent visiting. As long as family support of some

---

[1] See Sarah Alexander Smith, *Natural Systems and the Elderly: An Unrecognized Resource* (Washington, D.C.: National Council on Aging, 1982).

[2] *The Senior Center: A Partner in the Community Care System,* book 3: *NISC/NCOA Informal Supports* (Washington, D.C.: National Council on Aging, 1982).

[3] Ethel Shanas, "The Family as a Social Support System in Old Age," *The Gerontologist* 19, no. 2 (1979), 169–74.

[4] See Shanas for further discussion on this subject.

kind exists, help from friends and neighbors appears to be supplementary to that provided by family members. In this supplementary role, however, neighborly help can become a valuable support in itself by relieving some of the burden on the family.

STRENGTHS AND WEAKNESSES

A complex set of values and some legislation regulate the informal system. Accountability for adequate service is obscured by the absence of centralized organization. Family patterns of responsibility may not be uniformly accepted by individual family members, including the older person.

Some older people are strongly motivated not to seek help from relatives. "I don't ever want to be a burden to my children" is an often-cited goal. However, when critical needs arise, these same individuals usually prefer that family be the first avenue of support. Thus one of the major strengths of the informal system is that it is the older adults' preferred response to their need for help. Levels of preference are evident. Grandma Parkinson, for instance, is grateful to a neighbor who stops by to see if she needs something from the store, and she accepts the volunteer visitor from the church who has her on her list. But she would prefer, above all, to have her son or daughter visit and take her shopping. Essentially, if the informal system is broadly defined, older adults are likely to see it as an important and positive source of support.

Another strength of the informal system lies in its very naturalness. The traditions of good neighborliness ("the Golden Rule") and family responsibility ("Blood is thicker than water") are well established. In addition, the need of the helper to be needed is satisfied by the opportunities to give assistance.

In these times, when financial considerations are often a limiting factor in personal and family decisions, the informal system offers an attractive alternative to expensive, formally organized services. The cost to the larger society is much less when assistance is provided by relatives, neighbors, or friends. The individual whose financial resources have been depleted over time by major health care costs will further burden the tax payer by requiring public reimbursement for nursing-home care or even home-health-aide care. If that care can be provided in part by an informal support network, the saving is obvious.

The prevailing weakness of the informal system is its unpredictability. No two communities are exactly alike in the resources for help provided by neighbors, volunteers, civic groups, or even churches. Families in different circumstances may have different notions of responsibility, some of which may stem from financial considerations. In other cases, the desire to be responsible may lead some supporters—and recipients—to expect too much and this eventually becomes burdensome to both sides.

One serious problem with informal support through the family is the inadequacy and resentment that grown children often feel when faced with the possibility, or necessity, of caring for an aging, infirm parent.

There is certainly a very strong natural and social stricture on what middle-aged sons and daughters can say when confronted, maybe, with a decade of geriatric care and nursing. The dread that this may happen is often so overwhelming that it begins to eat away at the respect and affection which the children have for their parents if they show signs of senility, or even long before. It is not just a reluctance to take on a burden which causes this corrosion, but the emotional shock and resentment at the reversal of roles. Many people suffer from a kind of indignation when they see what looks like an abdication of parental care.[5]

It may seem particularly unfair that the children are now imprisoned in caring for their parents just when it seems the parents cannot provide the support and advice they have always given before.[6] The emotional and financial costs of family support of older relatives may thus become enormous. The need of some to be the "givers" and "helpers" may lead to overprotection and invite greater dependence. In these and other cases, family members can become so overburdened that the extended family actually resorts to abuse of the older person. Abuse can be verbal, physical, or financial; in any case emotional abuse results.

Common assumptions in our society contribute to the unhappiness that this situation can bring. We must learn to see through the myth that in the past the extended family was the sole and ultimate source of care for the elderly. The documented fact is that only in modernized nations with increased longevity can the "norm" of a multigenerational family be found. We must also keep in mind that family relationships do not remain constant over time: what seemed a comfortable interdependent arrangement to a middle-aged couple and their young adult children may not be a harmonious solution twenty years later.[7] And not all families have related happily from the start. "Too often," warns one expert in the field, "family is treated as a 'sacred' institution whose virtues are taken for granted and whose weaknesses are hidden. In our rush to emphasize the positive aspects of family life, we overlook and ignore its negative aspects."[8]

Even the best-meant and most affectionate plans can go awry when parents and children expect too much of each other. For example: Mrs. Carmichael's husband died after thirty years of married life, during which she never worked and saw herself as the family homemaker, uninvolved in the financial aspects of the family economy. The idea of living alone was intolerable to her, and she chose to move in with her daughter's family, rather than accept a similar offer from her sister, mainly because she believed that her son-in-law could provide the "strength" she had relied on in her late husband. For the first few months, Mrs. Carmichael enjoyed living

[5] Ronald Blythe, *The View in Winter: Reflections on Old Age* (New York and London: Harcourt Brace Jovanovich, 1978), 22.

[6] Blythe, 22.

[7] Bertram J. Cohler, "Autonomy and Interdependence in the Family of Adulthood: A Psychological Perspective," *The Gerontologist* 23, no. 1 (1983), 24.

[8] Harold L. Orbach, "Aging, Families and Family Behavioral and Social Science Perspectives on Our Knowledge, Our Myths, and Our Research," *The Gerontologist* 23, no. 1 (1983), 37.

with them. But the lifestyle of the daughter and son-in-law was not what she expected. Both worked outside the home, sharing financial responsibility for producing income and making decisions about spending. When it became obvious that Mrs. Carmichael expected the son-in-law to manage her affairs completely and to spend long hours doing so, difficulties arose. The son-in-law chose to avoid her rather than discuss and deal with the problem. Mrs. Carmichael complained to her daughter about the way she was being treated. The daughter felt trapped in the struggle.

How many versions of this situation can be found in families facing day-to-day tensions they do not know how to resolve? Mrs. Carmichael's story has a happy ending. The daughter was urged by a friend to attend a lecture and book review on "you and your aging parent." The lecturer also wanted to recruit people for a support group. Mrs. Carmichael's daughter and son-in-law both joined the group, and in addition to meeting others in similar circumstances, they benefited from the advice and encouragement of the professional writer.

PROFESSIONALS' RELATIONSHIP

The helping professional relates to the informal system to encourage or supplement the provision of care by families and to intervene when a level of care is needed beyond the capability of the informal system. Professional people should work to increase the ability of family, friends, and neighbors in the provision of appropriate care. Helping professionals stand as the secondary level of support to older adults when the focus of their relationship is support of those who make up the natural or informal system. A professional identifying the resources of family and friends must include an evaluation of the extent to which this constellation is able physically, emotionally, and perhaps even financially, to provide what is needed. Further, the worker should include consideration of whether the older person will accept not only the informal resource supports, but the fashion in which they are given.

For example, Mrs. Wilson chose to go into a nursing home after her hospitalization for repair of a fractured hip. She freely discussed with the professional worker the reasons. Two daughters, both married with several children, were each willing to take her home immediately. For one, it would have involved no strain, because of the ample financial resources, to surround Mrs. Wilson with the physical and medical aftercare she needed. For the other daughter, it would have meant a disruption since she was employed and her family income was so modest that employing help would have been difficult. "I would prefer to be at Gloria's house rather than at Grace's, but Gloria would have to stay home or let Grace pay someone to come in for awhile to help," explained Mrs. Wilson. "Oh, Grace would do it, but I can hear her now—she'd go on and on about why I didn't just go to her house where servants could take care of me. Well, I like the atmosphere at Gloria's, and I figure if I stay in the nursing home for a short while it will be easier for all concerned when I choose Gloria's." Then, in a breathless afterthought, Mrs. Wilson admonished the worker, "Please don't tell the girls what I've said. They are both good to me, and I appreciate what they do, but I know I'd be happier at Gloria's."

Many checkpoints are raised in the confidential exchange between Mrs. Wilson and the worker. Was the situation as she described it? What biases in favor of creature comforts versus feelings of warmth might the worker have to overcome in his or her own approach? How compelling could the worker afford to be in pushing Mrs. Wilson to allow some discussion with her family in order to circumvent the nursing-home placement as part of the plan?

Ironically, in this instance, the worker faces problems not because of a lack of natural supports, but because there is a definite choice expressed by the client where the supports are abundant.

In another situation, the worker faces a different task. Mrs. Trumbo took an early retirement from her secretarial job expecting to marry a sales representative about her age. Her two sons maintained frequent contact by phone and viewed her plan to marry as providing a relief from her expressed dissatisfaction with the attention she received from them. When Mrs. Trumbo had a severe heart attack, marriage plans were abandoned, the groom-to-be was seen less and less, and the family rotated visits to the hospital on a daily basis. The worker became involved when the sons requested information about nursing homes in the area after the physician decided that Mrs. Trumbo could not be alone at home. In a visit to Mrs. Trumbo, the worker was told categorically, "I will not go to a nursing home. I know my sons would not want me to do that. I could stay with one of them until I can go home."

The messages were clear. The physician says the patient requires care; the sons look to an institution for the answer. Mrs. Trumbo has expectations for the family that they are not willing to meet. This worker did not give up the possibility that compromises would provide some satisfactory solution. Would Mrs. Trumbo be willing to go home if care could be provided there? Would the physician approve a plan involving a variety of resources? Would the family survive the partial burden? Were there other natural or informal supports that could be tapped? What community-based services from the formal system could be secured?

Whether a professional person is responsible for working with individuals, groups, or in relation to all the older adults in a community, the knowledge of the community's informal support system can be helpful in any service plan. The tasks for the professional who uses the informal system creatively require considerable professional skill.

Identification of the community system and, if working with an individual, of the configuration of supports of that individual, is only the beginning. Those systems must be evaluated for their worth in relation to the need being addressed. To assume that any of the possible parts of an informal system can be accepted on face value could lead to an inadequate service plan.

Information dissemination in a variety of forms including door-to-door outreach, media offerings, central information telephone numbers, and formalized classes, not only bolsters the quality of performance of the informal system but reinforces the backup function of the formal system in the event of crises beyond the capability of the informal system.

Assessing the individual's ability to accept this informal source of support is as important as identifying and evaluating the informal supports that exist in the community. Relatives and neighbors are probably the closest, most accessible help, but the older adult's need to feel some control over the situation will often determine whether or not that kind of assistance is feasible. This need for a sense of control can consciously bring the older adult to reject needed help from either informal or formal system sources.

Here is an example of the importance of the acceptance of informal help. In the development of a telephone reassurance system, volunteers were recruited from a service organization. The volunteers agreed to make daily calls to persons who lived alone and indicated they would like to have someone check to determine that nothing had happened to them. The volunteers set a time to call each day. If there was no answer, the names of two neighbors were on the registration card for the volunteer to contact. Such neighbors had agreed to physically check out the older adult.

An initial group of twelve older adults and six volunteers was selected. After the first month, five of the older adults had dropped out. Three of the volunteers had requested a conference regarding the "situation" in which their telephone friend lived. Obviously the service needed evaluation.

Interviews with all participants—volunteers and older adults—revealed two major problems. The value system of the volunteers promoted a lack of acceptance of the lifestyle of some of the older adults and a need to change their environment. The older adults felt compelled to satisfy the schedule set by the volunteers and often their unthinking intrusion into the older person's life. A nap, a bath, or an unexpected trip to the store with someone who might extend an offer at the last moment, had to be scheduled so that an absence and an unanswered phone would not trigger the alert system. The older adult was not in control.

A partial solution could have been to set up some volunteer training to include understanding of the result of their requirements in scheduling calls and in the implied or explicit criticism of the older person. The reluctance of the volunteers to accept the training brought a different solution. A simple check system—called Sen-Cit Check—has survived for many years. Older persons register the same as before, with two neighbors agreeing to be called to physically check. From there on, the senior citizen is in control. A call must be made by 3:00 p.m. in the afternoon to a central phone where a list is maintained with space for checking off each day's calls for a month. If any calls have not come in by that time, a call is placed to the older person's phone, and then, if there is no answer, a neighbor is called.

Matching the level of need with the appropriate resource is demonstrated in this example. An agency determined that older adults, whose functional ability did not require help, would benefit from the assurance that someone would know if they did need help and would trigger a response from channels designed to provide what was required. The options for meeting that need included a plan to initiate a technique using volunteers who could function with little cost in actual dollars, or in administrative or supervisory time. In assessing the feasibility of the plan, the professional uncovered unanticipated problems. The reluctance of volunteers to accept the training that would have adjusted the conflicting value systems, and the need of the older adults to retain control, became key factors in a decision to abandon the informal system and use the resources of the agency directly. It is important to point out that this example does not suggest that a telephone reassurance service using volunteers is to be viewed negatively. Across the country many such services are in place and meet the requirements of the locale in which they exist.

The assessment of the capacity of any plan to use the informal system as a resource is the key to maximizing the strengths and overcoming whatever weaknesses may exist. In some instances, the informal resources may be preserved by the support provided by the formal system. In other instances, the decision may have to be against its use.

With the increasing emphasis on the use of family, friends, neighbors, and volunteers to supply the responses for care, the social agencies and workers are challenged to seek ways to assure that the informal system does, in fact, provide the care and caring. It should be examined for its limits, both physical and emotional, and for economic considerations, as well as for the benefits of its naturalness. Agencies are finding their arena of professional knowledge addressing the need of the informal system for support.

USING PEERS TO SUPPORT ONE ANOTHER

The value of sharing experiences related to successful techniques of handling problems or stressful situations is realized through groups. Groups range from those consisting of members with health-related conditions themselves to groups of family members and care-givers who benefit from knowledge about the older adult's condition and from the realization that they are not alone in the feelings and struggles being experienced.

For example, Reverend Peterson, a minister whose schedule of funerals for male church members was particularly heavy during a month, started a widows' group. In addition to those recently widowed, he called upon an almost equal number of women who had gone through the early adjustments to the loss of husbands. He eliminated one possible member whose withdrawal was still a problem and another who was so talkative he feared she would dominate the discussion. A call from a church member asking to join the group because she thought she "still had a lot to learn" prompted Rev. Peterson to put a notice in the church bulletin.

In planning for the venture, he dismissed the options of prestructuring the format too rigidly and of training those who had already gone through adjustment to act as counselors. The first meeting went very much as expected. Rev. Peterson's wife had made cookies and these, with coffee and tea, provided a social atmosphere in which members learned of one another's situation. He was surprised, however, at how easily the group accepted the expressions of sadness and even tears. The short "business" part of the meeting set "helping one another" as the purpose of coming together as a group. The members agreed to come together at least four times before deciding what should happen after that. They brought up the issue that transportation for some of them, not only to meetings but to any church affair, was a problem. They also agreed that each would come to the next meeting with something that she felt might be discussed, and that group members would take turns in bringing some refreshments. The last to leave said very quietly, "Reverend Peterson, I didn't like Margaret much—she seemed so different. Today I see we have a lot in common. I'm so glad we're going to continue this."

These informal support groups differ from the groups professionally designed to achieve specific treatment objectives for particular group members. Indeed, using groups to achieve clear-cut treatment goals is a distinct and discrete helping methodology used by many professions as a means to provide services more effectively. The kind of group illustrated by Reverend Peterson's represents an informal support activity inasmuch as Reverend Peterson is providing the environment in which individuals can come together and direct their own group. In this instance, the professional person does not direct the group, but rather the professional makes it possible for a natural, informal system of mutual support to develop.

In the next four meetings, feelings of anger at being "left," loneliness, and fear of living alone in a house, concern over whether to move in with a relative, and anxiety about handling finances were areas touched upon. The group decided to continue without Rev. Peterson present but available to help if needed.

PROFESSIONALS RELATING TO SUPPORT GROUPS

Support groups with peer communication and development of coping skills find valuable assistance from agencies and workers in the formal system.

The proliferation found within the peer group support movement is wide-ranging. From Alcoholics Anonymous to the Alzheimer's Family Support Groups, most recently in national prominence, the idea that persons with like problems can be helpful to one another is well-established. The professionals, who see such groups as beneficial, enhancing the ability of the citizenry to cope successfully with problems and diminishing the demand on the formal and more costly system, welcome this development.

A variety of organizational patterns of support groups provides a diversity of ways for the workers in the formal system to relate to such groups. In fact, some of the organizations are more clearly identified as part of the formal system. In any case, the professional worker's relationship could span such tasks as identifying potential group members; enabling activities as mundane as finding a meeting place, or as technical as finding appropriate speakers; or, in rare instances, acting as a group therapist. Workers must be willing to promote aggressively and to train group members to assume leadership roles, recognizing the strengths within the members, in order to make the informal system effective.

Peer support groups are often initiated by professional persons, or such groups may call for assistance from them. Professionals, working in organizations mandated to provide services and, therefore, part of the formal system, may find helping roles

part of the informal system. For example, Myra Barnes is a public health nu
tive in her church. The minister sought her help in forming a group that would
bring together family members who were the care-givers for relatives recovering
from a stroke. Myra agreed to act as convener of such a group, to be invited by the
minister. She was able to use the knowledge she had as a professional, as well as the
link she provided to the public health department, to secure informational materials
and appropriate professionals as resource information persons. She functioned as a
support to the group, which remained in the informal system. One of the professionals she introduced was a speech therapist who designed a special training course for
the group and established it as part of her work for the agency. The speech therapist
remained in the formal system role, providing assistance to the family members
interested in becoming more skilled in their care giving.

The core of the informal system of support for older persons consists of family, friends, and neighbors. Beyond that core, there are resources that fall between
the informal and formal system. Civic organizations, professional associations, and
church groups constitute the main source of this type of support. During the 1971
White House Conference on Aging, this type of support was categorized as "voluntary organizations," and efforts were started to bring the helping potential of such
groups to bear on the needs of older adults.

NATIONAL VOLUNTARY ORGANIZATIONS
FOR INDEPENDENT LIVING FOR THE AGING

When planning for the 1971 White House Conference on Aging, Arthur S. Flem-
ming, who was U.S. Commissioner on Aging, and others began to view independent
living as the most desired and appropriate arrangement for most older persons. Prior
to the conference, the commissioner convened a group of representatives from
national health, welfare, professional, and civic organizations that provide services
to older people to discuss in-home services for the aging.

A steering committee of National Voluntary Organizations for Services to
Older Persons Living in Their Own Homes or Other Places of Residence was organized at the conference and elected Dr. Ellen Winston to chair its meetings.

Each of the 125 voluntary organizations (NVOs) that then comprised the
steering committee membership was called upon to sign a pledge to devote a new or
renewed effort to the committee's goals of promoting independent living for the
aged through increased voluntary sector involvement in planning in-home and supportive services.

Using the channels of communication available through national voluntary
organizations to their local units, the steering committee directed its efforts toward
encouraging communities throughout the country to provide new and expanded in-
home and supportive services for older persons. Staff support was provided to the
steering committee through funds made available by the Administration on Aging.
Part of the money was given as a grant to the National Center for Voluntary Action

for the purpose of providing staff services to assist the steering committee in these efforts. The Administration on Aging made staff available in its own offices to provide secretarial services for the steering committee and its officers and subcommittees.

In 1974, the steering committee shortened its name and became National Voluntary Organizations for Independent Living for the Aging (NVOILA) and became a program unit of the National Council on the Aging. The Administration on Aging provided a three-year grant to NCOA for NVOILA to develop a project entitled Operation Independence (OI).

The project was called Operation Independence because (1) its principal objective was to demonstrate and document, in a systematic way, the circumstances and conditions under which the voluntary sector (that is, NVOILA's membership of national voluntary organizations and participating community coalitions), working in collaboration with the public sector, could initiate and expand in-home and supportive services to increase the possibility that older persons could live more independently in their own homes, and (2) the project period embraced the nation's bicentennial year, 1976, the 200th year of independence for most Americans—with the notable exception of the frail elderly. Recognized as a National Bicentennial Program by the American Revolutionary Bicentennial Administration, the OI project cited eighty-seven communities and twenty-seven voluntary organizations for exemplary efforts in initiating and implementing new or expanded programs designed to promote independent living for the aging.

This project made clear that neither voluntary nor public service agencies are sufficiently aware of the wide range of resources available in voluntary organizations, professional organizations, civic, social, and fraternal clubs, and religious organizations. As groups, they have manpower resources, programmatic and organizational know-how, facilities, and funds that can contribute enormously to the provision of services to older people.

By April 1980, NVOILA had grown in membership to 226 national voluntary organizations. NVOILA has served as a catalyst, educator, technical resource, and convener for the voluntary sector in its ever-increasing contribution to the planning and provision of in-home and community-based supportive services designed to promote independent living for the aging.

WORKING WITH VOLUNTEERS

Professionals are being encouraged and even pressured to include the use of volunteers to provide or help to provide services needed by older adults. Within the federal government the Action agency funds local programs to stimulate the use of volunteers. The Senior Companions program links older adults with other older adults who require or can benefit from social interaction. The Retired Senior Volunteer Program (RSVP) was started to encourage and expand the recruitment of older people as volunteers. Volunteer Service Bureaus, first begun during World War II, were greatly expanded during the late 1970s as the National Voluntary Action Association encouraged a Voluntary Action Network across the country. These developments have already increased the use of volunteers in service to older adults as well as those of other ages and promoted the use of older adults as volunteers. This effort to provide older adults a role as contributors of service to others can be viewed also as a service to the older adults in that it fortifies the feelings of self-worth of those older adults who volunteer.

Volunteers come in all sizes and shapes, ethnic identities, religious persuasions, and cultural, educational, and income levels. More importantly, they have a variety of reasons or motivations for offering their time and effort without monetary reward to help others. Without a doubt, the use of volunteers can expand the quantity of services available to those in need. What is often questioned is the possible effect on the quality of services if volunteers are used too extensively. Professionals may even feel that the use of volunteers will reflect negatively on their claims to the need for a level of expertise in service provision that is beyond that which most volunteers possess. It is not surprising, then, to hear volunteers often complain that the jobs offered by agencies looking for volunteers are more likely to require low skill, such as handling the reception desk or stuffing envelopes.

What can be done to overcome these barriers to the use of this valuable resource of helping persons? How can professionals sharpen their skills in working with volunteers?

The view that the major reason to use volunteers is to expand services needs to be examined. If this is the way professionals relate to volunteers it invites the fear of replacement mentioned earlier. On the other hand, if volunteers can be viewed as providing what professionals cannot provide, it could lead to a better relationship. Two major areas can be suggested. Volunteers, no matter what specific tasks they perform for an agency, can take a positive image into the community to support the need for, and the quality of, the work being done by the agency. As part of the public relations of the agency, volunteers who speak for the agency not because they are paid, are viewed with greater credibility by those outside. Most often these are administrative volunteers in the nonprofit private agencies who serve on boards of directors or in the committee structure of the board.

Another example of how volunteers may perform differently from the professionals is found in a direct service volunteer functioning as a friendly visitor. The older adult who is visited by a paid staff member is receiving a needed service, aware that the worker is not only paid to provide it but that the worker has a busy schedule and is compelled to cover the needs of many people. A volunteer gives a different picture that offers the older adult being served the immediate perception that what is being done is done because the volunteer wants to do it and not because it is a paid job. This perspective on volunteer versus professional needs to be fully examined for complexities and refinements. The mention of this different way of approaching the use of volunteers is offered here as a way to overcome one barrier to their use.

Despite this suggestion of volunteers as important for good public relations, volunteers do, and should, provide expansion of services. Good practice in working with volunteers has been identified and should be used by professionals. It starts with *identification of volunteer jobs* and a *written job description.* A written description for a volunteer is just as important as a written job description for a paid worker. It makes possible a clear understanding of the expectations that both the volunteer and the agency can have of the tasks to be addressed. It also provides a way to evaluate the volunteer and his or her growth into a job requiring a higher skill level. *Recruitment* of volunteers may need to be done by the agency in which the volunteer will serve, or there may be a central volunteer service in the community available to provide the recruitment. No matter who does it, a variety of recruitment avenues can be used. Notices through the media, newspapers, radio and television, and church bulletins and appeals to groups within the church structure, civic clubs, schools, and professional associations are all possible ways of attracting volunteers. Those who are already serving as volunteers can be most effective in recruiting others.

    Assignment of volunteers is an important step. Careful interviewing to determine the capabilities of the prospective volunteer as well as his or her motivation (as mentioned earlier) are as important to determine as the time they are willing to give and when they are available. Prospective volunteers may be screened out for many reasons just as applicants for a paid job would be screened. Unlike screening paid-job applicants, it is difficult to reject someone who is offering service without financial considerations. Too often professionals will accept an unsuitable volunteer because of their inability to reject the person, only to find problems later on. For this reason, volunteer bureaus and central volunteer services are helpful because the prospect can be returned for a different placement in a job match that is more suitable.

    Orientation and training get the volunteer off to a good start. This should include a review of agency policies, a clear description of the job, the assignment of physical space (a place designated may be an office or at the very least a place to put personal belongings) which also indicates respect for the volunteer, and introductions to staff. *Supervision* based on the job description and, when possible, inclusion in staff meetings will produce better quality of work and greater satisfaction for the volunteer. *Recognition* of some sort can range from the informal commendation by other staff to the yearly formalized recognition ceremony with certificates or pins or some tangible evidence of praise. An often overlooked form of recognition is promotion or change of job to a more complex or higher-skill one.

    This review has focused on the volunteer who serves within a formal agency and the considerations that professionals should be addressing in working with them. The volunteers who are part of the informal system and therefore not within the authority of the professionals are important in those instances when professionals are developing service plans for clients. Neighbors, friends, and church and civic club members may be regarded as volunteers in the informal network of support available to provide service. As such they should be regarded by workers as a significant resource. Therefore, part of the orientation to the community that any professional serving older adults should undertake would include an *identification of what community-wide volunteer efforts exist.* Does the Lions' Club provide escort assistance for the blind? What churches schedule transportation for church activities? Is there a club or group with a fund to be tapped for purchase of prescription drugs? Who does friendly visiting in the high-rise for the elderly and handicapped? Does the local scout leader look for volunteer projects bringing the young into contact with the old?

Another consideration for a professional in regard to the community is gaining an understanding of the prevailing values of responsibility of neighbors. Is it prevailing practice for people living in a neighborhood to help one another? Or do people barely speak to residents living next door? Is there a neighborhood watch program?

Knowing the attitudes of concern will help the worker in assessing the resources that might be available in working with an individual or family of older adults. But the worker must use this information as background and verify the supports available to the immediate service need of the one or ones being assisted. Is the neighbor next door, like most of the community, willing to be of help; or is that neighbor unwilling or perhaps unable for a variety of reasons to be at all involved?

Unpaid workers, or volunteers, are valuable resources in providing services to older adults. Professional workers can utilize this resource to its maximum potential by developing the skills necessary to achieve that potential.

SUMMARY

The informal system is the natural helping system preferred by most older persons and by society at large. Its weaknesses of accountability and incapability to meet demand require support in order to maintain it. Intervention by the formal service delivery system may occur as a support to the informal system or as a substitute for it. Methods that a professional might use include identifying the informal community support system and those of an individual being served, disseminating information to the informal system, assessing the acceptability of the informal supports to the older adult, and matching the level of community or individual need with the appropriate resource in the informal system.

CHAPTER TEN

THE FORMAL SYSTEM

Agencies and organizations made up of a range of incorporated or public bodies may be categorized as a formal system, as distinguished from an informal system of helping persons made up of relatives, neighbors, or friends. This distinction is made sharply to place any incorporated body with a stated purpose into the category of a formal system of helping persons. It must be noted, however, that the exact definition of a formal organization varies in the literature describing services and activities. Club groups and especially church-sponsored support kinds of activities are sometimes considered and reported as part of the informal system.

Volunteers supervised by professionals, working as friendly visitors in a nursing home or providing outreach services from a senior center, are considered part of the formal system. On the other hand, the "visitation committee" of a church can be viewed as either formal or informal depending on the scope and range of activity included under the charge accepted by the committee, the links to other community services, and the accountability built into the method of operation. In general, organizations in the formal system are easily identified and have a corporate structure as a base of organization, whereas the informal system is made up of a more fluid base that is largely relational (as described in Chapter 9). By discussing a wide range of organizations providing services, the importance of strong links—communication, mutual support, cooperation, and coordination—between and among the variety of helping efforts is made clear.

This chapter examines the broad system related to providing assistance in satisfying the needs of older adults for a quality of life that assures not only the basic necessities of food, shelter, clothing, and health care but goes beyond these to the recognition of social and psychological needs.

A brief review of the two major types of organizational structure will aid in understanding how a professional within the formal system is utilized in helping older persons. A more detailed description of the structural levels in the "aging network," spanning federal, state, county or area, and community, is found in Chapters 6, 7, and 11.

PUBLIC AND PRIVATE ORGANIZATIONS

Twenty-five years ago it was a simple matter to differentiate between a public and a private agency. An agency mandated by law and supported by tax funds was a public agency; an organization formed by a group concerned with a special interest, supported by voluntary contributions, and authorized by articles of incorporation was a private agency. A private, for-profit organization, like any business, was supported by owners—single, partnership, or corporate stockholders—whose goal of providing service related to the primary purpose of one organization. Accountability was clear. Each organization was responsible to its source of financial support. The public agency was accountable to the taxpayers, as represented by their elected officials, the private agency to its contributors or owners.

An accepted characteristic difference between public and private nonprofit agencies was the private agency's flexibility to engage in experimental or innovative approaches, and literally any relevant social activity that its contributors thought was appropriate. Policy decisions rested with different types of bodies. Public agency boards or commissions were usually appointed by the appropriate elected officials; private agency boards were elected by some type of membership. A few organizations existed outside this dual structure. The American Red Cross, mandated by law, was and is a membership organization supported by voluntary contributions. Public Housing Authorities have boards appointed by legislators, but their budgets are not subject to approval by those officials. In each case, for different reasons, these organizations constitute a quasipublic status.

During the early 1970s one familiar distinction between public and private organizations started to change. Contracts for services, paid for by tax dollars, were equally accessible to private, nonprofit agencies as to public agencies. Private agencies were often required to include an appointed public representative on a board of directors as a part of the agreement for funds. A variety of policies have been influenced in the private sector because of the grant or contract process. Most usually required for federal funds are commitments to provide barrier-free access, civil rights compliance, and even affirmative action plans. Another effect of this practice was greater uniformity in service provision and development of standards and guidelines for practice in private agencies. Further changes can be expected as the trend to block-grant federal funds to the states becomes more widespread. Anticipated reduction in tax dollars allocated to human services has already promoted a plea for greater cooperation between public and private support.

In looking at the formal system of social services it is well to remember that it grew out of the informal system. As a body of knowledge based on experience emerged, the "professional" helper developed. The trademark of the formal system is this professional approval. Philosophy, ethics, and standards of practice changed over the years as a result of awareness of the importance of a national policy in regard to those in need. A study of legislation in this country provides documentation of shifts and change. The three major White House Conferences on Aging give further evidence of a continuing struggle to formalize commitment and priorities for attention. The democratic process makes for slow change, but change it does promote.

The formal agency service system was obligated to respond to changing times beyond its control. Economic, cultural, and ethnic diversity, family patterns of mobility and, as important as any other factor, the lengthening of life expectancy (particularly for women), along with the educational attainment and health status of the older adult brought challenges to all formal organizations.

THE CHALLENGE OF LIVING ARRANGEMENTS

Of all the challenges facing the formal response system of organizations and the helping professionals working in them, the environment in which people live and the impact of that environment has been too often ignored by helping persons. Separate professional perspectives for planning of physical structures and such allied concerns as zoning, sanitation, utilities, streets and highways, and for health, financial, and social concerns, known as human services, have developed. This tends to obscure the interrelationship of these perspectives in addressing the needs of the total person. The professionals, whether serving in agencies mandated to provide health or social services, find that living arrangements influence care plans. The purpose of this section is to examine trends that have shaped the development of living-arrangement options for older adults.

Where people live has an important bearing on their ability to function. Conversely, ability to function influences the decision about where to live. A recently widowed woman, living in a rural farm area in a household with children and grandchildren and with other children and their families living within several miles, will have little difficulty remaining in the home despite failing eyesight. By comparison, another widow, whose only child is a married daughter living hundreds of miles away, will face some hard decisions about remaining in her home alone as her eyesight fails. The section on housing at the 1981 White House Conference on Aging brought a clear message that every effort must be made to provide choices of living arrangements appropriate to the needs of the individual.

INSTITUTIONAL VERSUS COMMUNITY LIVING

The term "community living" refers to any and all arrangements available to or provided for individuals who are not in a hospital, nursing home, or mental institution. Living arrangements in the "institutional category" include homes for the aged, and group living called "rest homes" in some states. Retirement hotels and high-rise public or private housing projects are not included.

Residences in institutions account for approximately 5 to 6 percent of the population over age sixty-five. The average age of those in nursing homes has risen and represents those now being categorized as the old-old, specifically those over age seventy-five.

The psychological aspects of living arrangements are very important to older people. Housing is a symbol of security. Pride of ownership of one's home is embedded firmly in the American heritage. Housing change is more apt to occur when the husband or wife dies, and moving, particularly after such a crisis, is more unsettling than moving in the younger years. Going into a nursing home is generally regarded by older adults as a terminal move. In the past, too often the older person was ignored and housing decisions were made by family or helping persons without a detailed look at all the possibilities. On the other hand, prudence requires that the level of care necessary should not be sacrificed in order to satisfy the older adult's preconception of institutional care as a terminal move.

Living arrangements other than institutions are clearly the preference of most older persons. These include, in addition to their own homes, apartments, including high-rises, boarding houses, shared living where several unrelated persons may divide the cost of housing, retirement hotels, and retirement lifetime care communities. A recent development, where a wide range of support services is included with the physical structure plan, is called "congregate housing." Congregate housing arrangements resolve the problem of wide variance of human capability and need by providing a somewhat modified environment. Basically, it is one model that incorporates services within the same physical structure in which individuals reside.

Housing projects for the elderly offer facilities dependent on the physical space available (office, kitchen and dining area, and program room) usually called community space. They are supplemented by agreements with other agencies mandated to provide services such as meals, housekeeping, information and referral, health counseling, and recreational activities. Frances M. Carp reviews the experience of housing projects for the elderly in relation to the residents' decreasing capabilities and increased personal needs over time. The prevailing practice of most projects is to admit only those who can live "independently." However, as residents grow older, many lose some of that capacity. Too often, residents are asked to vacate when their ability fails to meet the standards of cleanliness in upkeep of the apartment or of personal care that are set by housing managers. Citing the supports provided for persons of younger ages, such as school lunch programs, counselors, and activity programs and employer-provided medical care and food service, Carp states that "the absolutely independent life style, if it ever existed, rarely does so today for persons of any age."[1] She further suggests an "add-on" model of project housing that would grow in scope of service delivery as the need of the residents increased with age. Four areas are suggested in the add-on process: extended and augmented health services, food services, cleaning services, and personal hygiene-related services, such as beauty and barber shops and foot care.

Another living arrangement being promoted across the country by formal organizations is "shared housing." Much shared housing occurs on an informal basis without involvement of any organization. Some arrangements are successful, others are not. Difficulties can be expected more often than not when one person is a long-time resident and probably owner of the house. Loneliness or financial considerations bring the owner to seek someone who will move in and share the responsibilities of residence. Even in those instances where a relationship over time preceded the arrangement, the potential for discord because of ownership inequality is possible. Formal, preplanned shared-living projects are sponsored by many different types of organizations and agencies. In most shared housing arrangements, older people require assistance from community-based services, as well as the support many may receive from others who share the housing.

Another version of shared housing has been patterned after child foster-home placement. Placing an older adult in the home of a younger family is gaining support as the concern for increased contact between and among generations is growing. Both public welfare departments and private or voluntary agencies are testing the feasibility of foster-home placement. This housing alternative is particularly attractive to mental hospitals seeking discharge of older persons who do not need hospital-level care. As with child placement, the importance of matching older persons with caregivers to insure a compatible relationship cannot be overstressed. Finding homes, preparing the older adult and the family for each other, gaining clear understanding of rights and responsibilities by all parties, and continuing supervision make this option more costly than might appear, even though many of the services an older person needs would be provided by the foster family.

This review of choices of housing arrangements that may be available to older adults reflects a national trend resulting from a policy clearly stated first in the 1971 White House Conference and reaffirmed ten years later. These conferences called for an end to institutional care except when the institution was appropriate financially and was matched with the older persons' physical and emotional abilities. Included in the review were indications of how helping persons share responsibilities for assisting older individuals in decisions about their physical living arrangements.

---

[1]Frances M. Carp, "The Concept and Role of Congregate Housing for Older People," in *Congregate Housing for Older People: An Urgent Need, a Growing Demand*, eds. Wilma T. Donahue, Marie McGuire Thompson, and D. J. Currens (Washington: Department of Health, Education and Welfare, 1977), No. 77-20284, 9.

THE RESPONSE OF SERVICE ORGANIZATIONS

The response of the formal service-delivery system to the White House Conference recommendations has been to develop community-based services designed to make it possible for persons to remain in community living arrangements whenever possible. Originally these were referred to as "alternatives to institutional placement"; the phrase has been modified more aptly to "alternatives to inappropriate institutional placement." The language sets forth a wide range of expectations for service organizations and professionals by recognizing the significance of residence in the lives of older people. Targeted for special attention is the 5 percent of the older population placed in residential institutional care. "Inappropriate institutional placement" usually occurs when an individual does not need the array of services or the level of care provided within and by the institution, but the informal or formal system in the locale does not have the capability to provide the care the older adult requires. Knowledge of what is available plays a part. Families and older adults cannot be relied upon to know what resources exist in their community. Fragmentation of services provided within the service delivery system, the varying eligibility criteria for service, and its corollary, the different funding patterns, all contribute to the difficulty of making appropriate placement decisions. Such complexities are an inherent characteristic of the formal system since each agency operates by specific policies, rules, or laws. Case management and case coordination may be the only way to overcome the complexities in the formal system. This technique of helping is discussed in detail in Chapter 8.

If where one lives is determined at least to some extent by what supports are available, and if older persons and national policy choose the community living pattern as opposed to institutional care, the idea of "community-based services" becomes an important objective for the formal service delivery agencies. Dr. Ellen Winston, a pioneer and prominent leader in the movement to establish in-home and community-based services, went even further than the projection of community services as alternatives to inappropriate institutional care. She stressed the point that the traditional system of care is family-based, with formal agencies relieving and supporting or substituting for the family; this viewpoint makes the institutional care the "alternative."

A DEVELOPING SERVICE CONTINUUM

The concept of a continuum of services evolves naturally from the national policy promoting the possibility of remaining in a community living arrangement. Far too many individuals have suffered on release from institutions, because the level of service they needed did not exist in their community. The idea of a continuum of care, or a continuum of services, is based on the specification of levels of support needed by individuals whose presenting profile ranges from complete personal independence to terminal illness. Most older people will need some assistance along this continuum at some time during the later years. Each individual will chart a different path, and not everyone will need all the services.

The goal of such a continuum of services should be to provide restoration to a level of less support when possible, and always to maintain an individual as long as possible at the lowest level of support appropriate to the individual's need. From the standpoint of any given community, the continuum of care represents a variety of services responsive to need, that is based on the desired choice of individuals, their physical, mental, and social condition, and their financial ability or the willingness of society to finance that desired choice.

In summary, the formal system of helping services provides resources that can be mobilized to enhance the quality of life for older persons. Community-based services expand the opportunities for older people to live at a satisfying level of interdependence outside an institution whenever possible, receiving the type of service appropriate to each person's need. Community-based services, as part of a continuum, provide a supportive foundation based on a philosophy that gives priority to care rather than treatment or cure. Thus, the philosophy underlying community-based services is as important as the formal services themselves. "The most difficult problem facing both professionals in the field and the children of older adults is how to care." This philosophy was offered by James T. Sykes, chairman of the Colonial Club in Sun Prairie, Wisconsin, and a former member of the President's Federal Council on Aging, at the National Council on the Aging (NCOA) Annual Conference in March 1983. Sykes provided specific suggestions, often overlooked, for establishing a caring environment.

1. Protect the dignity of the parent.
2. Differentiate thoughtfully between the rhetoric of independence and the reality of unexpressed needs.
3. Guard against erosion of the parent's right to decide.
4. Separate personal well-being from the well-being of parents.
5. Share responsibility and care with all family members.
6. Personal presence and attention rather than gifts are essential.
7. Recognize the wealth of experience that parents have, and *tap* that wealth.
8. Invest the time necessary to know what agencies in the community do, for whom, and how well.
9. Freedom is having a choice. Explore alternatives such as living together, moving, staying put, maybe even circuit-riding.
10. Make it easy, even unnecessary, for parents to ask for help.

Although Sykes addressed these comments to children of older persons, they have direct relevance and can be translated as guidance for the nonrelative helping professional.

THE PROFESSIONAL'S RELATIONSHIP

The helping professionals, no matter what specific discipline they may represent, are challenged to regard the older adult as a total person. The physical, social, and emotional aspects of the individual, as well as the living arrangements and available support system, are important. In this sense, the highest integration of the formal and informal system is not only possible but imperative. In order to achieve that integration, the professional must be able to identify pertinent parts of both the formal and informal systems.

Human service professionals in the formal system cover a wide range of discrete disciplines. Nurses, social workers, clinical psychologists, adult educators, physical therapists, ministers, therapeutic recreators, occupational therapists, nutritionists, lawyers, speech therapists, nurse practitioners, physician assistants, health educators, and physicians each represent a unique perspective and body of knowledge. If older Americans are to be served in a fashion that presents quality and efficiency of service as well as caring, each professional must seek ways to better understand other professional disciplines and to work in cooperation with them.

A mix of professional skills is needed. Interviewing, counseling, and case management can be identified as core techniques. This aspect of professional responsibility has been explored in depth in Chapter 8.

All professionals share a responsibility to assure inclusion of older adults in planning and decision making whether this relates to organizational and administrative issues or to individual problems. The concept of working "with" the older population recognizes the capabilities of this age group. This concept recognizes and is modified to allow for individual differences in ability. The helping person may span roles of listener, advisor, information giver, enabler, and even enforcer of regulations with different older persons.

SERVING IN INSTITUTIONS

Although the prevailing choice of older persons is to remain at home to receive the care they may need, for some the appropriate place to secure the level of skilled care they require is an institutional setting. Many professional persons serve older people in these settings. For professionals, working within an institution requires a different approach to some aspects of service provision because the institution itself determines the available formal services.

The worker in an institutional setting may find differences in responsibilities based on the level of care provided by the institution, its size, and the total staffing pattern. Large institutions are able to offer a narrow scope of tasks and show a wide range of specializations. In a small institution, the worker may find the job description covers not only services to an individual and that individual's family, as well as a close relationship to the treatment team, but responsibility for a variety of resident group programs. Group programs, in such settings, may range from purely recreational pursuits, such as birthday or holiday parties, bingo games, and passive events like concerts for the patients, to therapy groups related to both physical and psychological needs. Perhaps the range of professional tasks is best illustrated by the following example.

Connie Gant arrives at the nursing home at 8:30 a.m., checks the roster for scheduled new admissions, and makes a quick swing around the forty-five bed facility. A stop at the nurses' station tells her that Mrs. Gordon will not be leaving today because she had an attack during the night. She hurries back to her office to call Mrs. Gordon's son, who was to pick her up at 10:30. Realizing she did not have details the son would want, she backtracks to get more information about the incident and Mrs. Gordon's present state. She looks into Mrs. Gordon's room and sees she is sleeping.

The call to the son is a lengthy one. The son had arranged to be off his job and was obviously irritated as well as concerned about his mother's condition. Recognizing her own mounting irritation with the son, she concentrates on assuring him that she will call the home health agency and cancel the order for an aide to come to the house in the afternoon, thereby relieving him of an unnecessary expense.

During the second call, the administrator of the nursing home comes in to inform Connie of a scheduled visit by the state evaluation team. They discuss the importance of patient records being current, the brief presentation Connie will give about activities, and the need for processing a request for Medicaid reimbursement for one of the patients who claims he cannot pay his bill.

Two patients are waiting to see her. One complains about her roommate, who played her radio very late, falling asleep with it still on; the other wants Connie to have a small ceramic dish she has made in the crafts class. The complainer is reassured that something will be done about the radio, and Connie makes a mental note to ask the nurses to request that the night nurse check the room and turn the radio off. Her decision is based on previous experience and the futility of appealing to the roommate.

The dish is a problem. Acceptance of gifts by staff had reached the point of concern for the administrator because of the escalating competition among patients to outdo one another. Institution policy was set—no acceptance of gifts. Connie struggles with the urge to accept this one because she feels the great need of the patient to be a "giving" person. She carefully admires the handicraft, refuses it citing the rule she would be breaking, and suggests putting it on the table in the hall for all to admire. She makes a note on her list of things to discuss in staff meeting about relaxing the strict policy.

After lunch, the quiet time in the nursing home gives Connie the chance to go over records, arrange for some optometry students to come in to adjust eyeglasses, and finalize plans for some of the patients to visit the nearby senior center when a concert is scheduled.

The rest of the afternoon is spent with patients. A visit is made to reassure Mrs. Conners that she is going home the next day and that arrangements have been made to continue her physical therapy; she has a chance encounter with Mrs. Gordon's son and daughter-in-law, repeating much of the morning telephone conversation; she compiles lists of items she will purchase for patients; she places some patients' jewelry in the safe in the administrator's office; she reads a letter from an out-of-state relative and dictates a reply. Before leaving for home, she makes a note to call the volunteer bureau to request a friendly visitor to replace the volunteer who has taken a full-time job but whose help with socialization, and such tasks as letter-reading and writing for the patients has convinced her of the value of volunteers. As she leaves the facility, she puts a note on the administrator's desk to remind her that she will not be in until afternoon the next day because she will be attending a training session on Reality Orientation.

In addition to the kinds of tasks shown in the example, discharge planning requires engaging the institution with other formal organizations. Knowledge of community resources and ability to work with the staff of these services for smooth referral are important skills for the worker to have. The individual discharge plan uses these ingredients in relation to the specific condition of the patient. This condition includes not only the physical, emotional, and financial profile of the person but the family or natural supports that may be tapped.

Professional helpers in the hospital setting are much more dependent on the relationship to the physician than is the worker in a nursing home. Many patients go home from hospitals without any involvement of nonmedical professional staff. The patient in a nursing home is more apt to be part of a discharge planning process with a helping person other than the physician. There is no attempt here to make a value judgment in relation to the practices. The acute care in hospitals brings physicians into almost daily contact with patients; the long-term care of the nursing home depends more heavily on nurses, social workers, and physical and occupational therapists to plan and carry out the release of patients. At this point in time, there is a movement to identify discharge planning as a distinct professional skill, and many large institutions may even include such a job category on the staff roster. The notion that discharge planning begins at the time of admission has promoted a different view of the process. Added to that view is the recognition that follow-up after discharge may be important to forestall reentry into institutional care.

SERVING IN COMMUNITY-BASED AGENCIES

A myriad of organizations and agencies make up the formal system of community-based services. Each has a purpose, organizational structure, staffing pattern, mandated constituent or service population, program of service or services, a planning and budget process, and some form of evaluation or accountability. Organizations vary from large multiservice public agencies to small private nonprofit ones offering a single service. Responsibilities of professionals vary to the same extent that agencies vary.

The report of one shared-housing program indicates the kinds of tasks the professional worker is expected to perform. The report outlines the importance of matching residents with formal support service agencies mindful of the resources that can be mobilized from informal supports. An interview determines what each individual wants and expects from the situation. A workable match is based on such terms as acceptability of location, mutual hobbies, time schedules, and interests. A meeting is set for prospective housemates to discuss the details of living together. Discussion includes such things as finances, cooking, laundry, smoking, use of the telephone, work schedules, and chores. This particular program goes beyond the matching stage to offer referral to community resources for other help, such as health services or even building repair. Professional involvement on a continuing basis to help insure that the homesharing experience goes smoothly is also built into the program.

This community-based agency, providing assistance to individuals interested in sharing a residence, is serving a need of that large segment of the older population which does not need ongoing supports. The professional workers are challenged to recognize the capabilities of these individuals and reinforce those capabilities by offering only the level of assistance needed.

A social worker and a nurse working as a team in a senior center find that their helping areas overlap as they share counseling of participants, or respond to calls for in-home services, or make assessments to verify need for home delivered meals.

An adult services worker in a large public welfare agency may be required only to determine the eligibility of clients, whereas a smaller agency may assign the work on the basis of a caseload that includes a variety of tasks, from eligibility determination to ongoing casework.

Workers in institutional settings use community-based services as referral resources in making discharge plans. Workers in community-based service agencies often bridge the gap between institutional care and community care as shown by the following case of a worker in a family service agency. It points up the difficulties encountered by workers as they relate not only to the patient but to family members. It presents a classic case of a family's coming to the end of its patience with a sick, old person and seeking the quickest solution to their problem. The helping person is not convinced that Mrs. Jackson needs the amount of institutionalized care the family is seeking. The helping person is convinced that Mrs. Jackson can be maintained outside the institutional level of care if the formal network can be made more effective.

> Mrs. Jackson is a seventy-year-old black woman admitted to the hospital with a severe stroke. At the time of referral, she was completely unresponsive to pain or any stimuli. Although discharge was not in the immediate future, the doctor felt that it was best to have someone in charge when the time came

for discharge. I saw Mrs. Jones approximately once a week during her hospitalization. I found that she would respond to simple commands, and that she seemed to be aware that someone was at her bedside. Due to her condition, she was being tube-fed, and she was catheterized. Mrs. Jackson has eleven children most of whom live in the local area, and they all insist on having a say in what happens to their mother. Mrs. Jackson was in such a condition that the doctor felt she would only be able to be discharged to a nursing home. Half the family did not want this to happen; yet no one volunteered to take her. There were many battles, and many times plans were changed. Finally, it seemed that Mrs. Jackson was going to be transferred to a nursing home. However, on the day of her transfer, the family decided they did not want to do this. The oldest daughter, Mrs. Brown, took charge and took her mother to her home. By the time Mrs. Jackson was discharged, she was no longer being tube-fed, and she was slightly responsive although she needed complete care.

I saw Mrs. Jackson in the home of Mrs. Brown once every two weeks for the next four months. I was really amazed at the improvement she made after going to Mrs. Brown's home. She went from a quite unresponsive condition to being someone who could say one or two words, smile, and understand what was being said. She could feed herself and could move from the bed to a chair with some slight assistance. The progress, however, was being made at the expense of Mrs. Brown, who was not getting any help from the rest of the family. Mrs. Brown and her husband and daughter took care of Mrs. Jackson; the rest of the family would come to see the old lady, but they would not offer to help Mrs. Brown in her efforts. She was also very concerned about her mother's Department of Social Services check, which she felt would be cut if Mrs. Jackson continued to stay with her, and she did not know if she could take any more money out of her own pocket. Mrs. Jackson had been living alone prior to her stroke, though only across the street from the family. Mrs. Brown kept hoping that her mother would improve to the point that she could go home. She also said that her mother had made the family promise that they would not get rid of the house or destroy her furniture should she become sick. This was a drain on Mrs. Brown's budget, and the Department of Social Services was not able to help out enough.

Even so, things seemed to be going along quite well at Mrs. Brown's, and, in March, I left the office for two weeks. During this time several developments occurred. Specifically, Mrs. Brown decided she was no longer going to keep her mother in her home. She said she simply could not handle the money or the nursing aspects without some help, and the family did not seem to be able to give that help. Although she had been a violent opponent to her mother's going into a nursing home, she now felt that it was the best idea. However, Mrs. Kerr, another daughter, now decided that she did not want her mother to go into a nursing home and was taking steps to prevent this. In March, Mrs. Jackson was transferred to a local nursing home. I called there to see how things were going and found that she had been removed from the nursing home by Mrs. McCall, another of her daughters, only two days after being admitted. Mrs. McCall said she would care for her mother in the home.

There were many phone calls between Mrs. Brown and myself regarding the fact that Mrs. McCall was not able to care for Mrs. Jackson, according to Mrs. Brown. She also said that Mrs. McCall's home was dirty and did not have the proper facilities. She felt that Mrs. McCall was only after the welfare check. On May 1, I went out to Mrs. McCall's home to see Mrs. Jackson. There were three very small children around the house, which was definitely rather dirty and shabby. Mrs. Jackson looked very good. She looked very clean, and seemed to be enjoying herself. She felt that she was getting along very well. She was able to carry on somewhat of a conversation, or rather to answer direct questions, and she said that she was very happy where she was and she enjoyed being around the children; they gave her a "lift," she said. Mrs. McCall said her mother had her good days and her bad days and, actually, they did not feel that it was too difficult taking care of her. They ate mashed foods and made other adjustments.

The doctor had seen her on April 28, and said that she was getting along fine. The public health nurse was coming to the home and performing catheter care, and Mrs. McCall said that her mother had not had an infection. They were hoping the catheter would be removed and that they would be able to get a physical therapist in to help get Mrs. Jackson up and walking with a walker. I saw the family again on June 30, and although Mrs. Jackson was not walking yet, she was able to transfer better. She could walk a little sometimes, but the physical therapist had not set up a program yet. Mrs. Jackson was eating all right and her speech was definitely better this time. I encouraged the family to call me if they needed me or had any questions.

On July 14, I saw the family again. Things were going fine, and the doctor, whom she had just seen, said Mrs. Jackson was doing well. She had good days and bad days, and her memory was not very good. However, she sat all day, read a large-print Bible, and listened to the radio or to the children. Mrs. McCall did not seem to be having too much difficulty taking care of her mother, and her mother seemed to be getting better with the individual attention. There were still family splits; however, they managed to keep this from Mrs. Jackson. I told Mrs. McCall, on July 17, that I felt she was getting along so well with her mother that I would not come back unless they specifically asked me to. Because Mrs. Jackson will have to be moved if she gets any worse, and because of the family problems, I feel we may be called upon in the future.

This case demonstrates that the interface of formal services in providing a caring and supportive environment for older people may be possible in face of great difficulties. The helping person in this case has been able to mobilize enough formal resources to enable the family to keep this person in a home environment.

Given the complexity of the family supports, Mrs. Jackson's formal services rested heavily on services provided by the public health nurse. In other situations, a different formal agency may provide a similar central service around which other supportive aids are arranged. It is important to consider exactly what services are needed for people like Mrs. Jackson and how the professional worker connects the person with the service in an effective way.

Professionals engage in face-to-face contact with older adults in a variety of different agencies that offer a variety of services either singly or in a grouping of services. Serving older Americans includes providing such services as information and referral, outreach, counseling, health screening, housing assistance, homemaker/ home health aide services, legal aid, employment referral, educational opportunities (ranging from recreational activities and discussion groups to skill-building classes), transportation, meal service, and nutrition education. The following sections examine more closely a select group of services for analysis.

IN-HOME SERVICES

In-home services are, in general, designed to provide assistance that may be necessary to support the older adults who continue to reside in the community at a meaningful level of self-sufficiency and independence. In many cases, as when there is no family, the formal services may be the only available alternative to institutional or nursing home care.

In a response to the national demand for reduction of high cost and inappropriate service delivery requiring residential placement in nursing homes and mental institutions, an array of formal, community-based services has been developing. As with all the formal community-based services, the array of in-home services grew as the need grew for substitutes for the informal or natural system. The array has developed in scope and complexity from a simple contact to assure that nothing had happened to an individual in a twenty-four-hour period, called telephone reassurance service, to a predetermined plan for personal and home care. As a response to individual and family needs, formal community support services are founded upon the preference of most individuals to remain in their own homes.

In-home services specifically cover a wide range of supports from telephone reassurance to adult day care. Even telephone reassurance service can show considerable variety, from the simple daily *check* to the volunteer-based, friendly *chat*. The service variety may be extensive. Home delivered meals, transportation for medical appointments and shopping, minor home repair, heavy cleaning or chore services, homemaker and a variety of respite care packages, and home health care, which includes nursing, physical, occupational, and speech therapy, nutrition counseling, and home health aide services, are a partial inventory of the services that are more frequently found as part of the formal helping service network.

Funding sources have been the most important factor in shaping the formal system that provides most in-home services. As sources of funds have increased, more service delivery organizations have developed. The rapid expansion of organizations suggests the need to require or promote cooperation and coordination. By tradition, the formal system has divided health and social services. A doctor's order is required for home care service funded by federal reimbursement for medical services, such as Medicare and Medicaid. Maintenance of homes in sanitary and safe condition, and some personal care are often funded from different federal sources, such as Title XX of the Social Security Amendments. The highest level of coordination occurs when these sources of funds are brought together in a purchase-of-services package, which can be either in the public or private sector, making possible one provider for services that are medical and/or social ones.

Home health services provide various forms of health care in the home. These services are carefully tailored to the needs of the older person. They require a strong administrative structure and a professional staff with well-defined responsibilities. These responsibilities include the assessment and selection of those situations in which health care in the home will be effective; the formulation of care plans; the use of appropriate, related resources; and the coordination and adaptation of services to meet changing needs. Added to these professional responsibilities is the responsibility that is unique to these services: the selection, training, and supervision of home health aides and their placement in the homes of recipients of services with concern for personal compatability while they perform assigned care tasks to achieve treatment goals. The following examples illustrate the use of home health services and some of the required professional responsibilities in providing these services.

> Mrs. Nelson was released from the hospital, after treatment for a stroke, with a service plan initiated by the hospital discharge planner in conjunction with the community-based home health agency. Doctor's orders for physical therapy and some personal care were on file at the agency. A specific service plan was made by the nurse and physical therapist who supervised the aide. The aide carried out the exercise program between the physical therapist's visits, as well as the bathing assistance, meal preparation, shopping, and light housekeeping duties needed. The nurse visited every two weeks, changing the aide's duties as Mrs. Nelson's recovery progressed.

> Mr. Stern's cancer is inoperable and terminal. Life expectancy is set at about two months. Mr. Stern's family has consulted the local Hospice agency because they wish to make his desire to die at home possible. The social worker has looked at two perspectives in relation to the situation—care of Mr. Stern and support of the family. A trained volunteer is assigned to work with Mrs. Stern and the Sterns' son and daughter-in-law, in whose home the Sterns live. Since both young people work, and Mrs. Stern is not physically able to manage some of the care alone, the family will pay for two hours a day, five days a week of homemaker/home health aide service.

As these examples demonstrate, the tasks of the homemaker/home health aide involve more than home management skills or supportive health care. The special feature of these activities is the presence of an intact, warm, healthy personality in intimate contact with the threatened family or individual in the environment of the home, supporting all that the term "home" implies: safety, familiarity, security, and shelter. For the elderly, especially, fears of incompetence may grow as their inability to cope with their failing health increases with age. Homemaker/home health aide services help allay such fears of incompetence. Many aged persons encountering failing health difficulties are faced with the choice between receiving no care at all or receiving total care in so-called *total institutions*—nursing homes, homes for the aged, and state mental hospitals.

While the familiarity and security offered by in-home services distinguishes them from institutionalized health and social programs, they cannot be seen as a substitute for formal services offered in an institution. In-home services do not replace the foster home, the hospital, or the nursing home. Such services are effective only when care in the home is appropriate. Together with the service provided in residential institutional care, and the full range of community-based services, in-home services become a reliable resource as part of a continuum of community services that are essential to comprehensive care for older people.

The National Home Caring Council has defined the tasks of the homemaker/ home health aide and the appropriate function of the agency administering such programs. The statement presented by the council establishes stringent parameters for the delivery of in-home services. Agencies providing such services must be part of the formal system of community public, voluntary, nonprofit, or profit agencies. Only qualified persons who have been trained may be employed. Doctors' orders may form the basis for referral. The appropriate professional staff of the agency (usually a nurse and social worker) establishes with applicants their need for the service, develops a suitable plan to meet the need, assigns and supervises the homemaker/home health aide, and continually evaluates whether the help given meets the assessed need of recipients.

Personal services provided by homemaker/home health aides include: bathing, toileting, feeding, assistance with prescribed exercises and medication, escorting when an elderly person's movements are unsure, teaching adjustments to be made in handling tasks of daily living, and emotional support to encourage continued coping. Aides also perform environmental services such as light housecleaning, cooking, shopping for food, and other home-management tasks.

The professional working in a homemaker/home health agency may be related in direct "hands-on" service to the patient. For example, physician's orders for certain injections require the nurse to administer them; or physician's orders for massage and/or manipulation of limbs require they be carried out by a physical therapist. A social worker in such an agency may be scheduling therapeutic counseling sessions with a patient who is experiencing emotional difficulties in coping with the loss of the ability to function.

In addition to these "hands-on" types of tasks, professionals should be making the assessments and reassessments for services, particularly those assigned to aides. Professionals form one link between the patient and the treating physician. Professionals also form links with other service agencies when they are needed in the service plan. As has already been indicated, professionals supervise aides and participate in the overall evaluation of the agency service. A social worker who works with a nurse as an in-home services team may have the kind of day described below.

It might begin with a review of the evaluations of service received from clients or families. The worker notes several areas that seem to need immediate attention; some evaluations suggest commendation of certain workers and others raise a question about the service agreement form currently used. A conference with the nurse is held before scheduled home visits are made. The conference determines that one home visit will center on the transfer of the client from a private paying status to Medicaid reimbursement. The social worker will do a reassessment of service need and discuss with the family the extent of support family members will be able to give. The other home visit is a routine monitoring scheduled at the time the home aide is working.

The worker reviews the files on the clients and checks out with the receptionist, giving a time for return to the office.

The reassessment process involved talking with the client who has had a stroke and with a daughter who works part-time. The daughter is concerned that the worker will expect her to give up her job to care for her. The daughter strongly pushes for the mother to be cared for in a nursing home so that "she can get physical therapy every day." The worker establishes immediately that the purpose of her visit is "to see how the mother can receive the care she needs" but proceeds quickly to reassure the daughter that there is help available that will permit her to share the responsibility of her mother's care and keep her job.

Workers are often faced with this dual relationship of responsibility to a client where the family presents a conflict of solutions because they feel threatened. By immediately establishing the focus on the mother, but recognizing that the cooperation of the daughter is essential in serving the interest of the mother, the worker removes the daughter's fears as a barrier to an appropriate plan.

The home visit includes some discussion of the service provided by the home aide assigned in the past, a discussion of the physician's recommendations that do not include skilled nursing care, and a financial review needed to establish eligibility for Medicaid reimbursement. The worker leaves, noting that some discussion with the assigned home aide of the daughter–mother relationship might produce more information about why the daughter suggested nursing-home placement.

The monitoring visit is brief and routine. The return to the office gives enough time before lunch for the necessary recording of both home visits.

After lunch, the worker arranges the conference room for the regular biweekly meeting of the home aides. In-service training for the aides is shared with the nurse. Today's session deals with the relationship of the aides to family members in the case of terminal illness. The worker will show a film, reinforce highlights, and conduct a group discussion aimed at developing coping skills, when faced with a terminally ill client, and techniques of helping the family deal with their own feelings. The worker is careful to stress the limits aides must observe and how to refer family members for help beyond the capacity of the aides.

Homemaker/home health aide services, nursing, physical, occupational, and speech therapy, and nutrition counseling form the basis for in-home services most usually in existence. Other services are developing, if not under the same agency, in close conjunction. One agency uses the services of a physical therapist to assess the home environment for modifications that would enable the disabled older adult to function more easily. A home repair team is accessible to add grip bars to the bathroom design or build a ramp or lower a kitchen counter. Some recommendations are as simple as "take up all the scatter rugs"; others call for ordering devices such as long-handled scissor tongs for reaching items on high shelves, or special eating utensils designed for easier gripping by arthritic hands.

Another service under the umbrella of in-home services is home-delivered meals. Though the service was started long before 1973 by volunteers working as part of a church-sponsored program, the amendments to the Older Americans Act of that year brought the possibility of federal funds to support provision of meals for the homebound. The number of persons receiving this kind of service continues to grow as both the private, largely church-supported programs, and public funds have increased. Public resources from the Older Americans Act and Title XX of the Social Security Amendments are being used not only by public agencies, but through contracts for service by private agencies as well.

The National Association of Meals Programs has been an energetic and influential force in keeping the emphasis on the involvement of volunteers. Many states require that home-delivered meals provided with Older Americans Act funds be delivered by volunteers. The obvious saving in cost adds to the desirability of this kind of community involvement.

Despite the emphasis on using large numbers of volunteers, professionals in such programs are needed for a variety of tasks. In addition to the responsibilities of administration, knowledge of nutrition and food handling is obvious. But even further than actual food preparation and distribution is the desirability of verifying circumstances and assessing the exact needs of the older person. Home-delivered-meals programs are recognizing the added challenge of looking at needs other than nutrition that may be presented by someone requesting meal service. Professionals may be called upon to train volunteers to go beyond meal delivery and a cheerful smile to identifying those requiring broader attention and, having those individuals identified, the professional may see these individuals at home for the kind of information and referral that looks at the total person's total needs.

ADULT DAY CARE

Sometimes included under the broad category of in-home services is adult day care. It is a fairly recent addition to the formal service delivery system. In 1971, there were few such programs in existence. Those that were, emphasized mental or physical rehabilitation. By 1980, adult day care had become firmly established, with states developing standards and a national organization. The National Institute of Adult Day Care was formed as a constituency unit of the National Council on the Aging. Delegates from most of the states in the union are working to set standards of practice for adult day-care services.

Wide variety is found in organizational structure, service population, cost, program size, staffing patterns, and even facility design of adult day-care programs. A conference sponsored by Duke University's Center for the Study of Aging and Human Development reported as many as five program models in existence. Principle funding for the particular adult day-care operation seems to be the deciding factor in the type of program provided. A medical emphasis is usually offered when funding is sought from Medicare or Medicaid sources, and a social emphasis is offered when funding is sought from Title XX.

Despite this range of programs, the common stated purpose of adult day care is to provide a community-based service that makes it possible for more older individuals to reside in their own or a relative's home when the capacity to care for themselves is diminished. Some degree of health service, social service, and emotional support is provided in all these programs, if not within the program directly, at least by referral. When care is provided during the day, these older persons can return home in the evenings.

Most adult day-care programs serve persons eighteen years of age and older, with a few programs to serve only older adults. Despite the possible age range, the overwhelming number of persons who use adult day care are older adults. Mental institutions have benefited greatly by the development of adult day care in the formal service delivery system. The use of tranquilizing drugs coupled with the availability of adult day care made it possible for many older adults, who were well enough to leave the hospital but not well enough to be completely independent, to return to the community. Adult day-care programs housed in, or sponsored by, mental health centers, are often called day-treatment programs. They provide monitoring of medication, group therapy, and social and recreational activities.

Socially oriented adult day-care programs have increased nationally because funds from Title XX of the Social Security Amendments can be used. Eligibility for the service is determined consistent with Title XX guidelines. Medical day-care programs, as such, cannot be funded from Title XX, but despite funding restrictions, most adult day-care programs are required to show a link to health care as needed by the participants in the program. Churches have responded to the need for facilities, and some senior centers have special areas designated for adult day care or a specified program plan for the "at-risk elderly."

Regardless of the type of day-care program provided, all programs must have professional persons who are skilled in administration, individual assessment, service plan development, program scheduling, and referral to other agencies if appropriate. Useful skills might include casework, group therapy, working with volunteers, and programmatic expertise such as leading group singing, exercise, teaching handicrafts, or personal care. A variety of organizations sponsor adult day care. Private, for-profit programs may be found as part of nursing homes or hospitals; or private, for-profit programs may be completely independent businesses. Nonprofit organizations such as churches, councils on aging, and senior centers may be adult day-care sponsors. A private, nonprofit corporation may be organized solely to administer a day-care program. Programs may be supported with public funds for those eligible as well as fees paid by participants or families.

Adult day care is an arrangement of services in the continuum of care offered by the community-based service agencies and provides another option in selecting the appropriate level of care needed by an individual choosing to live at home rather than in an institution.

PROTECTIVE SERVICES

Another form of community-based service to older people is protective services. Every state in the union has some central state agency responsible for attention to persons over age eighteen who are incapable of self-care and who have no family able to be involved. In twenty-eight states these programs are mandated in law. Adult Protective Services is a social service with medical and legal components, provided to individuals with certain identifiable characteristics who are found in circumstances and situations which are considered to be harmful or dangerous. They are generally administered by a social caseworker who acts as the coordinator of these diverse services and is the central direct service worker with the individual clients.[2]

The professional worker who provides protective services faces the pressure of time as an additional factor in the development of a care plan. In many states assurance of prompt action is built into the guidelines for service if not into the law itself. Knowledge of services and/or resources and a timely assessment of the older adult's physical and mental capabilities must be brought into the highest level of legally supported practice. Protecting individual rights in protective services work is a basic responsibility for each worker. States have struggled with laws proposed to protect individuals from themselves or community residents from the behavior of some individuals, often offending the rights of those they seek to protect.

The right to personalized life styles, reflecting ethnic and/or cultural differences or even simple preference, has been and will be debated in our courts. Some measures have been so drastic that the plea "protect me from my protectors" has been hurled at legislators who, in good faith, have devised laws insensitive to individual rights.

Appropriate protective service activities vary widely from place to place. A worker in one state, investigating a report of a "bag lady" who has no address, depends on local merchants for food, and spends the spring, summer, and fall days on a favorite bench singing the songs of her childhood, decides not to take any interventive action. Another worker might choose a different course of action and begin a process of commitment to institutional care. Which one is correct? Each might argue the older adult was best served by the action chosen. There is little guidance from state laws, which vary in the extent of specifics regarding the point at which an individual's need for "protection" is justified. More than in any other helping situation, the worker who deals with potential protective-services clients must have a clear understanding of their values and even further must be able to accept behavior reflecting values that might be totally opposite to those of the worker.

Some situations are clear and pose no struggle over whether to intervene. Other situations may be quite touchy. A man who has lived for many years in a

---

[2]*Protective Services for Adults* (Washington: Department of Health and Human Development Services, Administration on Aging, Spring 1982), 7–8, 211.

boarding home and who begins to give away his money rather than pay bills, stops eating regularly, and stays in his room with the curtains drawn definitely needs help. A man who has been told he has terminal cancer and refuses to take medication may be a different story. A study done in 1962 at the Benjamin Rose Institute of Cleveland has served as a landmark for the shift from concern mainly for protection of property holdings to more emphasis on protection of the person.[3] The study identified the array of services that are most likely to be needed in protective-service cases as medical, financial, homemaker/home health aide, nursing care, psychiatry, and legal services. Social casework was identified as the core service. Butler and Lewis suggest that whenever possible the following principles are crucial to protective services:

1. Client or patient must have decision making power.
2. Trust and rapport must be established before all else; do not violate the trust.
3. Do things carefully and without haste.
4. Do not kill with kindness.
5. Work with assets.
6. Respect resistance.
7. Do not move people if it can be avoided and if it is against their will.[4]

SUMMARY

Older Americans are served by professionals, nonprofessionals, and volunteers working in public and private agencies and organizations that make up the formal service delivery system. This service delivery system includes care provided in an institutional facility and from community-based organizations and agencies. National goals support the desire of older adults to remain in their home environment whenever appropriate and possible and encourage the development of a continuum of services to achieve the goal.

A wide range of services under the sponsorship of many different organizations is funded by federal, state, and local governments, as well as by private contributions and fees. Many different professional disciplines are represented in staffing the service delivery. In order to keep the focus of purpose for the system on the older person, greater attention to team relationships and coordination must occur. This coordination includes the linkages and mutual support between the formal and informal systems.

[3] Margaret Blenkner, Martin Bloom, and Margaret Neilson, "A Research and Demonstration Project of Protective Services," *Social Casework,* 52, no. 8 (October 1971), 483-99.
[4] Robert N. Butler and Myrna Lewis, "How to Keep People at Home," *Aging—Mental Health* (St. Louis: C. V. Mosby, 1973), Chapter 10, p. 205.

CHAPTER ELEVEN

SERVING THROUGH INDIRECT ACTIVITIES

Service delivery is usually and easily regarded as direct application of some assistance to individuals or groups in order to meet a need as validated by public or private sources of help. Serving older Americans through indirect activities acknowledges those organizational bodies and operations that create, shape, and support the face-to-face or direct services described in the preceding section.

How these sources of help are created, organized, and function is important. Awareness of policy formulation, laws, guidelines for legislative implementation, and some knowledge of change mechanisms should be part of the helping professional's background. This chapter reviews the historical development and presents those parts of the system not so visible to the recipients of service but certainly a crucial factor for the professional.

Other chapters have dealt extensively with policy development. This chapter focuses on the planning and coordinating mechanisms mandated and promoted by law and private support. The purpose is simply to give some understanding of the operational system behind the direct service delivery of the agencies designated within the formal system.

PLANNING, COORDINATION, AND SERVICE

The Federal Level

The Older Americans Act, first passed in 1965 and amended in 1968, 1973, 1978, 1981, and 1984, provides the blueprint for the indirect activities of a network that covers national, state, and local levels. The legislative process itself can be regarded as an indirect activity serving older Americans when the laws pertain to that age group. The identification of issues or problems, the drafting of legislation, the search for criticism that may lead to change in law, and campaigning among colleagues for support are all tasks to be performed. The process involves not only the elected officials but the professionals who staff the committees. Both national congressional bodies, the House of Representatives and the Senate, have committees related to concerns of the older population. The professionals who staff these committees are responsible for gathering information from a variety of sources. A composite day spent by a staff member of a congressional committee may help illustrate the indirect activities undertaken by those involved in legislative matters.

Monica Bennett found a note on her desk from Congressman Appleby. It said very simply, "Happy Anniversary, I appreciate having the benefit of your work with the committee for all these years." It was a thoughtful gesture and the kind of consideration that helped overcome some of the stresses and frustrations of a job she wouldn't exchange for any other—well, almost any other. She had finished the draft summary of an oversight hearing on employment for older adults the night before and given it to the secretary for typing. It had been a tedious hearing with long, repetitive testimony by the witnesses. Monica reflected on the witnesses she had suggested to the congressman, wondering if a different list of persons might have produced a better-balanced and more complete view of the problems. In addition to staff briefing of factual information and statistics related to whatever the committee agenda covered, the hearings were designed to include various points of view brought by those who gave testimony. She resolved to be sure the next letters of invitation would be sharper about submitting written testimony and presenting a summary at the time of the hearing. Professionals would be more sympathetic to the need for brevity, she thought, but the temptation to give "full" testimony at the hearing was often too compelling even for them.

The secretary gave her several telephone messages, noting one from another congressman wanting information about the status of a bill presently being discussed by the committee. The secretary noted the time the call came in, wondering when a certain congressman who called regularly, even before office hours, "ever slept." Monica chose to make those calls that might be urgent or from the congressman's district, and gathered the materials she needed for the meeting of the full committee scheduled to go over a subcommittee mark-up of a bill and produce a final mark-up. "Would there be coffee this morning?" she wondered. The full report she would write needed to be an accurate reflection of the intent of the committee in relation to the law, and the coffee might help keep her sharp.

In preparation for the meeting, Monica had worked with other staff members to compile facts that were pertinent and had minutely examined the wording of the bill for ambiguity and hidden pitfalls. Staff had "called around" seeking information about opposition to the bill, and she was pleased to report to the congressman that they found very little. "It should be a short session," she thought. She was correct, and the meeting adjourned, work completed, for a late lunch. She ordered coffee first and settled into a discussion, reminiscing with other committee staffers who were celebrating her anniversary date with her. They talked about close calls in committee votes and excellent testimony given by some witnesses in hearings, and teased Monica about the skillful way in which she handled a lobbyist who offered not-so-subtle favors.

Only one item was on the calendar for late afternoon, a meeting with a group of older adults who were concerned about budget cuts affecting the transportation service in the town back home. "Perhaps today I can catch up and return all the calls that have come in," she thought. Each day produced at least a dozen calls from other congressmen and their staffs regarding pending legislation, requests for co-sponsoring resolutions or bills coming up on the floor of the House of Representatives, complaints from lobbyists or representatives of special interest groups seeking commitment for support or no support for bills in which they had an interest, and requests for meetings such as the one later in the afternoon. Most calls completed, Monica headed for the meeting with the older adults. She thought about her reputation of skillful handling of such groups and realized it was rooted in many reasons. Monica really enjoyed older persons. She chuckled as she remembered some who were characterized as difficult. She had made it a point to go beyond the knowledge provided by her political science degree and take some courses on the process of aging and read material in the field to help her understand what the older generation faces. She found the group she was meeting, like most she saw, was made up of a distinctly vocal few who were leaders and the quieter ones who were willing to have the activity centered in the leaders. She felt the challenge and desire to stimulate these to speak.

The group had asked to speak to the congressman, and her first approach was to apologize for his absence. The House of Representatives was in session, and he was needed for an important vote. She hoped she was convincing in giving the facts behind his absence and reassuring in stating the congressman's wish that he could be with them. Monica listened; she had learned that lesson well over the years. It was prompted not just by courtesy but by the realization that the seat of federal government was far from the everyday lives of people. She jotted down a few notes in the meeting, explained the status of a bill that would bring the services the group desired, assured them she would convey their message to the congressman, and urged them to contact other uncommitted legislators.

Returning to her desk, Monica found a message reminding her of a professional association conference and her scheduled meeting with some of the leadership the next day. She debated about writing the report of the meeting she had just had and the record for the congressman. "It would just have to be done tomorrow," she thought. "This evening is mine."

The illustration reveals one of many whose activities indirectly promote service to older adults. The elected official, functioning as a legislative or study committee member, the professional staff of such committees, the citizens who testify at public hearings, the professionals and others who respond to invitations for input on proposed laws, regulations, and guidelines all contribute indirectly.

A different set of activities is carried out at the federal level by the Administration on Aging which was established by the Older Americans Act of 1965. The responsibility of the Administration on Aging to address the needs of the older adult population of the United States requires that it recommend national policy, implement legislation, allocate certain resources, develop linkages with other federal departments, and serve as advocate for the interests of older persons. Ten federal regional offices serve as extended arms of the central office. Direct responsibility for consultation, technical assistance, and monitoring the state units within the region is included in the scope of their responsibility. The following conjecture about a day spent by a deputy commissioner of the federal Administration on Aging illustrates the scope of indirect activity that might be provided by this professional.

Carl Masters takes pride in his many years of service in the federal Administration on Aging. An undergraduate degree in sociology and a master's degree in health education had served well as the political experiences of various level jobs were added. As deputy commissioner, he had shifted job responsibilities to some degree as each commissioner chose to define the sharing of responsibilities with some differences.

Other staff members had secured his promise to see what he could do about night meetings that this particular commissioner was scheduling, more often than not with little notice. Carl was counting on his good relationship with his chief to seek some relief from the practice. It was the first thing on the list he had prepared for the conference with the commissioner that would start his day.

Commissioner Josephson had come to the position with definite ideas of what he would like to see accomplished. The administration's secretary for human services also had an agenda. The two were not always compatible. The deputy was not only aware of the struggle, but knew that the commissioner relied on him to bring factual information into the compromises they hoped the secretary would foster with the present administration. After dealing with the staff concern, and the understanding Carl knew the commissioner would have, they discussed the meals program for older adults. Pressure to change the eligibility requirement of the noon meal in nutrition sites from a contribution by participants to a means test was the issue. Carl brought information from the ten regional offices regarding the amount contributed across the country and the average individual contribution this represented. They reviewed the objectives for the meals program, which had been prepared earlier, and agreed to seek no change in the law or the regulations.

Carl had worked long hours with staff and the office of the assistant secretary of human services on the current regulations. It was not his favorite task. The publishing of regulations always brought protest from someone or some groups. It was impossible to satisfy everyone. The rationale for the current suggested regulations regarding the contribution versus income eligibility would be the main topic of the meeting in the afternoon with the secretary.

Back at his desk, he called the general counsel, ostensibly to remind her of the meeting; but he also used the opportunity to get support for the position decided upon in the meeting he had just left. Two stacks of papers on the desk forced a choice. Telephone messages and letters and reports to be signed were a never-ending chain. The temptation to sign correspondence quickly had to be overcome. The time saved in not carefully reading could allow responses that might be inappropriate or conflict with policy. Oversight was part of the job. The first letter was overdue, and made the choice for him. As he read and signed, he noted on his calendar for the next staff meeting that staff members must be reminded that correspondence to be signed by him or the commissioner needed to be delivered sooner than had been done in the past. Before he had completed the signing, his secretary buzzed his phone. It was a congressional committee staff member. Taking the call, he found it was a request for his personal opinion about a legislative proposal. The committee staff member knew better. It would be risky to give a personal opinion not supported by the administration's policy. As diplomatically as possible he hedged the question.

The unfinished correspondence prompted a refusal to go to lunch with one of the unit staff. Carl ate at his desk, and eventually the letters were ready to go out. Commissioner Josephson, the unit staff member working closest with the meals program, and he went to the meeting together. The commissioner would make the presentation, and he felt somewhat relaxed as he realized his role was that of a listener, observer, and helper supplying answers to questions if needed. The push for an income means test was not strong. The secretary recognized that the contribution method for meals recipients as opposed to a fixed fee based on income was rooted in law. To change it would alter the intent of Congress, and a major battle would have to be waged. Another matter discussed at the meeting centered around the assistant secretary's request for a program initiative related to senior centers and the published regulations mandating qualifications for funding. These qualifications included a seven-day, twenty-four-hour response availability and had opened the floodgates of opposition. It was agreed that these needed revision and relaxation of the time factor.

Carl dropped off the commissioner and staff member and headed for a meeting with the chief of the Farmers Home Administration. As he waited to be seen, he wished he had thought to bring the agreement signed by both the Administration on Aging and the Farmers Home Administration outlining commitments to be mutually supportive. The chief, in true advocacy fashion, was looking for support from AOA in the form of a directive to area agencies to provide extra services to the rural areas. Carl listened. The head of the Farmers Home Administration was someone he respected for his knowledge and experience in the rural housing field. They needed to work together. He decided that cooperation was the strongest approach, and the meeting ended with each making a commitment to send informative directives to reach the local levels. Carl left the meeting satisfied that as much as possible had been accomplished. It was late, and he decided not to go back to the office. Tomorrow would be a day in which he would have to relate to three time periods. On his calendar there was a meeting at the Office of Management and Budget for early discussion of the budget two years ahead, a testimony before Congress on the next year's budget, and a staff conference related to administration of the current year. "Maybe cloning will help the future professionals," he thought as he pulled into his driveway.

These are but two examples of indirect service at the federal level. Other federal departments and private advocacy organizations are also part of the effort behind the face-to-face support provided at the local level. Between the federal and the local levels, two major structures stand out, the state units on aging and the area planning agencies.

State Units on Aging

In addition to establishing the federal Administration on Aging, the Older Americans Act established separate state units. Each state agency is responsible for (1) the development of a state plan, (2) implementation of the plan, (3) a list of priorities for services, (4) designation of planning areas and area agencies on aging in each, (5) advocating on behalf of the older population in the state, and (6) providing technical assistance, training, and monitoring for area agencies.

The compelling reason to create or name a state unit is that no funds from the Older Americans Act can be received by a state without such designation. The Older Americans Act provided states great flexibility in the designation of a state unit. State units can be any governmental body at the state level. The array that has developed shows a wide range from cabinet-level aging department to subunit within a department of human resources to authority given to a state department of social welfare.

A program representative working in a state unit on aging may spend a major portion of time in the field, attempting to insure compliance with the state plan as mandated by the Older Americans Act. In order to understand the professional skills needed for planning and coordination at the state level, one needs to consider some of the activities of one state agency worker.

John McKay has scheduled three days for a site visit to one of the area agencies. In preparation, he has reviewed the area plan, the contracts for services let by the area agency, and the statistical reports of service providers. The first day is spent with area-agency staff. Because of the recent turnover of the chief planner, John McKay includes a session with the new staff member in order to acquaint him with the assistance provided by the state agency. In a session with the full staff, he reviews the relationship of the state unit to the area agency and the scope of responsibility of the area agency and sets a schedule for his future visits. Throughout all the contacts, emphasis is placed on the mutual goals of the state unit and area agency and the kinds of assistance the state staff stand ready to provide.

A portion of the afternoon is devoted to the way in which statistical reports can be used by area-agency staff to monitor service contracts. Training needs for contract staff providing services are identified and possible training leadership suggested. The next day is scheduled for visits to some of the agencies with which the area agency has contracts for service. Included in the schedule is a council on aging providing information and referral, counseling, transportation, and outreach services, a senior center providing a noon meal service and a legal aid agency. Each visit is critiqued with the area-agency planner and/or staff. Possible problem areas and some remedial measures are identified.

A meeting with all the contract representatives in the area has been scheduled at their request. John hears about difficulties the contractors experience when funding checks from the state are late in arriving at the area agency, making subsequent checks to the service providers also late. He promises to consult with the state's fiscal officer and recommend earlier mailing of checks. His last conference at the area agency includes not only the aging staff, but the executive director of the agency that sponsors the area agency. Most of the time is spent on securing agreement about what is meant by advocacy and how the area agency can comply.

The head of a state unit would have a very different schedule. A day for this professional might also be spent out of the office but would be related to state-level planning and coordination.

Assistant Secretary of Human Resources Evelyn Pyler was appointed by the governor to head the Division of Aging. On this day, she stops by the office briefly to check the mail, read over the suggested proclamation for Older Americans Month being sent to the governor, instruct her secretary to secure plane and hotel reservations for the National Association of State Units on Aging Conference, route a letter received in the mail complaining about conditions in a nursing home to the nursing home ombudsman on staff, and approve the final copy of a brochure on homemaker/home health aide services to be used across the state. She is late for the meeting of the Study Committee on Aging of the state senate, and mentally notes the importance of speaking to the chairperson after the meeting to soften the irritation he will have at her lateness.

The meeting focuses on the mandatory retirement of state employees, and Evelyn has been invited to testify. Her material is factual, showing what other states have done and the results of abolishing the policy of mandatory retirement at any age. After the meeting, the conversation with the committee chairperson includes his compliment on her presentation, and she is assured that any irritation at her lateness is overcome. She leaves the meeting room with the legislative representative of the American Association for Retired Persons, who proposes that a plan for advocacy for older persons include a "silver-haired legislature" program that his organization had tried successfully in another state. Essentially, older adults would serve as state senators and representatives in a mock congressional session. They make a date to talk further after Evelyn receives material the AARP representative promises to mail.

Lunch is to be all business. The state legislature had passed a bill making it possible to use school buses to transport older persons when they were not in use for the children. Despite the enabling law, no arrangements for the use of the buses had resulted. Lunch with the director of the state department of education was designed to provide an atmosphere conducive to cooperation. Evelyn believes that the department head could be influential in gaining local agreements for the sharing of the vehicles. The meeting took an interesting turn, and one she did not foresee. In addition to the reluctance to share the vehicles, it appeared that the financial consideration of insurance was a barrier for all communities. She resented the arrogant and condescending manner in which she was being treated and struggled to hold back the sarcasm that surfaced in retaliation to the frustration. She realized that part of the problem was her own lack of preparation for the meeting, and she had to bear the blame for it. The meeting ended as well as she could expect, with each one promising to seek a way to overcome the financial roadblock. Leaving the restaurant, she bought an afternoon paper to see if it contained the news release about her appointment to an advisory committee on aging for one of the foundations located in the state. She was delighted not only with the appointment, but with the fact that the foundation was, in fact, committing attention to aging concerns. She hoped, and even expected it would bring financial support.

The afternoon schedule included a meeting of the advisory committee to the department of aging followed by a staff conference with the coordinator of training. The advisory committee went smoothly. The chairperson had been in the office the day before to make up the final agenda and be briefed on the various items. A lengthy discussion of the need for preretirement programs resulted in a recommendation for the development of a state-wide plan for promotion of this kind of training within business and industry. In anticipation of this recommendation, Evelyn had scheduled the staff conference with the training coordinator.

The advisory committee chairperson joined the conference session, suggesting that a subcommittee of the advisory committee be the structure for developing a plan. The three formulated the subcommittee charge or purpose statement and talked about subcommittee membership. The training coordinator pointed out how important it would be to include representatives from industry so that it might be easier to implement the plan once it was developed. This led to a discussion of the qualities that would be desirable in the subcommittee's chairperson. All agreed on a person from the advisory committee who was not part of industry or of training but who would promote discussion and move the deliberations along by a periodic summary of recommendations. The day ended with the advisory committee chairperson and the secretary dividing the list to be called for appointment to the subcommittee and the training coordinator accepting responsibility for staffing the subcommittee and immediately beginning to gather material on preretirement training.

These two examples point up some of the activities carried out by state-level staff professionals. The benefit of these indirect activities to older adults is found in the enriched service provided, not only to those older adults with problems, but to the total older population in the state. Those who serve at this level include the elected officials and their professional staff members, the state unit on aging staff and board or advisory committee members, and other state departments with which the state unit forms linkages.

Area Agencies

The 1973 amendments to the Older Americans Act created regional planning bodies, called area agencies, prohibited from providing direct services without documentation of the lack of any feasible way to contract for those services.

State units are responsible for selecting and designating area agencies. Any agency or organization, public or private nonprofit, may be chosen. Minimum size is stipulated by guidelines calling for at least 100,000 persons in the planning area. Large metropolitan areas can, and some have, set up a mix of agency types. Thirteen states have received approval for the whole state to be designated as the planning area. Other states have elected to group counties, often following a previously established geographic division for planning related to physical planning concerns such as land use, water conservation, housing, and so on.

The area agency is responsible for (1) assessing the needs of older adults in the area, (2) setting priorities for services, (3) focusing the awarding of grants and contracts for social and nutrition services on older persons with the greatest economic and social need, (4) planning and coordination of existing services, (5) development of new services, (6) acting as advocate on behalf of the older adult population in the service area, (7) providing technical assistance, training and monitoring for service providers in the area, and (8) designating "focal points" for service delivery.

The area agency must submit a plan to the state agency, which sets forth goals and objectives to be met during a three-year period and the steps to be taken to achieve these goals. Objectives are set, not only for service provision to be achieved by contracts, but for area-wide activities such as specific training for staff in service-providing agencies.

Assessing the needs of older adults in the area can be and is done in a variety of ways by different area agencies. The simplest and probably least reliable is the public-hearing method. An announcement is made of date, time, and place for those who wish to present problems and their ideas of what is needed to assist the older population to enjoy more satisfying lives. Staff attend as "listeners," compiling the information into a priority listing to be used for planning. More objective methods of community needs assessment techniques have developed. One such technique is the nominal group process, in which a select group randomly lists areas of need and reviews them several times to rank the needs and produce a final prioritized list. More sophisticated techniques involve prior identification of a list of barriers or situations producing problems and the current incidence of the problem. A series of rankings and group consensus scores produce a priority listing. In all instances, the assessment technique includes the older adult as the major character in the decision process.

The area agencies are the conduit for funds allocated under Title III-B and III-C of the Older Americans Act to reach the service-provision level. In order to satisfy the responsibility to see that these funds are used to benefit the economically and socially needy, the area agency must devise plans to identify where that population is and what needs must be met. Statistics showing demographic information about population areas should include numbers of older adults whose income is at or below the poverty level, the numbers living alone, the amount of substandard housing, and the percentage of minority residents.

Planning and coordination of services starts with needs assessment and priority setting. The coordination mandate stems from Congress' concern for the ability of older adults to negotiate a service delivery system that is made up of so many different agencies that it is difficult to know which may be the one to respond to the specific need presented by an older adult. In an effort to overcome this barrier to service accessibility, area agencies are charged with identifying all agencies mandated to provide services to older adults in the area and must work to pool these resources into a comprehensive service package. Contracts for the funds administered by the area agency are lent to organizations in order to fill gaps in the array of needed services or to expand the quantity of service available.

Advocacy is easily understood when one person assists another, as with a worker pleading a case for a client whose disability checks have been terminated. It is more difficult to define how a worker in an agency involved in indirect service to older adults performs as an advocate. Committees formed as part of the area-agency structure provide opportunities for advocacy. When representatives from other agencies or resources are included as committee members, their involvement in activities, whether planning or implementing plans, promotes the interests of older adults. For example, an area agency committee on employment that includes not only a representative from the state employment or job service, but personnel directors from key industries and business, brings the needs of older adults for jobs and benefits to the attention of employers who hire them. In another instance, a group of health professionals are brought together for the primary purpose of working on an informational series of presentations about chronic diseases. The focus on older adults and the greater visibility of their health needs results in more attention for the older age group as these professionals go back to their own agencies. Encouraging a variety of ways to celebrate Older Americans Month by local agencies, presenting certificates of appreciation to media members who produce positive images of older adults and help publicize events of interest to or involving older persons, appearing before local funding sources such as city or county officials and United Way budget committees to help local service providers secure funds, and arranging for older adults to give testimony at public hearings are some other examples of advocacy activities.

Monitoring of service contracts that have been awarded by the area agency is part of the work required throughout the aging network to assure accountability. Area agency staff periodically review the progress toward contract goals and implementation plans with the contractors. Technical assistance in the form of suggestions for improving both the quality and quantity of performance may be a part of the monitoring visit. In instances where more than one contractor may show a need for skill development or advice on method of operation, training can be scheduled.

The Older Americans Act charges area agencies with the designation of "focal points" for services and stipulates that senior centers be designated where "feasible." This activity strengthens the ability of the area agency to realize a higher level of coordination of services within its planning jurisdiction. Reactions to the provision in law for service focal point designation is mixed. Guidelines originally published the criteria for designation, but after they were protested, they finally emerged with such ambiguity that lack of uniformity has resulted. Use of phrases like "in each community" and "colocation of services" without defining "community" or "colocation" brought a variety of interpretations. Despite the confusion experienced by the area agencies and service providers, methods for determining where designations are warranted, based on criteria developed by the area agency, have resulted in an increase in the visibility and access to service provision.

A composite day for an area agency planner might start with a staff meeting. The planning area is multicounty, with a population of 60,000 older persons over age sixty. Three professional staff carry the responsibilities, and each performs a variety of tasks. The major part of the staff meeting deals with finalizing the criteria for focal point designation to be presented to the advisory committee for approval. Material such as the wording in law and guidelines from the federal administration on aging is consulted to make sure that the criteria comply with these requirements. In addition, the recommendations of a subcommittee of the advisory committee are checked to be sure that they are included. The quarterly statistics showing the number of persons served by the service contractors are reviewed. Weaknesses such as failure to meet projected goals of minority participation and a drop in the average financial contribution made by those receiving services are noted for investigation. A date is set for the public hearing on the revised area plan, and responsibility for issuing a news release about it is assigned to one of the staff.

The area agency planner rushes off to attend a meeting involving selected area planners in the state, to discuss the state-wide conference to be held as a multi-tracked training session for professionals and lay leaders of service-providing agencies. The hour's trip gives him time to formulate the basic points of a letter to a disgruntled older adult who claims that services are being denied to her. The meeting lasts through lunch, which gives an opportunity to talk with other planners about the process they are using for focal point designation. The conversations are reassuring in that other regions have not found their advisory committees as helpful in setting criteria or in willingness to be team members in site visits to facilities requesting focal point designation.

On returning to the office, the planner finds a backlog of calls, which he returns. A contractor has not received the monthly check, a county commissioner wants to know if the purchase of vehicles is allowable under the contract for services, a student wants an interview and a possible placement in the area agency, and a United Way community planning director wants a copy of the needs assessment process, results, and priorities. Signing letters and dictating a reply to the complaining older adult and a letter to service contractors pointing out the drop in contributions are hurriedly completed. The day ends with a meeting with the advisory committee chairperson to complete the agenda for the next meeting of the committee. Part of the meeting is devoted to a briefing about agenda items and a discussion of vacancies on the committee.

For almost ten years after the area-planning level was created, tension existed between the state units and area agencies. The national associations related to these two levels, the National Association of State Units on Aging (NASUA) and National Association of Area Agencies on Aging (N4A), have worked together at the national level to bring closer understanding and cooperation. By 1981, state units had relinquished most direct contact with service providers. State units now hold area agencies responsible for needs assessments that determine priorities for service in their area, a service plan, contracting with service providers, monitoring contracts, forming linkages with noncontracting agencies, and using the advisory committee technique to gain representative input into all aspects of the area agencies' operation.

THE SENIOR CENTER AS A FOCAL POINT

The senior center occupies a unique place in the aging network. As a concept, it is a service delivery technique that satisfies the need for better access to services and is therefore part of the indirect services category. As an operating mechanism, it is a service provider of many of the face-to-face services. Senior centers started and grew as a natural support system for older adults. At present the number is estimated to be over 8,000. They present a complex profile.

Historically the early centers of the 1940s and 1950s were membership-based, with a strong organizational allegiance by members. In 1973, the amendments to the Older Americans Act included a separate title for nutrition programs. Contracts for nutrition programs were seldom let to traditional agencies such as health departments or social welfare agencies that were not equipped to handle this kind of group service. Some senior centers welcomed the expansion of their food services; others shied away in fear of intrusion by federal regulations and the inclusion of a poor or needy population. Nutrition sites sprang up, partially as a result of the indifference or rejection of some existing senior centers, but also because area agencies perceived that a system started by them would be easier to administer and control. The aging network at every level, federal, state, area planning agency, and local service delivery, would struggle with this problem of senior centers and nutrition sites duplicating services and competing for a client population. In many areas of the country the struggle continues; in others the 1978 amendments to the Older Americans Act, which not only mandated area agencies to designate "focal points" but stipulated that senior centers be designated where "feasible," has brought greater coordination and cooperation. The picture is even more complex when close examination shows that some senior centers may be club groups or providers of one service such as recreation, and some nutrition sites have quite complete programs going far beyond meal or nutrition education provision.

Beginning in the early 1970s, senior center field practitioners and professionals concerned with the development of a meaningful response to the total needs of the total older population began work on the development of a philosophy, a definition, and standards for the senior center. Through the National Institute of Senior Centers of the National Council on the Aging, a senior center concept was developed. This concept is related to a geographic service area, as opposed to a closed membership base, with the promise of involvement of older persons as decision makers, paid and volunteer staff, participants in activities, and recipients of services. The concept also includes the responsibility of providing the other agencies in the service delivery system a way to extend services to older adults in a more accessible and acceptable way.

The following examples show some of the variety of people a center might serve.

> Mr. X's blood pressure is taken each week and recorded on a card shown to his doctor at his regular appointment. He began having difficulty with his hearing but was fearful of going to a new clinic. An appointment was arranged by the center, and he was escorted to the clinic, where his problem was solved.

> Mrs. Y has Alzheimer's disease and is often confused. But with the center's help she lives at home, is picked up each morning, spends the day under supervision, and is returned to her home at night. This service enables her to stay in the community and out of a mental hospital or nursing home.

> Mrs. Z, a retired teacher, is a diabetic who spends each weekday with her new friend, a former household worker, sharing common diet information during their noon meal at the center.

> Mrs. R is losing her sight. She now reads large-print books from the rotating collection in the center, but she knows that a cassette and tapes will be available to her if and when her sight is completely gone.

> Mrs. K has suffered a stroke and lives alone. Three times a week an aide arrives at her house to do household chores, help her with the exercises prescribed by her doctor, shop for groceries, and pay bills. The aide was trained for two months and is supervised by professional center staff.

> Mr. H is fifty-six years old, retired because of disability from a job that was not covered by social security. His disability is not sufficient to meet eligibility requirements for Supplemental Security Income. The center employed him

as a community services staff worker, which enabled him to be covered by social security.

Mrs. L's father, who had a stroke, lives with her. She attended a center workshop for families of stroke victims and found answers to questions that she had hesitated to ask busy health professionals. She also found she was not alone in the frustrations and swing of emotions that she experiences about her father. Her gratitude has encouraged her to start a support group that meets regularly.

There are also those who play cards. Mr. and Mrs. F attend regularly. Although Mrs. F is in a wheelchair, she has no problem in getting to the game because a van with a hydraulic lift transports them to the center.

Mr. J is a daily morning coffee customer. He arrives at 8:30 and waits for his friends and the coffee. Each Monday he brings some milk just in case the milkman may be late. He quietly informs the early arrivals that there is milk for their coffee. Here, then, is a man who again feels useful. His need to be a "giver" is satisfied as he receives other benefits. The relationship of interdependence, which is a comfortable feeling, is mutually acknowledged.

There are the sixty-year-old women who attended Women's Health Day and learned the technique of breast self-examination and discussed body awareness, and sexuality.

There are the representatives from twenty-seven club groups who marched down Main Street to celebrate Older Americans' month, and the hundreds of older adults who have appeared at public hearings reacting to state, area, and local plans for funding aging programs or protesting rate increases in services no longer regarded as luxuries.

There are those who attend yearly forums on such topics as transportation, housing, nutrition, benefits, and services, and in doing so, establish a dialogue between the older adults and service providers.[1]

The National Institute of Senior Centers of the National Council on the Aging has adopted the following definition.

Definition of a Senior Center

A Senior Center is a community focal point on aging where older persons as individuals or in groups come together for services and activities which enhance their dignity, support their independence and encourage their involvement in and with the community. As part of a comprehensive community strategy to meet the needs of older persons, Senior Center programs take place within and emanate from a facility. These programs consist of a variety of services and activities in such areas as education, creative arts, recreation, advocacy, leadership development, employment, health, nutrition, social work

[1]The Senior Center Role in Serving the At-Risk Older Person, NCOA/NISC Seminar, January 7, 1980, Washington, D.C.

and other supportive services. The Center also serves as a community resource for information on aging, for training professional and lay leadership
and for developing new approaches to aging programs.

Several points need emphasis. The center is not a service in the traditional use
of the word. It exists as a mechanism whereby services are provided in such a way
as to afford the older adult greater access to them. The center thus cannot be classi-
fied as a group service, since its program could include such services to individuals
as information and referral; counseling related to health, employment, income, legal
matters, and personal problems; transportation; health care from screening services
to clinic primary care and so on.

The center should be regarded as serving a designated service-area population
that includes all older persons whether they are to come to the center or need services that are part of the center package but delivered outside the facility. Such
services could include home-delivered meals, homemaker/home health aide services,
home repair, friendly visiting, shopping escort, and so on.

Obviously, the senior center concept presents the possibility of the highest
level of coordination of services, excluding only those that represent residential
treatment, such as hospitals, nursing homes, and mental institutions. One factor
that makes the senior center so desirable as a coordinating mechanism is that
through colocation of services no existing agencies are undermined, but rather these
agencies are actually supported and brought into a complementing package that enhances the ability of the other agencies to fulfill their mandate. Furthermore, the
senior center can add economy and efficiency to its reasons for attracting cooperation from other agencies.

A look at what the chief staff member of a senior center might include as part
of the workload will help to show the dual responsibility of a center relating to indirect and direct service delivery.

The director of a senior center finds great variety in each day. The head of a
center might start the day at breakfast with a local legislator who has agreed to
champion a request for additional funds to provide the local match for federal dollars available to purchase vehicles. In anticipation, the worker has prepared information related to the federal requirements and the limits of what can be done with
the money, the report of a public hearing on needs as expressed by the older adults,
existing resources in the worker's agency and others, and a projection of what
impact the expansion of service will have. The meeting ends with a date to be present at the meeting when the legislator will introduce the request. By agreement with
the legislator, the director will bring several older adults to the meeting.

After checking the schedule of activities for the day, reinforcing instructions
to the maintenance worker and several volunteers helping to arrange rooms as required by the schedule, a telephone call is made to the chair of the center advisory
committee, presenting a report of the breakfast meeting and the need to identify
appropriate older adults to attend the meeting. Together they discuss who might be
best to include, and the chairperson agrees to contact persons and report back.

The receptionist has a list of calls that have come in while the director was busy. Calls are returned to the following individuals: the health department nurse who wishes to be sure there will be a projector set up for the film on diabetes she will show at the beginning of her regular weekly group session; the daughter of a seventy-two-year-old center participant who was hospitalized and ready to be discharged; the area agency planner, who wishes to set a date for monitoring the contract for noon meal service; and a center participant who is complaining about the personal hygiene of another participant.

The assurance to the public health nurse that the projector will be ready gives the director an opportunity to discuss the evaluation of the educational sessions and a report to the board of directors covering not only the sessions but the individual health counseling, periodic health screening on various aspects of need such as foot, eye, and mouth examinations, and also the family of stroke victims support group shared by the nurse and director as a team.

The daughter of a center participant is concerned about placing her mother in a nursing home. The hospital has a social services department and the referral is made to the hospital worker. The daughter is given general information about services that might be used if it is thought possible for her mother to receive the care she needs at home. The contact is noted on a daily log of information and referral services, with a date for a follow-up call set.

The conversation with the area agency planner moves into a discussion of area-wide training for staff and current legislation being proposed at the state level. A legislative study committee is scheduling hearings, and the need for input directly related to the law is resolved by an agreement to continue talking after the director sees the piece of legislation being proposed. The conversation ends with the area planner reporting the results of the service-needs assessment done for the coming year and the priorities set for the area.

The call to the participant sets a commitment for discussion of the issue raised after the noon lunch the next day. The director recognizes the emotional depth of the complaint and the need for support without compromising values of acceptance of differences. A call is made to the public health nurse to check on what direct experience she has had with the reportedly offensive person. Registration records showing family, health information, and scope of participation in center activities are reviewed for both the complainer and person complained about.

After lunch, a conference with the bookkeeper covers a review of the current level of expenditures and reveals a need for budget changes that must be presented to the board of directors for approval. The change is a simple shift from one line item to another, and they decide it can be presented orally with a blackboard used for the amounts involved. The conference ends with the approval of mileage reimbursement for volunteers, who transport participants to medical appointments in their own cars, and the signing of checks for approved budget items.

The director slips into a meeting of a club group which schedules their monthly meetings at the center. During the meeting, the president of the club asks for information about the status of a piece of federal legislation. After the meeting, a commitment is made by the center director to make a formal presentation about federal and state legislation at the next meeting.

SENIOR CENTER STANDARDS AND PHILOSOPHY

The challenge of achieving quality performance by center staff in carrying out the definition of a center was accepted by the National Institute of Senior Centers of the National Council on the Aging. Work on a set of standards to be used as a guideline for performance was begun.

The Senior Center Standards, as a document, includes a definition of a senior center, a statement of philosophy, nine principles or ideals to be achieved, explanatory background pieces related to the principles, and the standards statements divided into the nine areas. The purpose of the standards is to explain and communicate the basic concepts and practices the senior center field believes to be important in the establishment and ongoing operation of that system known as senior centers. They were intended for voluntary use to promote and guide effective operation.

The standards identified the following eight major areas: purpose, organization, community relations, program administration and personnel, fiscal management, records and reports, facility, and evaluation.

Principles were developed as the first step in the task to be accomplished. Each of the major areas grew out of a statement of a principle. For example, the first of the nine principles states: "A Senior Center shall have a written statement of its purposes consistent with the Senior Center Philosophy and a written statement of its goals based on its purposes and on the needs and interests of older people in its service area. These statements shall be used to govern the character and direction of its operation and program."[2] Based on this statement, the standards themselves specify how those involved may proceed to attain the idea expressed.

This first principle, related to *purpose* of a senior center, refers to a philosophy. The existence of such a philosophy, although articulated in fragments or various forms, was crucial to the successful completion of universal standards. The philosophy, from which the principles and standards statements flowed, had to exist if there was to be any commonality in the field. The senior center field developed over many years. It grew opportunistically with meager funding available in many instances not growing to potential because of lack of funding and the lack of leadership skill and the understanding of good programming, sound practices, and administration.

Despite the differences in size, services, activities, sponsorship, and quality of management, the basic philosophy existed. It is now a recorded one to which all can refer. The philosophy clearly affirms a belief in the capability of older adults to be involved as decision makers. The philosophy recognizes the humaneness and

[2] "Senior Center Standards: Guidelines for Practice," NCOA/NISC, June 1978.

vulnerability that older adults share with persons of all ages. The philosophy challenges staff and leadership of centers to create and maintain a climate responsive both to the skills and capabilities of older adults and to their need for assistance on occasion. The philosophy projects the senior center as a social utility—needed, wanted, and supported by our society.

The principle related to the purpose of a senior center recognizes that despite the universal philosophy, the *exact* purpose of any one center may differ from that of another. The notion of a designated service area is important to create the identity of a center as responsive to a population that can be clearly described. Just as designated service-area populations may differ, so may a center's purpose. The standards make no attempt to say what that exact purpose should be. Consistent with the intent of the standards to communicate practices believed to be important to quality, program, and management, the standards stipulate that the purpose of a center should be written, consistent with the senior center philosophy, developed by board, staff, and participants, in a form suitable for distribution, reviewed regularly in a way that involves participants, and modified as appropriate. Standards related to other areas, such as facility and program, are handled in a similar way to those related to a center's purpose.

State and area agencies have used the senior center concept, including the standards, as a basis for developing focal point criteria. The future of senior centers as focal points, providing one type of access point to services, cannot be predicted. At this time, there is no parallel for coordination of direct services and, with already limited resources for human services diminishing, it seems unlikely that any significant replacement for the senior center, as projected in the existing standards, will emerge. Serving older Americans goes beyond care given in the informal and formal networks—beyond the information, maintenance, and intervention services. To serve older adults is to work for greater understanding of leisure, need for productivity, and desire for involvement in community affairs from the unique perspective of the older adult, for most of whom the workplace is absent. To serve older adults is to help them build and then support social and health institutions that satisfy their unique needs. The senior center is one such institution. The Older Americans Act amendments of 1981 stipulate the designation of focal points for service delivery and recognize the importance of building on the network of senior centers that older adults and their advocates developed over many years.

SUMMARY

In reviewing the aging network that is composed of federal, state, and area agencies engaging in indirect activities of planning and coordination to achieve heightened service delivery, both in quantity and quality, the place for professionals is clear. Professionals from many disciplines are found in the network. The social work profession is quite visible. In 1981, President Reagan appointed Dr. Lennie-Marie Tolliver as Commissioner of the Administration on Aging. Dr. Tolliver resigned a faculty position at the University of Oklahoma School of Social Work to accept the appointment. Deputy to Dr. Tolliver is Gene Handelsman, a graduate of the Tulane University School of Social Work, with many years of experience in the social welfare field. In at least one of the ten federal regions, the director of aging is a social worker with a professional degree. Frank Nicholson, in Region IV based in Atlanta, heads a staff whose knowledge in the administration of a human service program must be of the highest capability.

Activities necessary to the planning and coordination mandates carried out by professionals at the federal, state, and area agency levels bring professionals into a variety of tasks including gathering of information, negotiation, advocacy, staffing committees, making assessments of older population needs, identifying and pooling resources to be used in service delivery, and monitoring and evaluating each level of activity in the network. The unique role of the senior center, as developed by recent standards, provides service-level coordination that combines older adults as decision makers, paid and unpaid staff, participants in activities, and recipients of services.

CHAPTER TWELVE

THE WORKING WORLD OF THE PROFESSIONAL PERSON

Serving older adults challenges each professional person. Every professional person will bring special helping skills into the service of older people, but something more is needed. The particular helping skills of each profession must be refined with respect to the particular ways of older adults. Perhaps more than anything else, professional people must approach the challenge of serving older people with reformed attitudes about older people and what is necessary to bring services to them. This text presents materials by which professional helping efforts can become uniquely suited to serving older adults.

The foregoing chapters identify many of the special circumstances of older people that professional people must recognize in their practice. Economically, older people are at a great disadvantage compared with the rest of the population. Their financial resources are limited and often locked into homes and other non-liquid assets. The economic mainstays for most older people are their homes and their social security checks. Yet despite these similarities, older people do not constitute a homogeneous group. Instead, cohorts of older people can be identified with respect to their exposure to life-shaping circumstances. For some older people economic security is most important, but for others closeness to family and friends may take precedence in their lives. As a result, all professional persons must evaluate carefully the total personal and social context of the older person before proceeding with professional assistance. In this view, promoting the quality of life becomes the crucial factor in helping older people.

Theories about aging have become more sophisticated in the past two decades. Earlier theories that emphasized the developmental processes of life tended to explain aging as a stage of life at the end of the line. But as social, psychological, and medical knowledge has expanded, reformulated theories of how people grow old are more frequent. Theories about aging now tell us that aging is not a chronological event, nor is aging necessarily a biological event either. Whereas there may be a maximum life span, there is increasing evidence that this maximum age does not have to be reached through a series of progressive physical, emotional, and social decay. Undoubtedly as knowledge increases even greater emphasis will be placed upon the healthy aspects of aging. Biogenetic research is moving rapidly to a point where the eradication of the diseases of aging will be a serious possibility.

Already the vast majority of all older people are living independently, taking care of themselves, and by most measures, living "normal" lives. Of course many older people live with physical or emotional conditions that are disabling in one way or another, but they are able to manage these conditions successfully. Understanding these things, professionals give service to older people that emphasizes a caring strategy. The philosophy behind emerging public policy stresses maintaining older people in their own homes and communities. This philosophy is entirely consistent with an emphasis on quality of life, which comes from an appreciation of the diversity of older adulthood. The philosophy is also consistent with the direction of emerging theory and the fact that the great majority of older people live at home.

Public policies on behalf of older people have contributed to new theoretical perspectives on aging and a greater public awareness that age and health do not define older adulthood. Older people have struggled for and obtained a wide range of public policies and programs that provide protection to older people during post-retirement years. As a group, older people are extremely active politically. Perhaps because many older people have firsthand political experience as politicians or as program administrators, older people are alert to the opportunities for shaping public policy to meet their needs. The political sophistication among older adults has been developed slowly and within a climate of changing family responsibility for the well-being of elders. Thus greater shares of public resources have been required as a response to smaller family units, greater geographic mobility, and decreases in intergenerational networks of mutual care.

Somewhat in contrast with the White House Conferences on Children and Youth, the White House Conferences on Aging have provided an important political platform for the review and development of policy for older people. The 1981 conference illustrated dramatically the ability of the older adult population to withstand institutionalized forms of political power. In this respect, the politicization of the older adult population represents an important democratizing force in American public life. The Older Americans Act is a reflection of policies designed to keep older people within the mainstream of American life. Despite such successes, however, older people still do not receive a "fair share" of the public resources.

Political, social, and economic ways of understanding older people are complicated by the beliefs held about older people. These beliefs produce stereotypical responses by professional helpers and public policies, and programs are limited in their efforts to bring effective services to older people. In spite of new understandings about older people and often because of new understandings, belief patterns persist in American society that may contribute to shabby treatment of older people. If, for example, a "work ethic" were promoted exclusive of other beliefs, older people would be in worse financial circumstances than presently. Likewise if a belief in "survival of the fittest" were promoted freely, many public policies would be less humane than they are. Professional ethics must be applied with respect to making choices as to how older people should be served.

Despite belief systems that might have restricted the development of effective public programs, the scope of public resources available for older people is impressive. Almost all older Americans collect social security, and some sort of income maintenance assistance is available for all elderly. These resources added to medical assistance, housing, and a wide range of supporting social services have produced a backdrop of public support that offers encouragement for professional persons in their service efforts. Often the helping activity is simplified when the proper resources can be brought into play with the problem the older person is experiencing. Knowing what programs exist and how they can be utilized is an important professional responsibility.

The better understanding of older people and a firm grasp of the resources that can be used to assist them must be brought together into some helping approaches that complement the specialized helping skills of individual professionals. The most important helping skills are those involved in working with the informal social support systems of each older person and working with the formal network of services provided through public and private sources. With respect to the social support system, professionals who work with older people have developed skills in effective identification and management of the resources available from family, friends, and community social networks. With respect to the formal network of services, professional workers have developed skills of case management and teamwork in bringing resources together in support of older people.

These professional skills come together most effectively in the specialized tasks of assessment and helping when the professional worker carries out activities in a cooperative relationship with the older person, rather than doing to or doing for the older adult. The senior center most often acts as a focal point for these helping activities. Because of its flexibility, the senior center extends the professional helping network to a wide range of older people and their needs. A philosophy of developing a system of care for older people pervades the specialized application of professional helping activities.

THE UNFINISHED AGENDA FOR SERVING OLDER ADULTS

The commitments that a nation makes to its citizens are only as meaningful as its national policies and programs. Any nation, and any government, undertakes obligations to its citizens. These commitments are expressed frequently in national mottoes and symbols. In the inscription on the Statue of Liberty, for example, America asks for the tired, the poor, the "huddled masses yearning to be free" and offers a "golden door" to those who come. The Constitution of the United States promises to "promote the general welfare." Such statements of national intent exceed accomplishments when measured by social products for older people legally assumed in national statutes. Despite the impressive strides in development of policy and progress to support professional helping efforts, the resources fall short of realizing public promises.

More ironic still, the American dreams reflected by these symbols are being challenged at precisely the time when the "American Dream" is being exported around the world and reemphasized at home. The development of income support and social and medical services for older people all represent hard-fought public achievements. Social security, Medicare and Medicaid, and the Older Americans Act were achieved from constant activities by persons committed to realizing the lofty ideals America has set for itself. But during the past five years, the very fabric of these important national commitments has become frayed, and the whole cloth may be in danger of unraveling. While these affronts to national commitments for older people have been blamed on the current economic misfortunes, the following discussion suggests the extent to which America presently rewards its wealthy at the expense of the poor and expands its military might at the expense of its domestic needs.

Measuring the National Commitment to Older Adults

A recent analysis of shifting priorities by the Congressional Budget Office offers sobering evidence of the shift in national priorities away from domestic commitments to the most needy. As Table 12-1 shows, shifts in national spending priorities have reduced overall spending most severely among the lower-income population groups. Table 12-2 shows that the national spending reductions have affected most severely those programs that serve older people. Thus the average 30 percent reduction in domestic spending since 1980 produces a double shock for many older people.

The aggregate impact on the aged of this national retreat is reflected in the recent hearings on public assistance and poverty conducted by the Ways and Means Committee of the United States House of Representatives. The striking fact about the data presented in Table 12-3 is how quickly the amount of poverty has increased, particularly among older Americans. Considering the length of time it took to reduce poverty in this country, the outlook for a quick reversal of these dismal statistics is bleak indeed.

But as dismal a view as these data on public spending and poverty present, a more insidious problem is emerging with respect to national commitments to older people. Although it cannot be demonstrated statistically, there is a growing mood among this nation's leaders that government has gone too far in its efforts to secure reality for America's lofty ideals. There has always been healthy debate about the

TABLE 12-1   Projected Changes in Federal Outlays Resulting from Legislative Actions for Selected Human Resource Programs.

PROGRAMS	TOTAL OUTLAY CHANGES, 1982–1985, RESULTING FROM LEGISLATIVE ACTIONS	
	IN BILLIONS OF DOLLARS	AS A PERCENT OF PROGRAM OUTLAYS a/
Retirement and Disability		
Social security b/	−24.1	− 3
Civil service retirement c/	− 2.5	− 3
Veterans' pensions and compensation	− 0.6	− 1
SSI	+ 1.4	+ 4
Other Income Security		
Unemployment insurance	− 7.8	− 7
AFDC d/	− 4.8	−13
Food stamps	− 7.0	−13
Child nutrition e/	− 5.2	−28
WIC f/	+ 0.2	+ 4
Housing assistance g/	− 1.8	− 4
Low income energy assistance	− 0.7	− 8
Health		
Medicare	−13.2	− 5
Medicaid	− 3.9	− 5
Other health services h/	− 1.4	−22
Education and Social Services		
Compensatory education	− 2.6	−17
Vocational education	− 0.6	−12
Head start	i/	j/
Guaranteed student loans	− 3.8	−27
Other student financial assistance	− 2.1	−13
Community services block grant	− 1.0	−39
Social services block grant	− 2.9	−22
Veterans' readjustment benefits	− 0.7	−10
Employment and Training		
General employment and training	− 7.4	−35
Job corps	− 0.1	− 6
Public service employment	−16.9	−99
Work incentive program	− 0.6	−33

Source: Congressional Budget Office, "Memorandum to House Ways and Means Committee" (Washington, August 1983), 27.

appropriate role of government in promoting social objectives. In great measure, differences in opinion about the responsibility of government have been decided issue by issue. Social security, medical insurance, and social services have been raised as issues over which debates have been conducted and conclusions reached.

TABLE 12-2 Poverty Rates and Numbers of People in Poverty for Selected Demographic Groups Over Time.

	1959	1966	1970	1975	1978	1979	1980	1981	1982
Overall number in poverty (in thousands)	39,490	28,510	25,420	25,877	24,497	26,072	29,272	31,822	34,398
Poverty rate (percent)	22.4	14.7	12.6	12.3	11.4	11.7	13.0	14.0	15.0
Aged:									
Number (in thousands)	5,481	5,114	4,709	3,317	3,233	3,682	3,871	3,853	3,751
Poverty rate (percent)	35.2	28.5	24.5	15.3	14.0	15.2	15.7	15.3	14.6
Children:									
Number (in thousands)	17,208	12,146	10,235	10,882	9,722	9,993	11,114	12,068	13,139
Poverty rate (percent)	26.9	17.4	14.9	16.8	15.7	16.0	17.9	19.5	21.3
Nonaged adults:									
Number (in thousands)	16,801	11,250	10,476	11,678	11,542	12,397	14,287	15,901	17,508
Poverty rate (percent)		10.6	9.2	9.4	8.9	9.1	10.3	11.3	12.3
Individuals in female headed families:									
Number (in thousands)	10,390	10,250	11,154	12,268	12,880	13,503	14,649	15,738	16,336
Poverty rate (percent)	50.2	41.0	38.2	34.6	32.3	32.0	33.8	35.2	36.2
Blacks:									
Number (in thousands)	9,927	8,867	7,548	7,545	7,625	8,050	8,579	9,173	9,697
Poverty rate (percent)	55.1	41.8	33.5	31.3	30.6	31.0	32.5	34.2	35.6
Whites:									
Number (in thousands)	28,484	19,290	17,484	17,770	16,259	17,214	19,699	21,553	23,517
Poverty rate (percent)	18.1	11.3	9.9	9.7	8.7	9.0	10.2	11.1	12.0

Source: U.S. Congress, House of Representatives, "Background Material on Poverty" (Washington: Government Printing Office, 1983), 46.

TABLE 12-3   Composition of Poverty Population for Selected Demographic Groups.

	(PERCENT OF POVERTY POPULATION)			
	1959	1966	1975	1982
Aged	13.9	17.9	12.8	10.9
Children	43.6	42.6	42.1	38.2
Nonaged adults	42.5	39.5	45.1	50.9
Individuals in female-headed families	26.3	36.0	47.4	47.5
Individuals in other families	73.7	64.0	52.6	52.5
Blacks	25.1	31.1	29.2	28.2
Whites	72.1	67.7	68.7	68.4
Other	2.8	1.2	2.1	3.4

Source: U.S. Congress, House of Representatives, "Background Material on Poverty" (Washington: Government Printing Office, 1983), p. 47.

But today national leaders want to reexamine the conclusions reached by those earlier debates on the grounds that the commitments made by earlier generations cannot be met in today's climate of economic scarcity.

Such reasoning, we have concluded, represents little more than poorly disguised efforts to mislead the American people about the true meaning of America's commitments to its own lofty ideals. It is hard to believe that today's economic climate is less hospitable to social security commitments than was the economic climate in 1935. Nor is it convincing to argue that our military and international commitments are more pressing today, and consequently require a reduction in domestic commitments, than were the commitments during World War II or the war in Viet Nam. It is true that our social commitments in programs such as social security have increased as the programs have been liberalized and as the size of the older adult population has increased. But it is also true that we have expanded economic growth, decreased our taxes, and promoted great tax savings for corporations and wealthy individuals.

It is true that the national debt has increased to a staggering amount, so great that the interest on this debt is greater than federal spending for health care. But the reason for this increase is not an overgenerous policy of domestic spending. The fiscal policy decreases that aggravated the severe economic recession of the 1980s are responsible for the large federal debt—not the commitment to domestic obligations. These fiscal policy decisions have dealt older people a double blow. On the one side are those efforts to get the economy under control by tightening federal spending. On the other side, older people have been disadvantaged as the economy forced many of them to the edges of economic chaos. There is no reason why older adults must be disadvantaged because of these fiscal policy choices except that Americans have lost sight of their national objectives in favor of their private desires.

The Professional Responsibilities

Professional persons cannot serve older people effectively if they do not understand older people, nor can professional people serve older people when negative belief systems are directed toward the older adult population. In the same view, professional people cannot serve older people when the resources are not adequate. Thus the question is raised as to the role of professional persons as advocates for and with older people to realize the social commitments that this nation has undertaken. Advocacy by individual professional persons and by professional associations is often viewed with disdain by the general public. "Feathering their own nests," the public often complains. Moreover, although professional ethics do not prohibit professional activism, professional ethics do not require it. Thus the question of advocacy is left without a clear answer.

As individuals, professional people are free to advocate for anything they wish and in just about any legal way they wish to do so. In this role, professional persons often make good advocates because they are well informed about the problems and have creative ideas about potential solutions. In the role of private citizen, professional people can join advocacy groups, such as those identified in Chapter 4, and pursue activities consistent with their personal philosophies. But the question of advocacy in the professional role is more complicated, and some guidance on professional responsibility to advocate may be helpful.

Advocacy to insure and promote standards of service is a clear professional obligation. Professional people have an obligation to provide professional services, and if the services are not consistent with professional standards, professionals must advocate for standards. The shame of nursing homes has been ameliorated in the past few years, particularly with the enforcement of standards by federal reimbursement requirements. Yet many nursing homes cut corners and boarding homes and intermediate care facilities are frequently operated without reporting requirements. In such situations, where older people may be unable to assert themselves to insure adequate standards of care, professional persons are obligated to do it for them.

Many states have developed ombudsman programs, and in some states there are laws that guarantee the rights of nursing home patients and provide for local investigative committees that can hear patients' complaints. The initiative for these efforts came largely from professional persons who worked with older people and found that, without some outside review, standards often slipped below acceptable levels. Beyond this form of advocacy, however, is the clear responsibility on the part of the professional who works inside an agency where standards are not acceptable, to work toward the development of appropriate standards of service. Such activities may appear controversial, and may bring criticism from administrators, but there is no doubt that professional responsibility requires appropriate measures to insure that professional activities meet established professional standards. Capable administrators will understand that such professional activities are not in conflict with administrative goals.

Professional persons also take advocacy roles, as professional people outside of their agencies. These activities are more controversial than those suggested above, and different professions may or may not sanction and encourage the practice. Often professional organizations, such as the National Association of Social Workers (NASW), will take a public position of advocacy on behalf of a group of people or an issue, and in this context professional persons may work together through the professional organization.

There are situations, however, where a professional organization may not have taken a position, and where the professional person may feel a professional commitment to speak out and act in behalf of an issue of vital importance to older people. In this context, the actions of the professional person may be questioned. Despite such questioning, if the professional person is acting in good faith, and with accurate information, acting in behalf of older people seems consistent with those responsibilities endorsed by most professions.

Professional Development

At the beginning of this text we shared the conviction that working with older people is professionally rewarding. Older people, their personal perspectives mellowed by experience, are able to use appropriate helping efforts with a spirit of appreciation. Thus as professional people spend more time with older people, the load of professional service is often lightened. The field of serving older people is broadening in its scope, as we observed in early chapters. Therefore, professional people are likely to find themselves in interesting job settings; for example, transportation firms are likely to need professional persons to assist older travelers.

We also discussed the professional diversity within the field of service to older adults. Different professionals are likely to work together in a variety of occupational settings. Such interdisciplinary activity lends additional satisfaction to this work. Interdisciplinary work offers opportunity for the exchange of helping skills among professional persons, setting a healthy climate for professional growth. Yet because the professional services to older people are changing rapidly, all professional persons require continued updating about new programs and new trends in helping methodologies. As the older adult population continues to expand, and as greater numbers of professional people will be needed in an increasing variety of occupational settings, ongoing professional development will become a more important problem for all professionals.

The continual potential problems of which professional people should be aware—tendencies to stereotype older people, and to deny opportunity for self-expression and self-determination particularly among frail older adults—along with efforts to reduce support for older people, require vigilance. Professional people should be alert for the subtle shifts in policy that may have long-range, detrimental effects on older adults. Working with older people presents challenges and offers ample rewards for service. America's older people certainly deserve high-quality care and attention and a share of public resources in some measure to the contribution that they made to build this nation. Professional people can begin to meet this challenge by understanding older adults for the kind of people they are, and by bringing them the right programs with professional competence. If this text helps in that process, it will have served a useful purpose.

BIBLIOGRAPHY

AKHTAR, A. J., et al., "Disability and Dependence in the Elderly at Home," *Age and Aging,* 2, (1973), 102.

ALTMEYER, ARTHUR, *The Formative Years in Social Security.* Madison: University of Wisconsin Press, 1968.

AXINN, JUNE, and HERMAN LEVIN, *Public Welfare: America's Response to Need.* New York: Dodd, Mead, 1980.

BAILEY, STEPHEN KEMP, *Congress Makes a Law.* New York: Columbia University Press, 1950.

BALL, ROBERT, *Social Security Today and Tomorrow.* New York: Columbia University Press, 1978.

BEAUVOIR, SIMONE DE, *The Coming of Age.* New York: Putnam's, 1972.

BLENKNER, MARGARET, MARTIN BLOOM, and MARGARET NIELSON, "A Research and Demonstration Project of Protective Services," *Social Casework,* 52, no. 8 (October 1971), 483-99.

BLYTHE, RONALD, *The View in Winter: Reflections on Old Age.* New York, London: Harcourt Brace Jovanovich, Inc., 1978.

BREMNER, ROBERT, *American Philanthropy.* Chicago: University of Chicago Press, 1966.

BRILL, NAOMI, *Working with People: The Helping Process* (2nd ed.). New York: Longman, 1978.

BROWN, JOSEPHINE C., *Public Relief, 1929-1937.* New York: Holt, Rinehart & Winston, 1940.

BUTLER, ROBERT, "Psychiatry and the Elderly," *American Journal of Psychiatry,* 132, (1978), 172-188.

_____, and MYRNA LEWIS, "How to Keep People at Home," chapter 10 of *Aging—Mental Health*. St. Louis: C. V. Mosby, 1973.

CARP, FRANCES M., "The Concept and Role of Congregate Housing for Older People," in *Congregate Housing for Older People: An Urgent Need, a Growing Demand*, eds. Wilma T. Donahue, Marie McGuire Thompson, and D. J. Currens. Washington: Department of Health, Education, and Welfare, 1977.

CHAPPATIS, JOSEPH, "Federal Social Welfare Progressivism in the 1920s," *Social Service Review*, 46, (June 1972), 118–37.

CHEN, YUNG-PING, and KWANG-WEN CHU, "Household Expenditure Patterns: The Effect of Age on Family Head," *Journal of Family Issues*, 3, no. 3 (June 1982).

CLOWARD, RICHARD, and FRANCIS FOX PIVEN, *Regulating the Poor*. New York: Vintage Books, 1960.

COHLER, BERTRAM J., "Autonomy and Interdependence in the Family of Adulthood: A Psychological Perspective," *The Gerontologist*, 23, no. 1 (1983), 24.

DERTHICK, MARTHA, *Policy Making for Social Security*. Washington: The Brookings Institution, 1979.

DOBELSTEIN, ANDREW, "In Quest of a Fair Welfare System," *Journal of Social Welfare*, 2, no. 2 (Spring/Fall 1975).

_____, *Politics, Economics and Public Welfare*, Englewood Cliffs, N.J.: Prentice-Hall, 1980.

DOWNS, CAL W., G. PAUL SMEYAK, and ERNEST MARTIN, *Professional Interviewing*, New York: Harper & Row, Pub., 1980.

DROWLEY, F. S., "Financing the Social Security Program—Then and Now," in U.S. Congress, Joint Economic Committee, *Issues In Financing Retirement Income*, pp. 21–158. Studies in Public Welfare, 18. Washington: Government Printing Office, 1974.

EISDORFER, CARL, and DONNA COHEN, "The Issue of Biological and Psychological Deficits," in *Aging and Society*, eds. Edgar Borgatta and Neil McCluskey. Beverly Hills, Calif.: Sage Publications, Inc., 1980.

ERIKSON, ERIK, *Identity and the Life Cycle*. New York: International Universities Press, 1959.

FAREL, ANITA, and ANDREW DOBELSTEIN, "Supports and Deterrents for Women Working Outside the Home" *Family Relations*, 31, (April 1982), 281–286.

FRIEDMAN, JOSEPH, and JANE SJOGREM, "Assets of the Elderly as They Retire," *Social Security Bulletin*, 44, no. 1 (January 1981), 16–31.

GALPER, JEFFREY, *The Politics of Social Services*. Englewood Cliffs, N.J.: Prentice-Hall, 1975.

GEORGE, LINDA K., "Models of Transition in Middle and Later Life," *Annals of the American Academy of Political and Social Science*, 464, (November 1982), 87–110.

HALLOWELL, JOHN, *Main Currents of Modern Political Thought*. New York: Holt, Rinehart & Winston, 1950.

HAVENMAN, ROBERT, and KEN YON KNOPF, *The Market System*. New York: John Wiley, 1962.

HOFSTADTER, RICHARD, *Social Darwinism in American Thought*. Boston: Beacon Press, 1965.

JORGENSEN, JAMES A., *The Graying of America*. New York: Dial Press, 1980.

KAPLAN, MAX, *Leisure: Lifestyle and Lifespan*. Philadelphia: Saunders, 1979.

KEYNES, JOHN MAYNARD, *The General Theory of Employment, Interest and Money*. New York: Harcourt Brace Jovanovich, Inc., 1936.

KRISTOL, IRVING, "Equality as an Ideal," *International Encyclopedia of the Social Sciences.* New York: Macmillan, 1968.

LAREAU, LESLIE S., "Needs Assessment of the Elderly: Conclusions and Methodological Approaches," *The Gerontologist,* 23, no. 5 (October 1983), 518–519.

LASCH, CHRISTOPHER, ed. *The Social Thought of Jane Addams.* Indianapolis: Bobbs-Merrill, 1965.

LASSWELL, HARROLD, *Politics: Who Gets What, When, How.* New York: Meridian Books, 1958.

LAWTON, M. POWELL, "Applying Research Knowledge to Congregate Housing," in *Congregate Housing for Older People.* Eds. Wilma Donahue, Marie McGuire Thompson, and William Curren. Washington: Administration of Aging, DHEW pub. no. 77-20284.

————, RALPH GREENBAUM, and ADAM LIEBOWITZ, "The Lifespan of Housing Environments," *The Gerontologist,* 20, no. 1 (1980), 56–64.

LEACH, RICHARD, and ANDREW DOBELSTEIN, "The Federal Role in Public Welfare Today," *Forensic Quarterly,* 47, no. 2 (May 1972), 69–84.

LOWI, THEODORE, *The End of Liberalism.* New York: W. W. Norton & Co., Inc., 1969.

MADDOX, GEORGE L., "The Patient and His Family," in *The Hidden Patient: Knowledge and Action in Long-Term Care,* pp. 87–113. Ed. Sylvia Sherwood. Jamaica, New York: Spectrum Publ., 1975.

MARTIN, GEORGE, *Madam Secretary.* New York: Houghton Mifflin, 1976.

MOON, MARILYN, *The Measurement of Economic Welfare.* New York: Academic Press, New York, 1977.

MORALES, ARMANDO, and BRADFORD W. SHEAFOR, *Social Work: A Profession of Many Faces* (3rd ed.). Boston, Mass.: Allyn & Bacon, 1983.

National Center for Health Statistics, *The National Nursing Home Survey: 1977 Summary for the United States.* Washington: Government Printing Office, 1978.

National Council on the Aging, "The Senior Center: A Partner in the Community Care Center," Book 3: NISC/NCOA, *Informal Supports,* 1982.

————, *Myth and Reality of Aging.* Washington, D.C.: National Council on the Aging, 1981.

————, "The Senior Center Role in Serving the At-Risk Older Person," NCOA/ NISC Seminar, January 7, 1980, Washington, D.C.

————, "Senior Center Standards: Guidelines for Practice," NCOA/NISC, June 1978.

NELSON, GARY, "Support for the Aged: Public and Private Responsibility," *Social Work,* 27, no. 2 (March 1982), 137–46.

NOVAK, MICHAEL, *The Rise of the Unmeltable Ethics.* New York: Macmillan, 1972.

ORBACH, HAROLD L., "Aging, Families and Family Behavioral and Social Science Perspectives on Our Knowledge, Our Myths, and Our Research," *The Gerontologist,* 23, no. 1 (1983), 112–138.

ROSOW, IRVING, *Social Integration of the Aged.* New York: Free Press, 1967.

ROUSSEAU, JEAN JACQUES, *The Social Contract and Discourses.* London: Everyman's Library, 1938.

SACHIE, K. WARNER, "Mid-life to Old Age," *American Journal of Orthopsychiatry,* 2, (1981), 119–126.

SHANAS, ETHEL, "The Family as a Social Support System in Old Age," *The Gerontologist,* 19, no. 2 (1979), 169–174.

SMITH, SARAH ALEXANDER, *Natural Systems and the Elderly: An Unrecognized Resource.* Washington, D.C.: National Council on the Aging, 1981.

Statistical Abstract of the United States, 102nd ed. Washington: Government Printing Office, 1981.

STEENER, GILBERT, *The Children's Cause.* Washington: The Brookings Institution, 1976.

SULLIVAN, HARRY STACK, *The Collected Works.* 2 vols. Eds. Helen Perry et al. New York: W. W. Norton & Co., Inc.

United States, Comptroller General, General Accounting Office, *Entering a Nursing Home—Costly Implications for Medicaid and the Elderly: A Report to Congress.* Washington: Government Printing Office, November 1979.

————, *The Well-being of Older People in Cleveland, Ohio: A Report to Congress.* Washington: Government Printing Office, April 1977.

United States, Congress, Joint Economic Committee, Subcommittee on Social Security, *President's Social Security Proposals.* Washington: Government Printing Office, 1974.

United States, Congressional Budget Office, *Long-Term Care for the Elderly and Disabled.* Washington: Government Printing Office, 1977.

————, *Work and Retirement: Options for Continued Employment of Older Workers.* Washington: Government Printing Office, 1982.

United States, Department of Health and Human Services, Administration on Aging, *Protective Services for Adults.* Washington: Administration on Aging, Spring 1982.

————, Office of Research Statistics, *Program and Demographic Characteristics of Supplemental Income Beneficiaries.* Washington: Government Printing Office, May 1981.

————, Social Security Administration, *Income of the Population 55 and Over, 1978.* Washington: Social Security Administration, 1981.

United States, Department of Housing and Urban Development, Direct Loan Branch, *Housing the Elderly.* Washington: Government Printing Office, 1983.

WATKINS, ELIZABETH L., and AUDREY E. JOHNSON, eds., *Removing Cultural and Ethnic Barriers to Health Care.* Chapel Hill, N.C.: University of North Carolina, School of Public Health, 1981.

WEBER, MAX, *The Protestant Ethic and the Spirit of Capitalism,* translated by Talcott Parsons. New York: Scribner's, 1958.

WELLS, THOMAS A., "Helpers' Perception of Clients," *Psychological Bulletin,* 85, (September 1978), 988.

WETKIN, STANLEY, "Cognitive Processes in Clinical Practice," *Social Work Journal of NASW,* 27, no. 5 (September 1982), 389–394.

White House Conference on Aging, 1981, *Final Report.* 3 vols. Washington: Department of Health and Human Services, June 1982.

————, Technical Committee on the Physical and Social Environment and Quality of Life, *Report.* Washington: Government Printing Office, 1981.

WITTE, EDWARD, *The Development of the Social Security Act.* Madison: University of Wisconsin Press, 1963.

INDEX